Erotic Beasts
and Social Monsters

Erotic Beasts
and Social Monsters

Shakespeare, Jonson,
and Comic Androgyny

Grace Tiffany

DELAWARE

Newark: University of Delaware Press
London and Toronto: Associated University Presses

Associated University Presses
440 Forsgate Drive
Cranbury, N.J. 08512

Associated University Presses
25 Sicilian Avenue
London WC1A 2QH, England

Associated University Presses
P.O. Box 338, Port Credit
Mississauga, Ontario
Canada L5G 4L8

The paper used in this publication meets the requirements
of the American National Standard for Permanence of Paper for Printed Library
Materials Z39.48–1948

Part of this book has appeared in a different form as the article "Falstaff's False Staff: Jonsonian Asexuality in *The Merry Wives of Windsor*," reprinted with kind permission of the editors of *Comparative Drama*, and as the article "'That Reason Wonder May Diminish': *As You Like It*, Androgyny, and the Theater Wars," reprinted with kind permission of *Huntington Library Quarterly*.

Library of Congress Cataloging-in-Publication Data

Tiffany, Grace, 1958–
    Erotic Beasts and social monsters : Shakespeare, Jonson, and comic androgyny / Grace Tiffany.
        p. cm.
    Includes bibliographical references (p.) and index
    ISBN 0-87413-550-8 (alk. paper)
    1. Shakespeare, William, 1564–1616—Criticism and interpretation. 2. Androgyny (Psychology) in literature. 3. Jonson, Ben, 1573–1637—Criticism and interpretation. 4. English drama—Early modern and Elizabethan, 1500–1600—History and criticism. 5. English drama—17th century—History and criticism. 6. Hermaphroditism in literature. 7. Sex (Psychology) in literature. 8. Comic, The, in literature. 9. Theater—England--London—History. I. Title.
PR3069.A425T54 1995
822.'309353—dc20   94-28403
                                                       CIP

PRINTED IN THE UNITED STATES OF AMERICA

To Amy, Lori, and Michèle
and in memory of Craig

"So we grew together,
. . . seeming parted,
But yet an union in partition."

—Shakespeare, *A Midsummer Night's Dream*

Contents

Acknowledgments

ἕκαστος ἡμῶν οὐχ αὑτῷ μόνον γέγονεν
(each of us is born not for himself alone)
—Plato, *Ninth Letter*

My revision of this book was greatly assisted by the comments of three readers: Jeanne Addison Roberts, David Bevington, and Ed Johnson. I want to thank all three for their thoughtful analyses, as well as for their generosity toward my arguments and toward me. Thanks are also due to my students and colleagues in Arts and Sciences 1119, an interdisciplinary course in Greek literature at the University of New Orleans—especially to Ed, Mary Fitzgerald, Richard Katrovas, and Mike Mooney. Without the opportunity to help teach and learn from that class, this book could not have been written. Last, I must acknowledge the family and friends who are my continual sources of inspiration and love. I thank especially the Tiffanys, Karen and Gary, Saadi, and a very small Monster who helped a lot.

Introduction

A clarification of terms is a good starting point. The word "andro-gyne" has been variously manipulated in the voluminous recent work on gender distinctions in Renaissance England, and the proper use of the word itself has been a valid topic of debate. Although much has been made of the difference between the words "androgyne" and "her-maphrodite,"[1] the fact is that Renaissance poets, playwrights, and even prose writers frequently used them interchangeably, as will I. With the exception of scientific or medical references, Renaissance literary invocations of androgyny or hermaphrodism almost always described a psychological and behavioral condition. It was the nature of that condition, and of the writer's attitude toward it, that varied according to the generic context of the reference. The larger distinc-tion to be made, then, is between the philosophical and literary con-texts that defined androgyny/hermaphrodism during the English Renaissance. The clarification of this distinction is a large part of this book's intent.

Although Renaissance attitudes toward androgyny were doubt-less as varied as Renaissance notions of what an androgyne was, re-cent scholars are probably correct in identifying two basic kinds of literary use of the gender-transgressive symbol: the positive and the negative. Phyllis Rackin summarizes the general distinction between these two categories of literary usage:

> The androgyne could be an image of transcendence—of surpassing the bounds that limit the human condition in a fallen world, of breaking through the constraints that material existence imposes on spiritual aspiration or the personal restrictions that define our role in society. But the androgyne could also be an object of ridicule or an image of monstrous deformity, of social and physical abnormality.[2]

By distinguishing the similar double uses of the androgyne in classi-cal literary and dramatic texts, I hope to clarify two traditions that meaningfully contextualize these divergent Renaissance attitudes

11

regarding androgyny, as well as our discussions of these attitudes. These traditions are particularly relevant to Shakespeare's and Jonson's radically different comic methods. Specifically, my project is to define and label more precisely the Renaissance models of positive and negative androgyny as "mythic androgyny" and "satiric androgyny" (or "mythic hermaphrodism" and "satiric hermaphrodism"), and to identify Shakespeare's and Jonson's elaboration of these models, as the models themselves were complicated and reshaped by their encounters with Renaissance culture.

Accordingly, my first chapter is devoted to a discussion of the distinct traditions of mythic and satiric androgyny as they occurred in ancient Greek and Roman literature, and as they were later adapted to Renaissance philosophies and literary forms. My second and third chapters, respectively engaging mythic androgyny in Shakespeare's comedies and satiric androgyny in Jonson's, work to illuminate these playwrights' specific borrowings from and contributions to their chosen traditions. My fourth and fifth chapters demonstrate Jonson's and Shakespeare's occasional play with what were for each of them unfamiliar comic principles—satiric androgyny for Shakespeare, and mythic androgyny for Jonson—as well as their particular play with each other's work. Jonson's and Shakespeare's responsiveness to each other's representations of androgyny—representations that were deeply embedded in each other's general comic ethos—was, I argue, evident in the heated intertheatrical dialogue that occurred in London between 1599 and 1601, now known as the Theater Wars.

Overall, my discussion will treat the mythic androgyne as the basis for all later treatments of androgyny. That is, even the anti-androgynous ethos that strips the mythic androgyne of its positive valence is secondary and responsive to the original myth. Classical myths concerning the androgyne, like those found in numerous other cultures, used him/her to demonstrate a principle of relatedness: of potent human connectedness and progress, or what the Greeks called "eros." Eros, according to the androgynous principle, is far more than sexual libido. It is a metamorphic power that compels human creativity, procreation, and personal and social growth through intimate connectedness. In the words of Laurens van der Post, "the spirit of Eros" is "a process of metamorphosis," of which "[a]ll of us . . . are not only capable . . . but driven . . . by the collective unconscious" that "unites all humankind."[3] In the mythic tradition, the image of the androgyne or the hermaphrodite was the central symbol of erotic power; hence its primary significance exceeds that commonly attributed to it: "the capacity of a single person of either sex to embody the full range of human character traits, despite cultural attempts to render some exclusively feminine and some exclusively masculine."[4] Although the mythic androgyne at times assumes this significance, its larger valence goes beyond its meaning for any "single person" and suggests the capacity—indeed, the compulsion—of members of both sexes to sacrifice private identity to powerful, progressive relationships.

The mythic androgyne's significance as an energy *between* individuals, rather than a psychic state locked *within* individuals, is implicit in the very word "hermaphrodite." "Hermaphroditism" in a mythic sense means the agency of Hermes, the messenger or connector, combined with the motivational force of Aphrodite, or erotic love. "Hermaphrodite" means, in effect, "connection of love" (a significance that is radically displaced by discussions of Shakespeare's androgynous characters simply as liberated women or sensitive men). The mythic androgyne is linked with originary myths of primal unity and embodies, among other things, an innate impulse toward recombination with the Other, whose alterity it radically questions. Thus the androgynous principle begins, but does not end, with a psychic condition: its full meaning is realized in our acknowledgment of our essential human relatedness and our location of our identity there, rather than in gendered isolation. So this androgyne's doubled gender needs to be interpreted not (or not primarily) as the broadness of his or her private personality, but as his or her necessary involvement with someone else.

Even the feature of physical hermaphrodism, where it occurs, indicates for the mythic figure not freakishness, but an implied relational identity. We see this when we attend closely to the way biological hermaphrodism was rendered in both classical myth and that myth's Renaissance revisions. While Renaissance emblems sometimes represented the mythic androgyne as a figure who was simultaneously both biologically male and biologically female, in poetry, narrative, and drama this was almost never the case. When the androgyne or hermaphrodite did possess biological maleness and femaleness, it alternated back and forth between male and female incarnations. (This was the case, for example, with Zeus, Tiresias, and Athene.) Spenser's emblematic verse image of the statue of Venus in *The Faerie Queene* is the exception that proves this rule: the figure has "both kinds in one, / Both male and female" (book 4, canto 10, stanza 41, lines 6–7)[5] only because she is the symbolic reification of a process that is properly realized in flux. The image of Venus here borrows from the description of androgynous Isis in the ancient Orphic Hymns (popularly revived among Renaissance Neoplatonists), who is "waxing and waning, feminine and masculine" and "whose motion is circular" (Hymn no. 9, "To the Moon").[6] The dramatic or narrative image of the alternating male-female represents mythic androgyny as a force that realizes itself in time, through the gradual progress of a culture, through human procreation, or through the growth of a relational unit. Like the alternating male-female, the occasional appearance of the mythic androgyne as a being with two heads, or a person sexually involved with a beast, or an erotically impelled, mobile beast-human, underscores the figure's relational valence and its involvement in the temporal as well as the spatial dimension.

The Renaissance mythic writers, including Shakespeare, made symbolic capital out of all of these classical images and motifs, but turned increasingly to naturalistically presented dramatic characters as central conductors of the androgynous principle. Most common in this tradition was the mythic androgyne who was a constant biological male or female, but who incorporated within his or her manner or appearance certain features socially ascribed to the other sex. This figure's theatrical context and its literal aliveness enhanced its symbolism as a human relational entity.

The satiric androgyne, in contrast, emerged from a masculine ethos of distrust in personal and social relationships, particularly in relationships with women. Both classical and Renaissance satiric comic and poetic traditions produced mocking portraits of aggressively sexualized and hence "masculine" women, or vain and dependent and hence "effeminate" men. In the plays, poetry, and prose of such satirists, the motivational force of eros is displaced by that of lechery, the presentation of authentic male-female psychic overlap (such as that between Athene and Odysseus) by the chronicling or staging of invalid gender transgression, and the symbolism of relational yearning by the charge of parasitism. The satiric context attempts to disable myth and render it inoperative. Satire, in fact, fashions its vain, morally reduced, and socially monstrous androgynes largely by a rational and skeptical attack on myth and myth's basic symbols, including the androgyne. Since satire derived from an ethos of authorial distance and difference from the corrupt society its author criticized, the primary focus of satiric attack in both classical and Renaissance literature and drama was the threatening myth of human experiential connectedness, with its implicit suggestion that the satirist was indeed a part of the whole. And since the connective myth's central image was the androgyne, he/she bore the brunt of both classical and Renaissance satiric scorn.

The English Renaissance theater was a particularly charged forum for the confrontation between rival androgynes, for—as in Aristophanic comedy—there they could meet in the flesh, on stage. The addition of humors comedy to the ancient genre of verse satire during the Middle Renaissance period in England contributed fundamentally to the increased tension—what Marjorie Garber calls the "cultural anxiety"[7]—surrounding the androgynous figure during the late sixteenth and early seventeenth centuries. Thus a discussion of the archetypal mythic and classical satiric androgynous figures as they emerged in the work of the two greatest Renaissance comic playwrights best discloses the distinctions between what I will call androgynous and anti-androgynous principles, and best demonstrates the relevance of those principles to ideas of erotic relationship in their time and our own.

Resituating the androgyny symbol within the methodological categories of myth and satire may enhance the clarity of our own analyses, both of the late sixteenth century's rapidly changing dramatic genres and of its confusing discourse of androgyny. One thing I hope my analysis will achieve is a revised perspective on Renaissance comic paradigms. The idea that Renaissance comedy is generally definable with reference to the categories of romance and satire[8] is, I would argue, insufficient to an analysis of most of Shakespeare's and some of Jonson's comic works. The term I use in this book to describe Shakespeare's comedy, "mythic comedy," is consciously chosen more effectively to distinguish his methodology and influences, particularly with regard to the staging of the androgynous principle. The distinction between Shakespearean mythic comedy and non-Shakespearean romantic comedy is crucial to my fifth chapter, which attempts to distinguish Shakespeare's comic mode from the Petrarchan/Ovidian ethos of many of his contemporaries, including (paradoxically) Jonson.

Most importantly, I hope in this book to shed light on our discussions of androgyny's symbolic uses and of the competing philosophical and literary contexts out of which images of the hermaphrodite are generated. The ethos of satire, with its habitually misogynistic modes of attack, is now generally acknowledged as having been a

powerful cultural force during the Renaissance, perhaps because of
its newly perceived likeness to the strengthening ethos of Puritanism
in the late sixteenth century,[9] and most likely because of satirists'
propensity to announce who they are, what moral principles they
hold dear, and what they expect their art to accomplish.[10] What
needs clarification is the ethos of myth, particularly as it constructs
the androgyny principle. For example, Rackin's influential study of
Renaissance theatrical transvestism, quoted above, begins by acknowl-
edging the positive valence of some mythic images of the androgyne,
in defiance of that figure's common condemnatory representations.
But Rackin then clouds this helpful distinction, describing what is
essentially a satirical perspective on gender difference by referring to
an ancient mythic symbol whose real meaning is antithetical to the
one she attributes to it. "In an androcentric culture," she writes, "the
female principle is negative, like the blank space that defines a positive pictorial image." This female "blankness," or "absence," Rackin
claims, "can be figured by the yin-yang diagram that symbolizes the
relation of male and female."[11] It is, in fact (as my first chapter
argues), the misogynistic satirical frame of reference that genders
femininity as absence. The model indicated by the mythic Chinese
diagram is quite different. The "blankness" Rackin identifies is actually the male or yang portion of the symbol, and is not empty, but
filled with light. The dark side is that of the yin, or female, and it represents not absence but a complementary presence. Further, Rackin
does not acknowledge a crucial part of the diagram, which is the
presence of a dark or "feminine" spot in the yang and a bright or
"masculine" spot in the yin, indicating the impossibility of fully separating the genders. Finally, her analogy leaves out the flow of each
symbolic half toward the other, describing—as do the figures of
androgyny in Greek classical myth—the essential inclination of the
separated sexes toward union.

   Rackin's inversion of this well-known symbol of heterosexual
parity to support her prior vision of "androcentric" Renaissance culture exemplifies a disturbing trend in contemporary scholarship: the
tendency to impose a methodological template on an age's textual
productions, so that preordained findings are safely confirmed, while
access to genuine discoveries about the subject matter is severely
restricted. To quote Brian Vickers, such critical approaches, rather
than "opening up a field to fresh inquiry . . . effectively close it
down."[12] In current Renaissance studies, the most prominent self-
validating critical approach is the one exercised by Rackin above,

which holds widely varying forms of literature hostage to the a priori assumption that patriarchal norms held universal sway over Renaissance minds, and that patriarchal values were therefore all that could be expressed. This assumption unhealthily and unrealistically prioritizes the misogynistic satirical ethos—one current in a turbulent river—as the determinant of mainstream social attitudes. Even more seriously, the assumption facilitates radical misreadings of age-old mythic symbols and terms that designate a cooperative human power, and that may bring us closer than does Elizabethan satire to an understanding of common Renaissance attitudes towards gender.[13]

This project is, then, like this introduction, devoted to a clarification of such symbols and terms, as well as to the invention of a few. Like the words "androgyne" and "hermaphrodite," certain key phrases will herein be used synonymously. My chapter on Shakespearean androgyny proposes that Shakespeare, like certain classical authors, used a variety of images—Shakespeare's include water, beast-humans, mazes, dreams, and androgynes—interchangeably to suggest the ever-shifting, metamorphic power of eros. Mainly to avoid repetitiousness, my discussion of this phenomenon depends on similarly interchangeable terms. Thus "androgyny myth" and "beast-androgyny myth," "erotic principle," and "androgynous principle," and "erotic relatedness" and "androgynous relatedness" are used respectively to describe the same idea.

The word "transvestite" is somewhat trickier. Marjorie Garber has been criticized for using this word too loosely in her recent *Vested Interests* "to mean the creature who comes into existence whenever any person of one sex is clad in any form or any part of the other's dress, in life or in art, for any length of time, and under any circumstances."[14] Like Garber, I call "transvestite" many characters who are not consciously attempting to cross-dress. My reason for so terming them, like my reason for conflating "androgyne" and "hermaphrodite," is simply that the authors with whom I am concerned present these characters as transvestite. In other words, the authors (or their characters) represent the subject garb in terms that gender it as masculine or feminine—i.e., as cross-gendering the wearer.

Finally, the reader will find that—in defiance of a contemporary taboo—I frequently conflate the words "male" and "masculine," as well as the terms "female" and "feminine." And again, the reason is that the texts I am analyzing so conflate them. I use these terms interchangeably where my discussion is actually centering on the *fact* of that conflation: that is, where I am demonstrating the gendering of certain qualities as "male" or "female." Thus, rather than making the assumption that "male" and "female" refer to biological fact, while "masculine" and "feminine" refer to cultural construction, the reader may take it that all of these terms where they are mine refer to cultural construction, except where my reference is to a real body (e.g., "the male actor's cross-dressed body," "the female poet whom Jonson attacked").

In writing this book, I became gradually conscious of a paradox: that despite their antithetical perspectives, satire and mythic literature share a deep alignment of intention. Although one tradition rejects the androgynous ideal and the other affirms it, both embody a longing for re-form: a quest for an originary human identity. The difference between the quests is that, both in classical times and during the Renaissance, the satirist withdrew into himself and away from his social environment to recover this originary ideal, while the mythic writer moved outward, seeking to realize a very different vision of selfhood in erotic and other relational ties with his community. And much cultural evidence might be collected to support the theory that, in gendering these countervailing impulses as "male" and "female," the satirist was right.

But this is not my thesis. This study is not primarily historical, sociological, or scientific, but literary: I am concerned with reading texts, not with "reading" the English transvestite. Thus my discussion involves information derived from a broad cultural context only insofar as this information illuminates literary function and ethos, and as it urges an awareness of the relationship of the literature I analyze to contemporary notions—valid or invalid—of gender difference, and to related ideas about heterosexual as well as same-sex relationship. It can be, indeed has been, said that the mythic androgynous ethos that affirms male-female connectedness, like the satiric ethos that distances itself from the "feminized" world, actually reinforces oppositional views of male and female nature. A symbol of male-female relationship that celebrates such relationship as the union of opposites may illuminate "maleness" in the female and "femaleness" in the male, but it inevitably reinforces a cultural model of natures that are essentially gendered.[15] With this thesis I would not, and will not, argue. What I will argue is that the Shakespearean mythic androgyne is properly seen as a symbol of the suspension of gender roles—whether these roles are biologically mandated or culturally invented—which may occur when individual identity itself is suspended in response to an inner erotic demand for relationship. Further, I will argue for a decisive distinction between such androgynes and the satirically inspired "anti-androgynes" of Renaissance social critics like Jonson: a distinction that locates these double-gendered or gender-transgressive symbols within the respective contexts of classical myth and satire, as these contexts were elaborated and transformed by Renaissance thought.

Finally, I would like to point out that the antithetical symbols of mythic and satiric androgyny are, as usual, powerfully present in our current cultural productions. Satiric androgyny is a rife and ribald motif in the visual media (any viewing of the popular television show *Saturday Night Live* will confirm this). Conversely, mythic hermaphrodism may be located in such contemporary dramatic characters as the central character in David Cronenberg's recent long-running play and 1993 film *M. Butterfly*, or the androgynous hero of Sally Potter's 1993 film version of Virginia Woolf's *Orlando*. As I earlier noted, an integral part of my argument regarding the androgynous principle concerns its relationship to erotic beast transformation myths, and the elaboration of both traditions in Shakespeare. I mention this here in order to contextualize another contemporary cultural phenomenon, which is the television and cinematic interest in dramatizing erotic beast encounters with humans. One example from recent years, the CBS television series *Beauty and the Beast,* is worthy of note in the context of this discussion—that is, in the context of contextualization—as is the still more recent (and far more stunning) artistic experiment in gender reversals, Neil Jordan's 1992 film *The Crying Game*. In the television series, a professional urban woman artfully negotiates an eroticized relationship with a man who is, mysteriously, half human and half beast. In Jordan's film, a heterosexual man artfully negotiates an eroticized relationship with a male transvestite. In both examples, the lovers are left in conditions of frustrated, partial fulfillment; the erotic consummation is either endlessly deferred or clearly impossible. Still, they are empowered and ennobled by each other's kindness. Further, the lovers' mutual yearning deeply informs, and in fact sustains, their problematic relationship.

This is the myth that the androgyne implies. In our contemporary culture, as in Renaissance England and classical Greece, the beast and the androgyne are relational symbols that give meaning to our stories of erotic striving. Symbolically, they propose a paradox, indicating both our ineradicable impulse toward total relational unity and our inevitable failure to achieve it. Most importantly, however, the myths of beast-androgyny propose a pattern for continuance: for the maintenance of our problematic human relationships. As such, they reaffirm, as did Shakespeare's mythic hermaphrodites, the impulse described in a fragment of Greek verse:

> I saw them, caught them in the act.
>   They could not slake, though lip
> was fixed on feverish lip in fury,
>   Their tyrannous thirst. They longed
> each to invade the other's heart.
>   Exchanging clothes, they eased
> the ache of impossibility.[16]

Erotic Beasts
and Social Monsters

1

Erotic Beasts and Social Monsters: Two Forms of Classical and Renaissance Androgyny

> There could be no relationship to that which is absolute other.
> —Joseph Campbell, "Love and the Goddess"

"Because life as experienced is fragmented," Robert Kimbrough writes, "androgyny, of necessity, looks beyond duality back to a time when personhood experienced innate wholeness and unity, a time 'back there,' 'once-upon-a-time,' 'in the beginning.'"[1] Kimbrough's words, intended to explain the baffling power of the androgynous characters who control Shakespeare's comic plots, also begin to define the larger, older, multivisaged mythic "character" who was a central inspiration for Portia, Rosalind, and Viola, as well as for Bottom, Benedick, Petruchio, and many other Shakespearean comic figures who in some sense defy conventional gender distinctions. The task of this book is to distinguish this ancient mythic androgyne and the nonindividuated human community it represents from the newer satiric androgyne, the literary and stage presentation of whom supports a militant and masculine individualism that attacks the transgressive presence of all gender-conflating behaviors and symbols. In Renaissance England, the satirically presented androgynous figure achieved its most colorful embodiment in the comedies of Ben Jonson, but the vision of masculine self-sufficiency that informs Jonsonian humors comedy derives from a misogynistic classical ethic that, as early as the seventh century B.C., confronted and warred with the older myth of the sacred androgyne.

The androgyne's originary status in numerous mythologies suggests its transcultural value as a symbol of the sum of human capabilities, primarily the capabilities for sexual interaction, procreation, and communal understanding. Cultures that were initially widely separated

23

accord central mythic importance to an androgynous figure who combines all human attributes in one state of hermaphroditic being. Like Christ, in whom Saint Paul tells us "there is neither male nor female" (Gal. 3:28), this genderless "god" is paradoxically both human and divine. It is human in that it is defined by its possession of all known "masculine" and "feminine" qualities, and it is divine in that, as a symbol of procreative erotic activity and thus of a broad self-renewing human community that exists beyond the separated, terminal lives of individuals, it is deathless. Thus a crucial characteristic of the androgyne is, as Kimbrough's remark suggests, its freedom from fragmentary experience and isolation. The androgyne's sexual doubleness symbolically represents the occasional human experience of transsexual connectedness, as well as a necessary location of identities in a heterogenous human community rather than in separated bodies. The Hindu creator god Siva (Shiva) is one such androgynous being, at times taking the form of (or actually becoming) the goddess Kama; his/her sexual incarnation is determined by particular erotic circumstances that require a sex change for the continual channeling of a procreative force.[2] Native American tradition also links androgyny with fertility and community: Winnebago legend features a quasi-divine "trickster" with an enormous penis, suggestive of powerful virility, who yet undergoes an educational journey during which he is required to turn female and bear children.[3] A similar character emerges among the legends of the African Yoruba, who tell of "a creature of great instinct and energy" who is "a spanner in the social works" and "a generating symbol who promotes change by offering opportunities for exploring what possibilities lie beyond the status quo."[4] Even the Judaeo-Christian tradition has linked androgyny and fertility to its creation myth. The third-century Christian theologians Philo and Origen believed "that the first and original man was androgynous; that the division into male and female belonged to a later and lower state of creation."[5] Origen interprets the Genesis verse "Male and female he made them" (1:27) as meaning that God originally intended humans to be androgynous entities who might "increase and multiply by the very accord among themselves" (1:14).[6] The Hebrew Midrash also stresses original androgyny (despite the "male, patriarchal bias," noted by Kimbrough, which it shares with Origen),[7] saying: "When the Holy One, Blessed be He, created the first man, He created him androgynous."[8] Conversely, a Chinese matriarchal myth finds human origin in a woman, T'ai Yuan: a "Great Original" who (according to Joseph Campbell) "combined in her person the masculine Yang and the feminine Yin."[9] Androgyny's best-known symbol is, in fact, undoubtedly the yin-yang diagram, which schematically represents all the sentient and gendered powers of the universe in indissoluble connection. The dark yin or female half of this round diagram both flows into and contains a portion of the bright yang or male side, and vice versa; the total symbol thus figures, among other things, the fertile and doubly sexed human community as an interconnected whole.

In Greek myth, as in the examples above, androgyny stands for a compulsory human relatedness, the work of erotic forces that (in Plato's words) "round out the whole and bind fast the all to the all" (203A).[10] For the ancient Greeks eros is not an option but a necessity,[11] and the vital communality that derives from its influence defines both the public and the secluded arenas of human experience. A variety of androgynous Greek characters personify different aspects of this dynamic relational state. The male-garbed Athene, for example, emerges as the Olympian god most closely associated with humanity through her idealized representation of a heterogenous Greek community and her frequent assumption of human form. Athene's incarnations are sometimes male and sometimes female; in *The Odyssey* she appears as Mentor in book 1, a young girl in book 7, and a shepherd and ultimately a woman in book 13.[12] Athene herself speaks of her close identification with Odysseus, the consummate Greek man (see book 13, lines 379–83), whose heroism is enlarged by his own tendency toward "feminine" emotional expressiveness (Odysseus cries like a woman when he hears stories of his lost companions-in-arms, "weeping the way a wife mourns for her lord" [bk. 8, line 561]). The prophet Tiresias, who according to Greek myth (and despite T. S. Eliot's "old man with wrinkled dugs") was not physiologically hermaphroditic but alternately male and female, is similar to the weeping Odysseus in that his androgynous experience indicates moral insight. Tiresias's inhabiting of both sexes is mystically linked to his personal longevity and his ability to foresee communal futures. In both Sophocles' *Oedipus Cycle* and Euripides' *Bacchae* Tiresias is "master of all the mysteries of our life" (*Oedipus the King,* line 341).[13] *The Bacchae*'s chief androgyne is, however, Dionysus, a man born from the "male womb" of Zeus's thigh (line 527) and himself inhabited and feminized by a god. Male but long-haired and girlish, the fertility god Dionysus confers his own androgynous symbolism on his worshippers, fitting the women with thyrsi (honey-spurting staffs whose phallic significance is obvious) and ultimately dressing Pentheus, the Theban ruler who has attempted to proscribe the Dionysian revels, in feminine attire (lines 916ff.).[14]

As "the bull-horned god" (line 101), Dionysus is invested with another element of Greek symbolism suggestive of divine sexuality and fertility: the aspect of the horned or hooved beast, repeatedly associated with erotic/procreative desire in Greek myth. "Bull-like" and "cow-eyed" are features traditionally described to archetypal divine parents Zeus and Hera, whose cult may have derived from the worship of real animals. The bull in particular suggests both desire and potency.[15] Like Dionysus, who temporarily assumes a bull's form in *The Bacchae*, Zeus appears as a bull to Europa; Pasiphae, sexually driven to couple with a bull, gives birth to the half-human Minotaur. In the *Hippolytus* of Euripides, Pasiphae's daughter Phaedra compares her mother's encounter with the bull to her sister's union with Dionysus and her own passion for Hippolytus, the charioteer who rejects her (lines 337–41).[16] Like the tragic denouement of *The Bacchae*, involving the sacrilegious Pentheus's dismemberment by the bull-god's charging worshippers, the catastrophe of *Hippolytus* employs the horned/hooved beast to dramatize the dangers of repudiating or suppressing erotic passion. Hippolytus, who like Pentheus regards sexuality with horror, is punished when his chariot is overthrown by "a monstrous savage bull" that, emerging from the ocean, maddens his horses (lines 1214ff.). These Euripidean tragic denouements argue that healthy eros demands acquiescence in one's own sexual nature: demands that we own, or acknowledge our possession of, a paradoxical human beastliness that, if distorted through denial, turns savage. As the comic mask worn by *The Bacchae*'s Dionysus suggests, erotic beastliness is essentially a comic, life-giving force, and turns destructive only when suppressed.

The powerfully sexual half-human centaurs and satyrs, like the Minotaur and the Euripidean bulls, associate human sexuality with the horned/hooved beast, as does Plato's allegory of controlled passion in the *Phaedrus*, wherein Socrates represents eros not as libidinous instinct but as human direction and control of an "uncomprehending, hardly submissive" horse that represents carnal desire (sec. 253).[17] Eros, in other words, is the hard-won but progressive cooperation of reason and desire. Ovid, whose *Metamorphoses* recounts the stories of Zeus's erotic beast transformations, revises Plato's *Phaedrus* metaphor in the *Amores*, presenting man as the reluctantly submissive horse and passion as the rider: "The mouth of the restive horse is bruised by the hard curb, and he feels the bridle less that yields himself to harness. More bitterly far and fiercely are the unwilling assailed by Love than those who own their servitude" (*Amores* 1:2, lines 15–18).[18]

Intriguingly, the allegorizing of human erotic activity as a human-beast confrontation or as a highly sexualized half-human beast is often accompanied by or conflated with the image of the hermaph-rodite. The hooved or horned erotic beast is, in fact, associated in classical myth, as it later would be in Shakespeare's plays, with the submission of the gendered individual to a double-gendered (and thus genderless) whole, representing sexual relationship *between* individuals. The fusion of separated identities figured by the androgyne is also represented by the stories collected in Ovid's *Metamorphoses* of a (usually) divine amorous beast and a human lover who alternately assume the powerful position of "rider." In the Europa myth, the maiden Europa first rides the bull Zeus before being sexually "ridden" by him. The myth of Io also baffles the image of Zeus as potent male beast, as the amorous god transforms, not himself, but the woman Io to a hooved animal.[19]

The link between gender confusion and the hooved beast emerges more subtly in the myth of Hercules as recounted in Ovid's *Heroides*. Here, Hercules' donning of his lover Omphale's garments curiously reminds his wife Deianira of a savage encounter between female horses and men. Deianira first makes a scornful remark: "You have not shrunk from binding your shaggy hair with a woman's turban. . . . And for you to disgrace yourself by wearing the Maeonian zone, like a wanton girl—feel you no shame for that?" Then comes the odd question, "Did there come to your mind no image of savage Diomede, fiercely feeding his mares on human meat?" (9:55–72).[20] These lines express a jealous woman's scorn for behavior that she regards as degrading to her husband's character. The Omphale episode, however, is in fact central to the myth that *creates* Hercules' character. It is mythically appropriate that the image of the super-masculine Hercules should be bound to the revelation of his androgynous potential, and that the episode that reveals this potential should describe the superman's erotic experience. In myth, the androgyne's gender-transgressive behavior is validated by the erotic context that inspires it, as well as by related images and symbols that deepen its meaning. The Hercules myth, which includes the tale of Hercules' tutoring by beast-human centaurs, his temporary gender switch with Omphale, and (in Ovid) his wife's confused mingling of images of his transvestism and Diomede's mares, creates an archetype for the consummately powerful male, whose selfhood paradoxically includes his potential for "beastly" erotic androgyny.

Androgyny and the erotic beast merge again in the Greek Orphic mystery religions, which involve the worship of the Egyptian goddess Isis and which date back to the first several centuries A.D. The Orphic hymns are consecrated to a bisexual creative force that "bellows like a bull" (Hymn no. 6, "To Protogonos") and is like the "bull-horned Moon" (Hymn no. 9, "To the Moon"). Although the hymns perpetuate the moon's mythic association with women (arising from the obvious fact that women, like the visible moon, undergo a monthly cycle of physical change), the hymns' references to the new moon's "bull-horned" aspect invoke the lunar symbol's equally ancient masculine gendering, emphasizing both sexes' involvement in the erotic process. Further references tie another hooved beast to the image of the androgynous moon: the fertile lunar force is not only "feminine and masculine" but—strangely—a "lover of horses" (Hymn no. 9).

A related instance of what might be called the "beast hermaphrodite" image occurs in the Roman Apuleius's second-century A.D. *Metamorphoses* (an important source for Shakespeare's *Midsummer Night's Dream*).[21] Apuleius creates a myth that combines beast-loving humans, androgyny, and a fertility ritual honoring Isis. His narrator, having been magically transformed into an ass, tells of a lady who "ardently yearned for [his] embraces" "like some asinine Pasiphae" (*asinariae Pasiphae*) (vol. 1, 10:19). His graphic description of their sexual encounter concludes, "[B]y Hercules, I believed that I did not even have enough to fulfill her desire, and that the Minotaur's mother might have had reason to take her pleasure with her mooing paramour" (10:22).[22] To refer to Hercules is, of course, to invoke the paradoxical association between supreme manliness and "feminine" behavior that resides in the Omphale myth; the gender-confounding reference is appropriate to this section of Apuleius's narrative, where the literally asinine narrator and the figuratively asinine woman merge identities in erotic foolishness just as they merge bodies in sexual unity. Apuleius's subsequent description of the participation of his protagonist, now restored to human form, in a procession celebrating Isis recalls the transvestite revels dramatized by Euripides' *Bacchae*:

> And now the prelude to the great procession gradually began to march by, everyone beautifully attired in fancy dress according

to his own choice and desire. One had strapped on a sword-belt and was playing the soldier; another, wearing a tucked-up cloak, was marked by his boots and spears as a huntsman; another, dressed in gilt slippers, a silk dress, and precious ornaments, had fastened a wig of curls to his head, and with a swirling gait was pretending to be a woman. (vol. 2, 11:9)

The association between playacting, transvestism, temporary bestiality, and erotic encounter forged by Apuleius's work calls to mind the merging of identities that occurs in both private and public location of identity in a sexualized community of two or of many. When private identity is displaced by erotic relationship or by communal selfhood, claims to individual ownership of sexual or social roles are overturned. Thus the language of Apuleius's narrative urges an imaginative correspondence between the asinine lovers as their erotic situation comically reverses their roles; unconventionally, the lady is the aggressor, demanding erotic contact, yet rather than riding the ass, she is ridden by it. The special function of the hermaphroditic beast encounter is to keep all identities in this kind of flux, and thus to deny an isolated or stable self to any of the participants. The participants instead derive identity from their shared sexual nature and the inclusion that nature promises in an erotic community. By this mythic antilogic it makes sense that Ovid's amorous speaker in *Amores*, identifying himself as the horse ridden by passion rather than as the passion-horse's rider, should invert the meaning of Plato's *Phaedrus* metaphor; it also makes mythic sense that Euripides' Pentheus, Dionysus's antagonist, should adopt the long-haired look and other feminine attributes of his bull-horned enemy late in *The Bacchae*, presenting an onstage image of their overlapping identities. Ironically, Pentheus's attempt to stable *The Bacchae*'s bull Dionysus only discloses the fluid instability of the sexual energy the androgynous god represents, and that energy's ubiquitous presence. Chained as a bull in one corner, Dionysus reappears as a man at Pentheus's elbow, rejecting not only a single gender role but any stable form or locus (lines 619ff.).

Water is often the medium for this type of unstable (and unstable-able) mythic figure, who dissolves sexual barriers and unites distinct entities into a human whole.[23] (Recall that the bull who destroys Hippolytus rises on a sea-wave.) Greek romances employed shipwrecks and tidal changes as standard plot devices in narratives celebrating separation and reunion by means of water. The bull-horned, masculine-feminine moon is, of course, linked to tidal ebb and flow.

The hermaphroditic aspect of Isis, whom Stevie Davies calls the "most inclusive" goddess, is inseparable from its association with the Nile, from which Isis "collects together the dismembered fragments of her brother-god, Osiris, makes them potent and impregnates herself with the recreated phallus."[24] Thus Osiris, Egyptian god of death, is made the source of new life through the action of flowing water and his wife's revival of his male potency. Greek-Egyptian epitaphs commonly included the blessing "May Isis give you cold water,"[25] indicating the hermaphroditic deity's link to the Nile's life-giving power. Analogously, the myth of Hermaphroditus as told by Ovid places the nymph Salmacis and her young man in "a pool of water crystal clear" (*Metamorphoses* 4:299–300). Here Salmacis "clings as if grown fast" to the boy (line 369) until the gods fuse the pair. They are "no longer two, nor such as to be called, one, woman, and one, man. They seemed neither, and yet both" (lines 371–79). Although Hermaphroditus laments the loss of his individual manhood, significantly, he does not implore the gods to restore it. Instead, he begs that his fate be visited on other men who visit the magic pool, willing the broad dissemination of his problematic androgyny.[26] Hermaphroditus's male-femaleness and his ultimate plea suggest, as does the Hercules-Omphale myth, the human necessity of the gendered individual's surrender, within eros, to his or her own watery dissolution: a paradoxical reduction that is also an enhancement of the self, as it allows the individual dynamically to combine with another self. As Gayle Whittier writes, the androgyne so created is one whose

> body seems . . . in motion, challenging the perceived world of settled objects, replacing stability with progressive activity. . . . That is why many representations of sublime androgyny place the androgyne near a pool or stream of water, fluid, elementally essential, and shapeless.[27]

The doubly sexed life force this androgyne represents is, according to the Orphic Hymns, "Father and mother of all . . . / ever turning the swift stream into an unceasing eddy. / Flowing in all things, circular, ever changing form" (Hymn no. 10, "To Physis"). Like the earlier-discussed descriptions of alternating beast and rider, images of fluid and changeable anatomies are appropriate for the representation of the erotic impulse, which seeks to obliterate the isolating distinctions between differently sexed human selves. In the Orphic Hymns, as in Euripidean tragedy, we see a cluster of such "androgynous" images—

water, sex change, and erotic beastliness (Isis, we recall, is the "lover of horses")—cooperating to represent the creative force of eros.

The most famous articulation of the mythic Greek ideal of fluid "beast androgyny" occurs, not in epic, tragic, or Ovidian poetry, but in the philosophical dialogues. Plato's *Symposium* not only offers a comic version of the hermaphroditic entity later described by Ovid, but is deeply structured so as to baffle and confound the gendered identities of its own characters in a way that bears out the myth. In *The Symposium*, a fictive Aristophanes gives a fanciful account of humanity's hermaphroditic origin, according to which men and women were originally physically unified but were later cut in two by Zeus, who feared the power of these undivided male-female beings.

> Now, since their natural form had been cut in two, each one longed for its own other half, and so they would throw their arms about each other, weaving themselves together, wanting to grow together. . . . Love is born into every human being; it calls back the halves of our original nature together; it tries to make one out of two and heal the wound of human nature. (191B–D)

Plato's image characterizes humans as naturally androgynous, but interprets androgyny not as an individual's self-sufficient display of both sexes' capabilities, but as the effort to create interpersonal relationship, and thus to reconstitute the original healthy hermaphroditic organism. Like the alternating beasts and riders of other erotically charged Greek myths, Plato's comical monsters are naturally mobile and continually shifting top position as they roll around. Their power-sharing is a crucial aspect of their identity, for like Hermaphroditus (who was formed, unconventionally, out of *female* erotic aggression), Plato's androgyne is a fusion of equal beings rather than an individual person with both sexes' characteristics. (The suggestion that relatedness itself rather than heterosexuality is the essential conferrer of human identity is clear from the Platonic myth's inclusion of original homosexual and lesbian as well as heterosexual double-beings [189E].) Humans, according to this androgyny myth, are not separate, but separated.

Thus, beyond a whimsical justification of the sexual act, Plato's two-backed beast embodies a complex vision of two properly joined sexes that, though sundered, retain psychological impressions of their absent halves. Each sex, in other words, contains an element of its opposite that it registers in its yearning for that opposite. (Again, the Confucian yin-yang diagram is a helpful visual register of this dynamic, with the qualification that this diagram represents a heterosexual paradigm.) Erotic yearning both justifies sexual relationship, with all its suggestions of human regenerative and procreative power, and constitutes the primary androgynous condition that makes such relationship possible.

The myth of "Aristophanes" is borne out by the gender confusion intrinsic to *The Symposium*'s subsequent dialogue between Socrates and Diotima. Here Socrates gives up his customary role of teacher/questioner—a definitively masculine role for the Greeks—to the woman Diotima and assumes the student's position. By means of their dialogue, love (in Greek, ἔρως)—the definition of which is the goal of this dialogue—is properly depersonalized and identified not as a beloved being but as an energy that flows between and unites lover and beloved, as well as an energy that unites humans to the divine. Like Hermes, Love is one of the "messengers who shuttle back and forth" between gods and humans, "round[ing] out the whole and bind[ing] fast the all to the all" (202E). Love as this connective intermediary force is personified by Socrates at *The Symposium*'s end; passing a cup of wine back and forth between the tragic poet Agathon and the comic playwright Aristophanes, he tries to convince the writers that their opposing genres require each other: that "the skillful tragic dramatist should also be a comic poet" (223D). The fact that Aristophanes falls asleep and Agathon "also drift[s] off" just when Socrates is "about to clinch his argument" (223D) gives comic life to another of Diotima's arguments about love: that the longed-for union between opposites, once found, "always slips away" (203E). So we need to keep chasing it. The pursuit of one's complement (an action which Diotima calls "Poros"), born of our need ("Penia"), is connective energy, or love (203C–D).

According to Diotima, this connective power is androgynizing, for it makes men as well as women "pregnant" with creative desire. "Pregnancy, reproduction—this is an immortal thing for a mortal animal to do"; it is "in harmony with the divine" (206C–D) and is "what mortals have in place of immortality" (207A). Diotima's emphasis on the androgynizing quality of eros points to the lover's necessary self-immersion in a sea of ongoing life that exceeds his or her terminal being. "It is for the sake of immortality that everything shows this zeal, which is Love" (208B). By fostering human immortality through procreation, love fulfills its intermediary purpose, linking not only male to female, but human to divine.

The androgynous quality of this binding power is again suggested in the image Alcibiades uses to describe Socrates near the end of *The Symposium*'s penultimate chapter. Tiresias-like, Socrates is "pregnant" with wisdom, like the popular Athenian statues of Silenus that, when opened, are seen to be "full of tiny statues of the gods" (215B). Silenus's mythic association with both Dionysus and the hooved beast is worth recalling here. We know fat Silenus as Dionysus's drunken, donkey-riding follower, the key figure in the fertility god's comic entourage. Thus Alcibiades' lines invoke the association between fertility celebrations and comic beast-riding, even as the lines explicitly link human wisdom (Socrates) to the androgynous image of Silenus's "male womb" (to recall the Dionysiac chant from *The Bacchae*). The final events of *The Symposium* further the work's emphasis on androgyny. Reversing Greek custom, the handsome youth Alcibiades defines *himself* as the erotic pursuer of the old, learned Socrates, and defines Socrates as a desirable feminized male (215E–19E).[28] Alcibiades' baffling reversal of expected erotic and gendered identities is consonant with the fluid nature of the mythic androgyne of "Aristophanes," the *Symposium*'s central symbol: a being whose very structure locates identity in a process and a relationship *between* individuals—all pregnant with the creative possibilities intrinsic to such relationship—rather than in the individuals themselves. The various androgynes of the *Symposium* are, in fact, analogous to Hermaphroditus, whose parentage reflects her/his importance as a joiner of individuals through eros rather than as a self in his/her own right. For Hermaphroditus is the offspring of Aphrodite, goddess of love, and Hermes, the messenger, literally the divine go-between.[29] Hermes, in fact, scurries not only between gods and humans, but between the living world and the underworld. Called "Lord of the Dead" in Aeschylus's *Libation Bearers* (line 1)[30] and "Escort of the Dead" in Sophocles' *Oedipus at Colonus* (line 1755), Hermes is the mythic restorer of Persephone (springtime) from Hades to the earth.[31] His name combined with Aphrodite's forms a verbal symbol analogous to the *Symposium*'s whirling androgyne. Both symbols suggest the all-inclusive, relational erotic process by which humans participate in perpetual life.

The mythic androgyne, then, presents a fluid, interactive model for human identity-in-relationship. This vision validates the erotic impulse that generates both "feminine" males and "masculine" females, using androgyny to represent love-yearning, defined by Plato as "our desire to be complete." The mythic androgyne allows both men and women a broad range of human behaviors, presenting overlapping gender characteristics as the demonstration of lovers' felt likeness and shared identity, born of sexual attraction. But the myth does not validate an isolated androgynous identity; instead it presents androgyny as the necessary impulse precipitating relationship. In Greek myth, sexuality *is* androgyny. The androgyne, as the fullest expression of human sexual completeness, embodies humanity, standing for social health and continuity through the agency of eros.

Dialogue, a verbal interchange by which conversation builds alternately and interactively on the words of more than one speaker, is a device deeply fitting for the stage or literary celebration of mythic androgyny. (It is therefore appropriate that Apuleius's celebration of its narrator's erotic adventures and conversion to the worship of androgynous Isis should begin with a dialogue between that narrator and Socrates [vol. 1, 1:1].) Claude Lévi-Strauss identifies myth itself as

> a dialectical structure in which opposed logical positions are stated, the oppositions mediated by a restatement, which again, when its internal structure becomes clear, gives rise to another kind of opposition, which in its turn is mediated or resolved, and so on.[32]

Weaving oppositional views into a larger synthesis, dialectic demonstrates in language the mythic process of androgynous relationship. The alternation of controlling speaking positions central to dialectic parallels the alternation of controlling roles suggested by the cluster of images with which Greek myth expresses erotic unity: the beast and rider, the beast/human, the fluid androgyne. Thus it might be expected that a deviation from the vision of communal identity that the mythic androgyne represents would be framed in language that also resists the equalizing properties of dialogue.

This is, in fact, the case in the rationally skeptical satirical tradition that, as early as the seventh century B.C., began to erect a defensive masculine ethic of individualism in place of the androgynous ethos of relationship. While mythic androgyny locates identity in heterogenous pairings and other forms of community, male-authored satire rejects emotionally based relationship-in-identity, and consequently rejects any "female" component of human selfhood. Satire, in fact, urges a cool distancing from the "feminizing" pull of emotion (emotion is "feminizing" simply because it urges connection with the female, and threatens the replacement of the individual male self with an eroticized identity derived from this connection). Instead, satire bases identity on a detached and rational observation of (rather

than an emotional participation in) the foolish activities of others—
in fact, constructs a vision of others *as* "Others"—and logically tends
to express this vision in a self-contained declamatory or epigrammatic style rather than through interactive dialogue. Satire insists on
the personal difference of the male writer from the group he describes,
a tactic that constructs "manliness" as a guarded verbal self-sufficiency. Thus the declamatory language of the satirist, avoiding effeminate dialectical zig-zag, is "clear, masculine and smooth" (quoting
the dictum of Swift's Brobdingnagian king).[33]

Stylistic and thematic emphases on forthright self-expression, militant defensiveness, scornful detachment from others, and misogyny
are evident in the epigrammatic verses of the seventh-century B.C.
Greek poets Semonides and Archilochus. Both poets use the relatively
simple conversational iambic form rather than the complicated verse
structures of the choral lyric;[34] both also avoid the elaborate metaphorical descriptions found in choral lyrics and in Homeric poetry,
and omit Homeric dialogue. Instead, they construct poems of varying length out of short, pragmatic, self-delivered sentences.
Semonides' long discourses frame detached observations on "the un-
profitable desires" that motivate human striving (no. 2, "The Vanity
of Human Wishes") and on the repulsiveness of women:

> She eats all day, she eats all night, and by the fire
> she eats. . . .
> . . . .
> For women are the biggest single bad thing Zeus
> has made for us; a ball-and-chain; we can't get loose.
> (no. 1, "An Essay on Women")

Many of Archilochus's verses, like Semonides' diatribes, bark out
short declarative sentences to construct a stance of self-removal and
an ethos of attack. "One main thing I understand," Archilochus
tersely states, "to come back with deadly evil at the man who does
me wrong" (no. 33). In other poems, Archilochus adopts a marginal
position from which to observe his fellows, rejecting his own self-
threatening emotional response: "I neither envy nor admire [Gyges],
as / I watch his life and what he does" (no. 6). Ironically, some of
Archilochus's fragmentary lyrics suggest a link between his speaker's
studied indifference and the painful experience of emotional turbu-
lence. The speaker can alternately "lie mournful with desire, / feeble
in bitterness of the pain gods inflicted upon me, / stuck through the

bones with love" (no. 24) and urge himself and others to seek out a
battle rather than "lie down on your bed and cry" (no. 9); to "act
like a man, and put away these feminine tears" (no. 8). Like Semonides' complaining "essay," Archilochus's satiric rejection of things
feminine seems motivated by the hated consciousness of emotional
bondage to the opposite sex. Thus these poets' blunt lines point to
the origin of satiric misogyny in erotic suffering (a connection to be
elaborated in a later chapter). Their resistance to erotic connection
is appropriately framed in a self-contained, nondialectical or "smooth"
verse style.

Antidialectical gestures are apparent even in the work of the later
satirist Aristophanes (the real one, not Plato's fictive persona), who,
as a comic playwright, had to employ dialogue. For example, Aristophanes' *Frogs* caps its dialectical action (involving a *poetomachia*,
or poets' dispute, between Aeschylus and Euripides) with a choral
epode emphasizing the frivolity of such processes, which it terms the
"no-good lazy Socratic dialogue."[35] Aristophanes' published version
of *The Clouds* moves further from the dialectical principle, including
both a written prologue that sets forth the play's moral in advance
of the play's dramatic conversation and a parabasis in which, halting
the play, the author delivers a sixty-line speech upbraiding his audience for their sexual depravity and bad taste in dramatic entertainment, and appeals over their heads to a readership of "men of true
taste" who will better appreciate his work.[36] Thus, like the plays of
some future Renaissance satirists, *The Clouds* offsets its own dialogue with compensatory prose written after the live performance,
delivered by the playwright in his own person and designed to assert
his moral control over the play's dangerous multivocality (including
the vociferousness of a rambunctious and "degenerate" audience).

The "prosaic rather than poetical" "satiric spirit"[37] expressed by
Archilochus, Semonides, and Aristophanes is habitually linked, as in
the above-cited *Clouds* speech, with the writer's refusal to surrender to
what Jonas Barish calls "the anarchy of the sexual instincts."[38] Since
myth depends on and symbolically expresses this erotic "anarchy"
through figures such as the androgyne, satirical skepticism is frequently framed as an attack on myth itself, primarily the androgyny
myths that express the deep correspondence between differently sexed
individuals. *The Clouds*, for example, ridicules not only unorthodox
sexual behaviors but the mystery religions that used androgynous
figures like Isis as symbols of divine unity. Its protagonist's bogus initiation into Socrates' "Thinkery," involving his stripping and ravag-

ing by bedbugs (pp. 60–61), is a careful mockery of the Eleusinian rites later celebrated by Apuleius's *Metamorphoses*. *The Frogs* attacks mythic androgyny by presenting Hercules' lion skin as the symbolic garb of the pansy, Dionysus as a cowardly nincompoop, and Euripides as an impious playwright who worships his own body.[39] Lucian's second-century satirical sketches treat Greek divine hermaphrodism with similar skeptical irreverence. In Lucian's "Zeus Is Indisposed," Poseidon is told by Hermes that the supreme god can't get out of bed because "he's just had a baby." Poseidon, *"roaring with laughter,"* replies cynically, "Do you mean to say he's been a hermaphrodite all these years without our realizing? But there wasn't any sign of pregnancy—his stomach looked perfectly normal. . . . What a splendid chap he is! He can produce babies from every part of his anatomy."[40] In another sketch, "The Pathological Liar," Lucian expresses similar skepticism toward the myths of erotic beastliness, calling the "talk about Zeus transforming himself for erotic purposes into a bull" a story "fascinating to children who still believe in the Bogy-man" (p. 197). Lucian's "Conversations in the Underworld: A Slight Change of Sex," recalling the underworld challenge of *The Frogs* to the Hercules and Dionysus myths, makes Tiresias the focus of its rational skepticism. In this satire a character named Menippus, visiting Hades to conduct "a scientific investigation into the factual basis of mythology," confronts Tiresias with a series of sarcastic questions: "So . . . do tell me which life you enjoyed most, a man's or a woman's? . . . [And] in course of time your uterus disappeared, and your vagina closed up, and your breasts got whisked away, and you developed male genitals and a beard?" To Tiresias's response, "You seem doubtful whether it ever happened at all," Menippus answers, "Oughtn't one to be a little doubtful in such cases, Tiresias? Wouldn't it be rather stupid to take them on trust, without inquiring whether they're actually possible or not? . . . all you so-called soothsayers are the same. You never actually tell us a word of truth" (p. 75).

These comic satiric treatments of myth subvert through omission the symbolic value of mythic androgyny. The satirist's rational approach to knowledge, prioritizing scientific inquiry and empirical proof over physical or spiritual experience, is incompatible with the nonintellectual "sense" of human connectedness to which mythic symbology is consecrated. Aristophanes' and Lucian's treatments of the androgynous gods are examples of what Matthew Hodgart calls the satirist's impulse toward "destruction of the symbol": the satirist "pretends not to understand [an image's] symbolic connotations, and presents with as much realism as possible the thing in itself: the flag is just a piece of cloth."[41] When the image of the androgyne is separated by the satirist from its mythic roots, it becomes simply this "thing in itself": not a multiform, polynomial, fluid symbol of multiple selves, but one single effeminate male or inappropriately aggressive, "manly" female who, so far from figuring communal wholeness, appears as an unhealthy impediment to the productive life of the community.

Given Aristophanic comedy's evident respect for feminine power, it may seem curious to categorize Aristophanes as an enemy of the "masculine" female. But the heroic women in plays such as *Lysistrata* and *Ecclesiasuzae* are not mythically androgynous; they remain fully feminized despite their temporary rebellions against patriarchy. These women do not arm or cross-dress and they conspicuously avoid "masculine" political debate, instead bringing to their governments the arts of weaving, cooking, and grocery shopping. Aristophanes' true androgynes are not "masculine" females, but satirically presented "feminine" males: not only the cowardly Dionysus of *The Frogs,* but *Lysistrata*'s powerless city commissioner, whose authority is symbolically nullified by the women's garb and mock funeral ceremony with which Lysistrata provides him,[42] and *The Clouds*'s lisping, jewelry-wearing Amynias, whom the manly Strepsiades terrorizes with threats of violence (pp. 126–27). Aristophanes' repudiation of mythic androgyny is perhaps best expressed in *Thesmophoriasuzae*, a play that seems initially to promise an expansion of women's social roles, including a validation of female aggressiveness, but which actually culminates in a satiric affirmation of cultural norms defining, limiting, and clearly separating genders. In *Thesmophoriasuzae* Euripides (the habitual butt of Aristophanes' jokes) is called before a jury of Athenian women to answer for slandering the female sex in his plays, but he hires his father-in-law, Mnesilochus, to cross-dress and join the assembly to argue in his behalf. The vehemence of Mnesilochus's defense precipitates his discovery (as in *The Clouds*, stripping is the means of disclosure and humiliation), and the women themselves attack him in language that validates traditional gender distinctions:

> Whence comes this effeminate? . . . What contradictions his life shows! A lyre and a hair-net! A wrestling-school oil flask and a girdle! What could be more contradictory? . . . Do you pretend to be a man? Where is the sign of your manhood, pray? Where is the cloak, the footgear that belong to that sex?[43]

Comically deriding the "contradictions" intrinsic to Mnesilochus's temporary androgyny (in despite of the contradictions intrinsic to their own impersonation by male Athenian actors), these women assert the satirist's characteristic resistance to mythic hermaphrodism in favor of a vision of isolated, stably gendered personhood and sexual difference.

A humorous song from *Lysistrata* inverts the myth of Melanion, pursuer of Atalanta, to create an extreme version of the isolated, stubbornly gendered satiric individual. As the old Athenian men of that play attack the women occupying the Acropolis, they taunt the women with "a simple tale . . . a sterling example of masculine virtue":

> The huntsman bold Melanion
>   was once a harried quarry.
> The women in town tracked him down
>   and badgered him to marry.
>
> Melanion knew the cornered male
> eventually cohabits.
> Assessing the odds, he took to the woods
>   and lived trapping rabbits.
>
> He stuck to the virgin stand, sustained
> by rabbit meat and hate,
> and never returned, but ever remained
>   an alfresco celibate.
>
> Melanion is our ideal;
> his loathing makes us free.
> Our dearest aim is the gemlike flame
>   of his misogyny.
>
> *(Lysistrata, p. 415)*

Ironically, Melanion is a mythic character intimately associated with erotic pursuit, not flight from women; he was the one man successful in catching (and marrying) Atalanta, the swift female racer.[44] *Lysistrata* does not, of course, endorse Melanion's misogyny, but in reversing Melanion's and Atalanta's roles[45] and the erotic intention of their story, it comically foreshadows the intensely misogynistic bent of Roman satire, and also provides an early model for that genre's inversion of the emblems of androgynous erotic connection. These emblems are appropriated instead for the justification of the satirist's social self-marginalization.

Like Aristophanes, the Roman and later Greek satirists drained the Greek mythic androgyny symbols of their irrational significance, using Odysseuses and Amazons as objects of scorn. Horace treats Tiresias and Ulysses as morally corrupt effeminates in a satire wherein Tiresias tells Ulysses he should pimp for his wife: "[F]reely offer / Penelope to Mister Big, volunteer her" (book 2, 5:75–76).[46] In Lucian, Tiresias's hermaphrodism becomes, not access to total human wisdom, but a symbol of transgressive female authority: Tiresias claims he enjoyed being a woman because "women can always boss their husbands around" (Lucian, p. 74). Juvenal inveighs both against such aggressive women, "monstrosities" (*monstra*) who "[wear] a helmet, [abjure their] own sex, and [delight] in feats of strength" (6:286, 251–53),[47] and effeminate Roman males: "One prolongs his eyebrows with some damp soot . . . another . . . ties up his long locks in a gilded net; he is clothed in blue checks, or smooth-faced green. . . . Another holds in his hand a mirror like that carried by the effeminate Otho" (2:93–99). Whereas in myth, the pluralized male-female monster symbolizes creative power and sexual potency, in Juvenal's satire individual sexual monsters are identified with social uselessness and even infertility: the effeminate Romans who pose as "brides" to their lovers "can't conceive, or give birth" (2:137–38), and the aggressive woman of Rome perverts both reason and sexuality, studying seduction rather than philosophy, but ultimately "inducing abortions, / Killing mankind in the womb" (6:596–97). Persius's satire 1 similarly presents gender-transgressors as impediments to procreation, as the women spend time "pig-sticking" rather than having babies and the "soft eunuch takes to matrimony" (lines 23, 22).[48] And Martial criticizes as inappropriately womanly the vain man who doctors himself with hair oil and cosmetics: "Give over, if you have any shame, making a sight of your wretched bald pate: this is wont to be done by women elsewhere, Gargilianus" (book 2, epigram 3).[49]

In *The Power of Satire*, Robert Elliott testifies to the fundamental defensiveness of such taunts, claiming that satire involves both "the will to attack, to do harm, to kill" and the desire "to control one's world."[50] In other words, the satirist's mockery of what he despises is, at bottom, an attempt to control himself: to secure his own integrity against the taint of the abhorred Other. Imitating the Greek model proposed by Archilochus and Semonides, the Roman satirist stands as *vir bonus*, a good and self-sufficient man defending his integrity against the world's feminizing corruptions. Logically, then, the satirist's vision of properly distinct sexes depends on a militant vigilance against any form of gender-blurring—of eliding or obscuring sexual distinctions—and this vigilance resolves itself into an attack on the satirist's sexual opposite. Thus the classical satirists claim for masculine sexuality the characteristic of violent, predatory rapaciousness. Passive (and nonsatirical) men are effeminate; sexually aggressive women are masculine. The only exemplary woman featured in Semonides' "Essay on Women" is she who "alone takes no delight in sitting with the rest / when the conversation's about sex": sexual interest is unfeminine. Martial calls the lesbian Bassa "a nondescript" whose transgression of sexual roles renders her monstrously formless, not so much because she desires women, but because her "portentous lust imitates man" (book 1, epigram 90, p. 85). And in Aristophanes' *Clouds*, the contrast of the masculine Strepsiades with the effeminate Amynias requires, not proof of Strepsiades' heterosexuality, but a demonstration that Strepsiades sees both men and women as sexual prey rather than as cooperative erotic agents. This is apparent when Strepsiades chases Amynias off stage with threats of sexual violence: "*Raising his phallus to the ready*," Strepsiades yells, "Git, dammit, or I'll sunder your rump with my ram!" (p. 127). For satirists such as Martial and Aristophanes, femininity and masculinity are defined not (or not primarily) as heterosexual orientation, but as acquiescence or aggression. This definition supports (in W. Thomas MacCary's words) a "unitary view of sexuality . . . in which there are men and non-men . . . but no women in and of themselves."[51] The abhorred feminine thing is, paradoxically, nothing—there is no real feminine "Other"—for femininity is simply the absence of male behavior; it is that which would passively permit penetration and usurpation. The male is he who usurps, and exists by usurping; if he does not usurp, he will be usurped and feminized. The classical satirist's construction of male identity is inextricably tied to this nightmare of self-loss. And since the mythic androgyne was a validation of the mystical gain inherent in self-loss—perceived by myth as the surrender of the self to a larger identity-in-relationship—the satiric rejection of such shared identity *as* identity involved denying this larger possibility, stripping the androgyne of mythic significance and thus of power by comically reducing it to a particular stage effeminate or humorous monster-woman. Crucial characteristics of the mythic androgyne had, after all, been its freedom from temporal and spatial boundaries and its plurality of names, suggestive of its representation of the possibility of linked identities: Pallas Athene is Minerva and (at times) Mentor and other people, Salmacis and her lover become Hermaphroditus, Dionysus is Bacchus and also Bromius, and Odysseus's aliases are legion. In contrast, the satiric androgyne is temporally, spatially, and socially located—"a female barber sits just at the entrance of the Subura" (Martial book 2, epigram 17, p. 121)—and carefully singled out by one specific name: Amynias, Gargilianus, Basso.

The classical stage and literary conflict between the mythic and the satiric androgyne was complicated by its reinterpretation by Renaissance authors. While the disciples of Aristophanic comedy and Greco-Roman satire tended straightforwardly to reproduce the rather uniform defensiveness and misogyny inherent in those genres, the revived tradition of mythic androgyny assumed a variety of forms, not all of them—despite their praise for "the feminine"—liberating for women. Although some writers were drawn to the vision of ever-circulating, ever-alternating powers-in-relationship suggested by the Orphic Hymns and by the "beast-androgyny" myths, others interpreted the myths and symbols of androgyny in a way that arrogated power and generativity to the male, gendering as female only passive, contemplative virtues.

Stevie Davies has written at length about Renaissance humanism's belief in "the coincidence of opposites and the existence of the whole in the part and the part in the whole,"[52] a vision that depended largely on the recovery of classical androgyny myths. To this end some Renaissance writers invoked the image of Hermes or Mercury, the go-between, to signify various forms of human relationship, often figuring his connective value by presenting him as "bisexual, or able to combine with other gods, as in Herm-Athene, or Herm-Aphrodite."[53] The Egyptian Hermetic tradition, itself influenced by the symbolism of Greek Hermaphroditus and the stylistically androgynous Platonic dialectic, influenced Marsilio Ficino and Pico della Mirandola, whose writings invoked not only Philo's and Origen's interpretations of Genesis but the Hermetic dialogues (named for the legendary Hermes Trismegistus), as well as the Orphic Hymns.[54] The pseudoscience of alchemy, associated with the Hermetic mysteries, used the "*Rebis*," or hermaphrodite, to designate "the apex of transmutation"; Edgar Wind writes of the *Rebis*'s "regular appearance in alchemical books."[55] Plato's myth of the androgyne was also influential, inspiring both iconographic and literary treatments. Many of these treatments of myth, to quote Davies, "put the female principle" of fertility and birth "at the centre."

But Davies also notes that during the Renaissance,

Most women still lived . . . undignified lives. . . . They had no vote, few rights, little choice and minimal education, and mostly died without knowing that divine hermaphroditism was available to be believed in, or that the female mystery religions of the Ancient world and the Greek Pantheon of powerful female goddesses had been disinterred from time and Platonistically reinvented for the edification of the modern world. . . . We have to read the myths of feminised power against the realities of power exerted . . . as it has always been exerted.[56]

It is worth noting (as Davies does not) that the Neoplatonic "reinvention" of classical myths often palliated the myths' images of "powerful goddesses" and, sanctifying a vision of feminine passivity, helped consolidate "the realities of power exerted."

Marsilio Ficino's interpretation of Plato's hermaphrodite myth, for example, validates (as do Philo's and Origen's writings) "bi-sexual" human nature—the existence of "feminine" qualities within the male and vice versa—but does so in a way that, like satire, genders active virtue as male.

Justice is called Bi-Sexual; feminine inasmuch as because of its inherent innocence it does no one any wrong, but masculine inasmuch as it allows no harm to be brought to others. . . . And since it is the function of the male to give and the female to receive . . . the sun, which receives light from none and furnishes it to all, we call Male; the moon, which receives light from the sun and gives it to the elements, we call Bi-Sexual, since it both gives and receives; the earth, since it indeed receives from everything, and gives to nothing, we call female.[57]

Ficino's erasure of the female role both in generation and social contribution is indeed partially derived from the *Symposium*, which includes some lines that suggest that the male's role in procreation is paramount.[58] But Ficino disregards the vision of alternating powers within a relationship implied by the structure and movement of Aristophanes' androgyne, as well as by the shifting "genders" assumed by characters throughout the *Symposium* (not to mention the destabilizing effect exerted by the Platonic dialectic on any one speaker's claim to truth). Ficino's example shows that Renaissance versions of the mythic androgyne could, no less than satirists' androgynes, deny "femininity" creativity and sexual power. Even some Renaissance interpretations of the androgyne myth that offered (in Davies' words) "a high valuation of the feminine and a wish to incorporate and emulate it"[59] identified as feminine only what was passive (albeit wholesomely passive): Ficino speaks of the "relaxed and cooler nature of Woman's passion and her gentle disposition,"[60] while Pico della Mirandola's *Heptaplus* interprets the Orphic Hymns as "designat[ing] by the terms *male* and *female* these two powers in the same substance, one of which is engaged in contemplation while the other rules the body"[61] (a view also expressed in Antonio Beccadelli's *L'Ermafrodito*).[62]

It is difficult to see how an image of feminine passivity could be derived from Orphic lines like "waxing and waning, feminine and masculine, / glittering lover of horses, mother of time, bearer of fruit" (Hymn no. 9, "To the Moon")—which gender the generative or "waxing" powers female—or from the following Orphic hymn of praise:

> resourceful mother of all. . . .
> self-fathered and hence fatherless. . . .
> Father and mother of all, nurturer and nurse,
> you bring swift birth, O blessed one, and a wealth of
> seeds and the fever of seasons are yours
> . . . .
> and, loud-roaring, you rule migh tily over sceptered kings.
> Fearless, all-taming, destined fate, fire-breathing,
> you are life everlasting and immortal providence.
> Since you fashion these things (you are everything)
> You are the all, for you alone do these things
> to bring peace, health, and growth to all.
>
> (Hymn no. 10, "To Physis")

Such interpretations were, however, one means by which Renaissance authors could subordinate the alien values of an ancient culture to the patriarchal norms of Christian Europe, while retaining the powerful pagan myths and symbols.

However, the raw idea expressed by the Orphic Hymns, as well as by original mythic versions of the androgyne—the idea of the robust power available through an enhanced "male-female" identity—was made available to a literate public by some authors, artists, and (in England) royal propagandists, who used images suggesting a creative and connective energy that was dependent on the fusion of sexes. In England, the nation's total symbolic embodiment in a female was stressed through Elizabeth I's occasional appearance in modified masculine garb, as when she allegedly addressed her English troops at Tilbury clad in symbolic armor.[63] The "masculine" political talent suggested by Elizabeth's androgyny was incidental to its real symbolism: her male-female appearance both figured and authenticated her political representation of a heterogenous English population. The image of Elizabeth as political androgyne both inspired and was furthered by Spenser's female knight, Britomart, in book 3 of *The Faerie Queene*; Spenser also re-presents the original Orphic image of the hermaphroditic goddess-queen in his description of the Temple of Venus in book 4. Spenser's Venus "hath both kinds in one, / Both male and female . . . / She syre and mother is her selfe alone" (10:41). A sixteenth-century visual rendering of Plato's hermaphrodite myth suggests, as do the above examples, the shared power available through transsexual union. A medal by the Italian artist Pietro Pomponazzi features a two-faced, double-sexed "beast with two backs" based on Plato's image. Pomponazzi's medal stresses

Medal of Pietro Pomponazzi: DUPLEX GLORIA. By permission of Faber & Faber.

the equality of the two figures: at first glance the male seems posed as a beast of burden, bearing the female on top, but a close look reveals that the female's arms serve as the man's front "legs," and that the female is also poised to flip over and reverse the posture of the "beast." Thus the medal offers an emblem of functional partnership as opposed to solitary self-sufficiency or self-obsession, a theme also represented in the works of numerous sixteenth-century painters' renditions entitled "Narcissus Opposed to Hermaphroditus."[64] The image of Hermaphroditus was, in fact, a popular emblem for the mutuality of marriage, as Jeanne Addison Roberts and Gayle Whittier have noted.[65] Emblems in Barthelemy Aneau's 1552 *Picta Poesis* and Johannes Sambucus's 1564 *Emblemata* each present a joined male-female planted in and growing, treelike, from a natural landscape.[66]

In sponsalia Johannes Ambii Angli & Albae Aoleae D. Arnoldi Medici filiae. Woodcut from Johannes Sambucus's *Emblemata*. Antwerp, 1564. By permission of the Folger Shakespeare Library.

Aneau's *Matrimonii Typus*, also from *Picta Poesis*, presents the herma-phrodite flanked by a human and a satyr, mingling, as does classical myth, the images of the hermaphrodite and the hooved beast-human.

Such image-mingling is fully appropriate to Renaissance revisions of the androgyne myth, since the original myths themselves mingled the hermaphrodite with the horned and hooved beast or beast-human.

Humano Origo et Finis. Woodcut from Barthelemy Aneau's *Picta Poesis ut Pictura Poesis Erit.* Lyons, 1552. By permission of the Folger Shakespeare Library.

Matrimonii Typus. Woodcut from Barthelemy Aneau's *Picta Poesis ut Pictura Poesis Erit.* Lyons, 1552. By permission of the Folger Shakespeare Library.

(And, as Davies writes, "The syncretistic tendency of the Renaissance scholar was not to substitute one image . . . for items in the existing collection . . . but to accumulate as many as possible.")[67] In fact, both the androgyne and the beast-human image are simply different symbols used to represent the phenomenon of shared identity-in-partnership, or relationship. By means of androgyny, men are empowered, beastlike, to undergo submission to a greater power, as when love "caused Hercules. . . . to spin on a rock, sitting among maidens in a woman's apparel" (noted approvingly by Elyot in *The Boke Named the Governor*).[68] Rather than effeminacy, men's "feminized" role-play connotes, in a mythic context, the courage to sacrifice individual will to the claims of a relationship, as the reasoning charioteer curbs his passion-horse in Plato's *Phaedrus*. Philip Sidney's *Arcadia* invests in this celebration of Herculean androgyny, presenting Pyrocles' female disguise as the transformation of "the very essence of the lover into the thing loved, uniting, and [like the Holy Spirit] incorporating it with a secret and inward working."[69] Thus numerous sixteenth-century emblematic and poetic treatments of various androgynous "beasts" managed to convey the equalizing symbolic properties of the mythic androgyne.

The stage offered a particularly charged forum for the representation of the mythic androgyne and its multifarious possibilities. The gender-blurring bafflement intrinsic to the Elizabethan practice of using boy actors for female roles has been amply noted by scholars.[70] Kent Cartwright has also recently described how the shift that sixteenth-century drama underwent from religious didacticism to the staging of "secular subject matter" had analogous baffling effects for theater audiences. Now, rather than articulating specific moral lessons to a listening audience, plays began to urge the spectators' imaginative interaction with the drama and to allow meaning to "derive at least partly from the nature of theatrical experience itself." In a sense, theater became heuristic, as "[f]or perhaps the first time in English drama, a play's meaning [hinged] upon the ambiguity of its acting."[71] This new theater's allowance of "enigmatic" and "playful" figures—figures of speech as well as characters—that challenged the "categories" and "absolutes" of Renaissance moralists[72] made it an almost inevitable home for the mythic androgyne. English playwrights including John Lyly, William Shakespeare, (more rarely) Ben Jonson and Thomas Dekker, and the collaborators Francis Beaumont and John Fletcher exploited the "baffling" capability of the transvestite boy actor by making mythic androgyny a central theme in their plays, suggesting a wealth of possible identities for androgynous, often cross-dressed characters. Shakespeare's stage androgynes, the focus of the next chapter, were deeply invested in the classical join-ture of the mythic androgyne and the erotic beast-human. In *The Taming of the Shrew, A Midsummer Night's Dream, As You Like It,* and *Twelfth Night,* among other comedies, the double-gendered "mon-strousness" of transvestite or otherwise androgynous characters sym-bolized the expansive possibilities of human achievement through identity-in-relationship. Shakespeare's vision of comic androgyny helped inspire Beaumont and Fletcher's *Philaster,* Dekker's *Roaring Girl,* and Jonson's *New Inn,* all of which feature virtuous and pow-erful transvestite characters.

But an earlier inspiration for Shakespeare's complex revisions of the beast-androgyne myths can be found in the work of Shakespeare's predecessor John Lyly, particularly in Lyly's 1583 *Gallathea,* which first staged the classical connection between erotic beastliness and androgyny. As an early demonstration of theatrical tropes that pro-foundly influenced Shakespeare's own androgynous principle, com-ically elaborated over three ensuing decades, *Gallathea* warrants close examination.

Gallathea, based on Ovid's myth of Iphis and Ianthe and the older myth of Andromda, is set in a vaguely English pastoral world, peo-pled with classical deities and a few gods of Lyly's own invention. Lyly's mythological innovations are grounded in the older mythical connection between divine erotic monstrousness, androgyny, sexual fulfillment, and social health. The play's opening dialogue between the maiden Gallathea, garbed as a male to escape a ritual sacrifice, and her father, Tityrus, invokes this paradox. Tityrus's recounting of floods that have ensued when local communities have neglected to re-vere Neptune includes references to monsters and monstrous inun-dation, yet his description of "ships sail[ing] where sheep fed, anchors cast where ploughs go," and "monstrous mermaids" on land only proves tantalizing to Gallathea, who calls the phenomena "sweet mar-vels" (1.2.34, 39–40).[73] Tityrus's immediately subsequent description of the present and impending ritual of virgin sacrifice to Neptune like-wise intrigues Gallathea, who begs for details of the event.

> TIT.   The condition was this, that at
>   every five years' day the fairest
>   and chastest virgin should be
>   brought unto this tree, and here

> being bound . . . is left for a peace offering
> unto Neptune.

GALL.   Dear is the peace that is bought
         with guiltless blood.

TIT.   . . . he sendeth a monster called the
         Agar, against whose coming the
         waters roar, the fowls fly away,
         and the cattle in the field
         for terror shun the banks.

GALL.   And she bound to endure that
         horror?

TIT.   And she bound to endure that horror.

GALL.   Doth this monster devour her?

TIT.   Whether she be devoured of him or conveyed
         to Neptune or drowned between both it is not
         permitted to know and incurreth danger to
         conjecture.

                                         (1.1.47–64)

This curiously elliptical description of the god-maiden encounter is
charged with erotic implications. Gallathea's reference to the "guilt-
less blood" of the virgin suggests violent dismemberment (Hebe, the
virgin later brought to the sacrificial spot, will imagine being torn by
"Agar, thou horrible monster" [5.2.59–64]), but the reference also
suggests the virgin's defloration by Agar or Neptune. The projected
encounter is further eroticized by its hiddenness and by the obliga-
tory silence in which it is shrouded. The Agar, which Fraser and
Rabkin describe as a name derived from "'eagre,'" meaning "the
'bore,' a high tidal wave caused by the rushing of the tide up a nar-
rowing estuary,"[74] adds an obvious phallic suggestion.

Further, this eroticized description's embedment in a dialogue between Tityrus and the theatrically hybridized Gallathea, dressed here
as a boy, begins to conflate the image of monstrous sexual desire and
the image of the hermaphroditic "monster." This conflation is furthered by Tityrus's and Gallathea's lines at the end of the scene, which
explicitly link with Gallathea's transvestism the Ovidian erotic metamorphosis of gods to beasts. "To gain love the gods have taken shapes

of beasts, and to save life art thou coy to take the attire of men?"
Tityrus asks her (1.1.101–3). Gallathea's rejoinder suggests a link between her recoil from the "hateful" male disguise (line 100) and her
revulsion from the image of beastly sexuality: "They were beastly
gods, that lust could make them seem as beasts" (lines 104–5).
Tityrus's ambiguous reply, "In health it is easy to counsel the sick,
but it's hard for the sick to follow wholesome counsel" (1.1.106–7),
though it seems superficially to characterize love/beastliness/herma-
phrodism as sickness (it would be hard for love-crazed gods to follow
your counsel, healthy, nonloving Gallathea), make more dramatic
sense as a complaining aside that characterizes love as health (it is
hard for Gallathea, sick in that she's never experienced love, to follow my wholesome counsel that she take a monstrous shape, like the
love-struck beastly gods). Heard the second way, Tityrus's lines fore-
shadow Gallathea's impending involvement with the play's second
cross-dressed heroine, Phyllida, and celebrate, as does the *Symposium*
speech of "Aristophanes," the *natural* hermaphroditic beastliness of
sexual love.

It is thus both ironic and symbolically appropriate that Gallathea's transvestism, a device designed for her escape from the eroticized encounter with the Agar/Poseidon, becomes the medium for
her amorous encounter with the similarly disguised Phyllida. For
Gallathea presents erotic love, culminating in sexual fulfillment in
marriage, as a natural and inevitable human experience.[75] Peter Saccio
has demonstrated that *Gallathea* argues the futility of defying the
gods: Gallathea and Phyllida flee Poseidon only to meet each other
and fall prey to Eros.[76] I would agree, and would further argue that
Gallathea presents Poseidon, Eros (here Cupid), and even the Agar,
the water-beast, as separate apotheoses of the same force, which is
erotic desire.[77] In other words, not only Eros but Poseidon and his
minister, the Agar, function as Eros in this play. The play's language
and action insist on this conflation, continuing to urge the correspondence between desire, divinity, beastliness, and androgyny, thus
repeating the suggestion of Tityrus's and Gallathea's initial dialogue.
For example, the nymph Eurota claims to have heard of "a beast
called love" (3.1.45); three scenes earlier Cupid himself has appeared
as an androgyne, dressed "*in nymph's apparel*" (2.2). Cupid's transvestism triggers a passionate outburst from Poseidon, which itself
links Cupid's hermaphrodism with that of Gallathea and Phyllida,
and transvestism in general with his own erotic beastliness and planned
disguise:

Do silly shepherds go about to deceive great Neptune, in putting on man's attire upon women, and Cupid, to make sport, deceive them all by using a woman's apparel upon a god? Then, Neptune, that has taken sundry shapes to obtain love, stick not to practice some deceit to show thy deity, and, having often thrust thyself into the shape of beasts to deceive men, be not coy to use the shape of a shepherd to show thyself a god. (2.2.18–26)

The sexual suggestiveness of "thrust" needs no comment; Poseidon's language adumbrates that of Shakespeare's later monster Petruchio, who will "thrust [him]self into [the] maze" of Padua "happily to wive and thrive" (*Taming* 1.2.55, 56).[78] Poseidon here fuses his own eroticism with that of Cupid, Gallathea, and Phyllida, and links sexual desire with the image of the transvestite androgyne.

As water beast-divinities, Poseidon and the Agar are fitting personifications of the force that dissolves gender boundaries and unites separate sexes into a fluid, interactive whole. The classical mythic androgyne's frequent medium and symbolic equivalent is, we recall, a river, sea, stream, or crystal pool such as Salmacis's pond. Attention to the thematic significance of water allows us to perceive how *Gallathea*'s Rafe, Robin, and Dick subplot, which Phyllis Rackin sees as incongruous with Gallathea's and Phyllida's story,[79] actually reinforces the play's prevailing image of boundary dissolution in love. In a sense, water is the medium for all of *Gallathea*'s action: the play begins on the banks of the Humber with descriptions of flood, concerns the appeasement of Neptune, and even involves its rustic clowns' activities and concerns with the action of water. Rafe, Robin, and Dick enter from the sea, bemoaning their recent wreck and near-drowning. But their complaint ends with a song celebrating the power of the ocean and, with bawdy puns, metaphorically representing the land as another "sea" that can be erotically navigated:

> 'Tis brave, my boys, to sail on land,
>   For being well manned,
>   We can cry, "Stand!"

(1.4.103–5)

The subplot proceeds to link its "water" references to the theme of alchemy (alchemy, as noted, was commonly linked in the Renaissance with the hermaphrodite symbol to figure the process of combining unlike elements into a magical whole). The Alchemist's servant whom Rafe encounters defends his craft by invoking the imagery of divine erotic transformation and rain, asking, "Didst thou never hear how Jupiter came in a golden shower to Danae?" (lines 106–7). And in 5.1, Rafe's description of how his astronomer employer "fell backward . . . into a pond" while watching stars (lines 8–9) constitutes a comic reference to water's encroaching, subsuming power, while continuing to develop the symbolic association between water and the alchemical arts. Act 5, scene 1, ends with Rafe's conflation of the image of water and the idea of erotic desire as he tells Robin, "*Venus orta mari*, Venus was born of the sea" (lines 54–55). Thus the subplot adds to *Gallathea*'s overall erotic suggestion, as, in fluid motion, its language and stage action continually combine, recombine, and re-present mythic symbols of connectivity and transformation: water, alchemy, the love-goddess born from the sea. In both *Gallathea*'s subplot and main plot, water is the metaphorical context for transformative erotic power: for the birth of the androgynous erotic beast, itself a metaphor for Gallathea's eventual marriage.

Poseidon's literal transformation of Gallathea or Phyllida (we are not told which) into a man so that their union can occur is, of course, the final element of the symbolism expressing the hermaphroditic character of marriage. As G. K. Hunter writes, Lyly is less "concerned with the integrity of his characters" than Shakespeare, and allows them literal metamorphoses.[80] This phenomenon, however, is merely Lyly's way of allegorically staging the process that Shakespeare's more naturalistic comedies will continue to suggest: the collapse of gender distinctions in the presence of eros.

I have analyzed *Gallathea* at some length in order to disclose the thematic foundation on which Shakespeare's more complex comic uses of beast-androgyny are largely based, as well as to provide what was, next to Shakespeare's works, probably the most faithful dramatic rendering in the Renaissance of mythic androgyny and its relation to the symbols of water and divine beastliness. In Lyly's work, as in Shakespeare's later comedies, the stage androgyne was the symbolic locus of an unbounded erotic power, signifying an impulse to challenge the parameters of gender and to manifest human synergy. It is *Gallathea*'s adaptation of this classical mythic "beast" to the Renaissance stage that, more than anything else, accounts for Shakespeare's sustained interest in the play, noted by both Leah Scragg and Kent Cartwright.[81] Lyly's and Shakespeare's mythic androgynes were, like those of Greek myth, symbols of transcendence, enabling the temporary suspension of the biological illusion of human separateness.

But the revived mythic androgyne of Lyly, Shakespeare, Sidney, Spenser, and others was confronted, as in classical Greece and Rome, with that other androgyne: what Phyllis Rackin calls the "object of ridicule" or "image of monstrous deformity, of social and physical abnormality."[82] In late-sixteenth-century England, this transgressive, abnormal, and impotent stage and literary monster emerged predictably and symmetrically from a militant, masculinist outlook derived largely from classical satire.

Some lines from John Marston's 1599 *The Scourge of Villainy* recall the classical satirist's propensity for deflating mythic images, particularly those that glorify androgyny. Referring to effeminate London "fashion-mongers," Marston's second satire complains that in contemporary English society, "Ganymede is up, and Hebe down."[83] Marston also repudiates the connective, androgynous power of Hermes, using "subtle Hermes" as a symbol of all that is wrong with the world. *The Scourge of Villainy* links the Hermetic spirit with Elizabethan dress styles that threaten to upend social (including gender) hierarchies; it sarcastically invites Hermes to "Advance, depose, do even what thou list" and mocks Hermes' "juggling fist" (satire 5, p. 17). (An anonymous sixteenth-century woodcut details the sartorial phenomena to which Marston objects, and also records this age's particular concern with female cross-dressing: out of the three figures representing social dress distinctions, only the woman wearing the man's hat is targeted as transgressive, through the epithet, "presumptuous woman.")

Subsequent satires in Marston's *Scourge* return doggedly to the mythic images of transvestism/androgyny, upending these so that, like the Hermes symbol, they become signifiers of social sickness:

> Curio, ay me! Thy mistress' Monkey's dead,
> Alas, alas, her pleasure's buried.
> Go, woman's slave, perform his exequies,
> Condole his death in mournful elegies.
> Tut, rather paeans sing Hermaphrodite,
> For that sad death gives life to thy delight.
> Yet Hercules true borne, that imbecility
> Of corrupt nature all apparently
> Appears in him, oh foul indignity,
> I heard him vow himself a slave to Omphale,
> Puling (ay me), o valour's obloquy!
> He that the inmost nooks of hell did know,
> Whose ne'er-craz'd prowess all did over-throw,

A Presumptious Woman

Wherefore gloriest thou in the Valleys: thy Valley floweth away, O rebellious daughter: shee trusted in her treasures, saying, Who shall come vnto me: THy feare and thy pride of thine heart, hath deceiued thee, thou that dwellest in the clefts of the rocke, and keepest the height of the hill: though thou shouldest make thy nest as high as the Eagle, I will bring thee downe from thence, saith the Lorde: Ieremiah: 49: 4: 16: How art thou fallen from heauen, O Lucifer, sonne of the morning: and cut downe to the ground, which didst cast lots vpon the nations: Isaiah: 14: 12: And Pharaoh saide, Who is the Lorde, that I should heare his voice, and let Israel goe, I know not the Lorde, neither will I let Israel goe: Exodus: 5:2: Herode made an oration: And the people saying, the voice of God and not of man: But the Angel of the Lorde smote him, because hee gaue not glory vnto God: Acts: 12:21: 22. 23.

Sixteenth-century woodcut featuring dress styles. By permission of the Folger Shakespeare Library.

Liest streaking brawny limbs in weakening bed,
Perfum'd, smooth comb'd, new glaz'd, fair surphuled. . . .
(Satire 8, pp. 80–82)

True to ancient Archilochan tradition, this satire conflates the idea
of emotional bondage to woman with the idea of sickly androgyny,
reductively employing the Hercules-Omphale myth to emphasize
male degradation (in clear contrast to Elyot's wondering acknowledgment of the power of love evidenced by Hercules' cross-dressing,
noted earlier). Marston's lines lend partial support to Jones and
Stallybrass's bold claim that "'heterosexuality' itself is effeminating
for men" in the Renaissance.[84] This statement is absurd when applied broadly to sixteenth-century England's predominantly heterosexual population, but the proliferation of Marstonian verse during
the late Elizabethan period suggests that at this time, the revived satirical connection between profound sexual attachment and emascula-
tion was at least a popular literary stance.

In a Marstonian vein, satirical Renaissance emblems such as "The
Deceyte of Women" presented man's loss of power to a spouse as a
shameful diminishment to servile beastliness, and depicted the
woman as inappropriately riding the man. Whereas the mythic writer
uses powerful horses, asses, and bulls to enhance the androgyne's
erotic charge and power—as "agents of revelation," to quote Jeanne
Addison Roberts[85]—the satirist uses animals as agents of ridicule.
The satirical beast, like the satirical androgyne, is a metaphor that
degrades its human subject. The Reader's Preface to Thomas Dekker's
1601 play *Satiromastix* provides an example of this negative use of
beast imagery; invoking Aesop, Dekker criticizes rival poet Ben
Jonson, saying, "[T]hou wilt sit as judge of all matters (though for
thy labour thou wear'st Midasses ears, and art *Monstrum horren-
dum*)" (lines 4–6).[86] Again we see the satirical use of the hooved-
beast metaphor, not as a vehicle of erotic power, but as a "scourge":
an instrument of moral condemnation. While the mythic beast/mon-
ster is something more than an individual man or woman, the satiric
beast/monster is considerably less. The mythic beast is semidivine;
the satiric beast is simply half-human.

When Renaissance satire uses the beast or monster image to de-
pict androgynous behavior, the trope is particularly degrading because
satire, unlike myth, does not locate selfhood in erotic relationship.
Thus satiric androgynous beasts never signify the necessary unity of
two (or more) persons, but only the illegitimate effeminization or

Woman Riding Man. From *The Deceyte of Women* (Anon.). London, [1561?]. By permission of the Huntington Library.

masculinization of one. We see the image of the hermaphrodite as a reduced rather than an enhanced human being in Joseph Hall's 1609 translation of a French satirical work, originally titled *Description de l'Isle des Hermaphrodites*, which tells of a dystopian land where lax living has caused the natives to degenerate into double-sexed beings.[87] Although these creatures have two noses and four eyes along with both forms of genitalia, they—unlike Hermaphroditus or Plato's androgyne—lack double souls, or selves. In contrast to the mythic androgyne, who is two-in-one, the Renaissance satiric androgyne is always some such solitary freak, figuring in deformed body, illicit dress, or self-degrading action a diminishment rather than a liberation of human potential.

Thus to Renaissance as to classical moralists, the most absurd human beast was the gender-transgressor. The cultural anxiety regarding shifting gender roles in Renaissance England has been exhaustively discussed by contemporary critics, most of whom focus, as did many Elizabethan moralists, on the danger to fixed gender boundaries posed by the institutionalized transvestism of the playhouse.[88] The derisive pamphlets of English Puritans and other social reformers focused obsessively on the theater's "feminizing" properties: its incitements to lewdness and the blurring of proper sex distinctions that occurred when male actors dressed as women. These writers' attacks on theatrical (and social) cross-dressing and other forms of androgynous behavior derived much of their authority from antiquity. Puritans quoted the biblical command that "The woman shall not wear that which pertaineth unto a man, neither shall a man put on a woman's garment" (Deut. 22:5), but also used the antitheatrical arguments of patristic Roman writers, notably Tertullian and St. Augustine, to bolster their complaints.[89] Like the classical satirists, these church fathers associated gender transgression with pagan myth, and resisted both. Jonas Barish writes of Tertullian's objection to the Roman theater on the partial grounds that it was consecrated to mythic deities.[90] And indeed, the Renaissance attacks on theater, like those of Tertullian, show the influence of the classical satirical (particularly the Juvenalian) tradition that used myth to symbolize social effeminacy. (Juvenal's third satire characterizes Greece as a womanish "nation of play actors," asking, "Could any actor do better when he plays the part of Thais, or of a matron? . . . You would never think that it was a masked actor that was speaking, but a very woman, complete in all her parts" [lines 93–100].) A mocking satirical edge, a Juvenalian antipathy to "feminizing" fashion, and a veneration for classical (old) knowledge is evident in a line with which the Puritan Anthony Munday launches his argument that plays are idolatrous: "This will be counted *new learning* among a great number of my gay countrymen, which bear a sharper smack of Italian devices in their heads, than of English religion in their hearts" (my emphasis).[91] In the focus and manner of their attacks, the antitheatrical diatribes of Munday, Phillip Stubbes, Stephen Gosson, and the later William Prynne exhibit the key features of classical satirical misogyny: defensive scorn for eros, disdain for dialectical encounter, a self-preservative ethic that constructs identity as fixed, immutable, and male, and a concomitant repudiation of plural or fluid identities through the fixing and stripping (what Stephen Greenblatt might call the "evacuating")[92] of the mythic symbol. Ironically, after the banning of verse satire in England in 1599, the comic stage itself began, in the manner of Aristophanes, increasingly (and schizophrenically) to display these satirical features.

Satiric resistance to the androgyne's metaphorical value is primarily evident in the antitheatricalists' refusal to distinguish between "street" transvestism—fashion trends that unsettled traditionally gendered dress distinctions in London society—and the symbolic stage transvestism necessary for the male actors' performances of female roles. For example, Philip Stubbes's 1583 *Anatomy of Abuses* describes stage cross-dressing as just one aspect of the general abhorrent "mingle mangle of apparel in Anglia,"[93] and William Prynne's 1633 *Histriomastix* ("The Player Whipped") conflates in one sentence the abuses of "wanton fashions, face painting . . . long hair" and "amorous pastorals" that require men to play the parts of women (to the accompaniment of "lascivious effeminate music").[94] Elsewhere, Prynne criticizes both the "beastly male-monsters" of the English stage and the "man-women English gallants" who "are metamorphosed into women in their deformed frizzled locks and hair," as well as "our English gentlewomen," who

> are now grown so far past shame, past modesty, grace and nature, as to clip their hair like men with locks and foretops, and to make this whorish cut the very guise and fashion of the times, to the eternal infamy of their sex, their nation, and the great scandal of religion.[95]

Prynne's conflation of female "mannishness" with "whorishness" demonstrates the satirist's customary dual condemnation of androgyny and sexuality, as well as his paranoid projection of lustfulness onto any available object. Music is both "lascivious" and "effeminate" to Prynne; similarly, Anthony Munday's diatribes recoil simultaneously from the female "harlots" in the playhouse audience and the feminized boy actors.[96] These double attacks on effeminacy and sexual licentiousness recall Marston's condemnation of Hercules, emasculated by amorous desire, as well as the Roman satirists' blasts at both effeminate males and sexually aggressive women. To the satirical mind, the erotic engagement that everywhere threatens males *is* femaleness. (As David Leverenz notes, "[T]he language of female contamination [in antitheatrical pamphlets] is associated not just with sexuality but with the overthrow of maleness itself.")[97] Prynne writes of lustful men within and without the theater who, dressing effeminately, "degenerate into women."[98] The classical satirist's nightmare of self-loss reasserts itself in this statement, along with the construction of femaleness as a diminishment or deficiency of maleness. The mannish haircuts that Prynne saw as women's contemporary "guise" were simply costumes covering their nothingness. The pretense to masculine identity constituted by these costumes was, to the Puritan satirical mind, identical with the feminine pretense to any identity at all. Androgyny seen from this defensive standpoint indicated, not fertility and a wealth of human capabilities, but encroaching sterility. (As Laura Levine observes, "[T]he male actor, dressed in women's clothing, seemed to lack an inherent gender, and this seemed to make him monstrous.")[99] From the Puritan's perspective as from the satirist's, femaleness appeared, not as an avenue to enhanced human power through relationship, but as a parasitic drain on self-sufficient male power. In Elizabethan and Jacobean London, femaleness continually threatened to erode men through gender-baffling costumes and erotic lures like music and spectacle. (Munday's "harlots" were, like the transvestite actors, "an object to all men's eyes";[100] much erotic danger lay in the likeness transvestite costume imposed—mythic writers would say "revealed"—between real women and their male counterfeits.) As Jonas Barish writes, the antitheatrical pamphleteers focused "obsessively on sexuality and effeminacy"—linking the two—disclosing a "fearful aversion to anything . . . that might suggest active . . . sexuality, this being equated with femininity, with weakness, with the yielding to feeling, and consequently with the destruction of all assured props and boundaries."[101] The protective masculinist construction of identity thus required that such threatening erotic/androgynous figures be continually mocked, their metaphorical garb stripped away until their inner hollowness became manifest. For such stripping, satire was a necessary tool.

This militant stance against erotic androgyny involved scorn for emotion, which might tempt the writer to imaginative identification with the abominable feminine (or feminized) object. The Renaissance antitheatricalists' rejection of emotion (except, apparently, anger) recalls the stoic detachment of Archilochus; the antitheatrical championing of intellect as an avenue to enlightenment parallels the classical satirists' privileging of scientific investigation as a means to truth. (Recall Lucian's challenge to the Tiresias myth: "Oughtn't one to be a little doubtful in such cases, Tiresias? Wouldn't it be rather stupid to take them on trust, without inquiring whether they're actually possible or not?") The resistance to "trust" in illusion—to that imaginative openness on which the success of theatrical metaphor depends—

demanded withdrawal into individualistic skepticism. This impulse for retreat from social community into private intellect is evident in the works of English satirists who consciously imitated Roman satire, as well as in the Puritan antitheatrical writings. The Puritans' disgust for the depraved London world echoes in the satirist Joseph Hall's lines, "'Mongst all these slurs of discontented strife, / Oh let me lead an academic life."[102] The world-weary disillusionment here expressed is fundamentally misogynistic in that it resists any other than scholarly, intellectual ties, and thus by definition spurns emotional engagement with members of the female sex.[103] The possibility of intellectual ties with women was generally (though not universally) dismissed by Renaissance satirists, as it was by their Roman forebears. Characteristically, these writers regarded educated (or would-be educated) females much as Prynne regarded short-haired gentlewomen: as shallow pretenders to masculinity. George Chapman ridicules women who "speak false Latin, and break Priscian's head,"[104] echoing Juvenal's criticism of female "monstrosities" who [lay] down definitions, and [discourse] on morals, like . . . philosopher[s]" (6:286, 436–37). Implicit in Chapman's and Juvenal's lines is the assumption that scholarship and philosophy are qualitatively masculine pursuits. Yet—ironically—rather than a genuine philosophical openness to inquiry, these "scholastic" satirists' outcry against learned women demonstrates an obsessive need to collect, store, and protect the conventional wisdom that holds such social innovations to be abominable. New knowledge, according to this view, is not knowledge at all. Thus the satirist's scholastic pose necessitates an entrenched resistance to notions or experiences that, if entertained, might dislodge firmly held views. This retentive impulse opposed the threat of what Barish has called "imaginative displacement, adoption of unfamiliar psychic hypotheses, experiments with untried states of feeling"[105]— all the things that erotic androgyny represented.

The discursive modes of Renaissance satirists and antitheatricalists—many of whom, as in classical Rome, were the same people— manifested the guarded mind-set that Barish describes. The antitheatricalists' choice of expository form, like the English satirists' sketches and epigrams, embodied a closed, retentive resistance to what Munday called "new learning," recalling the classical satirist's characteristic resistance to the threatening "openness" of dialectic.

Raman Selden marks the distinction between the Horatian style, which compromises its satirical edge and avoids "direct moral reprehension" through "the interplay of dialogue," and the Juvenalian (similar to the Old Testament) model of biting philippic, noting the preference of Renaissance satirists (despite their frequent citings of Horace) for the Juvenalian mode. English satire, like that of Archilocus and Juvenal, aimed at "'masculine' vigour and intellectual toughness."[106] This toughness demanded not only a resistance to florid speech-figures but to the balanced idea-sharing implied by the dialectical form. Thus the antitheatricalists published their arguments in expository pamphlets or long-winded tomes that vigorously asserted the author's identity against the threatening presence of those who might think otherwise ("This will be accounted new learning among a great number of my gay countrymen"). Analogously, verse satirists such as Joseph Hall, George Chapman, Everard Guilpin, John Marston, and Ben Jonson expressed themselves in epigrams and, for the most part, nondialectical sketches suggesting their intellectual independence from the effeminate world they described. Marston's *Scourge of Villainy* opens with a long poem that, conflating amorousness with effeminacy, rejects "feminine" courtly costume and romantic conversation, condemning "Each satin suit, / Each quaint fashion-monger, whose soul / Rests in his trim gay clothes," and who "Ne'er in his life did other language use, / But *Sweet Lady, fair Mistress, kind heart, dear cos.*" Against the amorous/effeminate language of courtly compliment, Marston, with repeated self-reference, asserts his harsh verbal individualism: "I, Phylo, I, I'll keep an open hall. . . . Gnaw peasants on my scraps of Poesy" (pp. 3, 4). Similarly, lines from Guilpin's 1598 *Skialetheia* demonstrate the English satirist's desire for detachment, born of the connection he sees between verbal ornament, prolonged social interaction, and effeminacy:

> Whose hap shall be to read these peddler rhymes,
> Let them expect no elaborate foolery,
> Such as hermaphroditize these poor times,
> With wicked scald jests, extreme gullery:
> > Bunglers stand long in tink'ring their trim say,
> > I'll only spit my venom, and away.

(epigram 2)[107]

Such stylistic isolationism occasionally caused the satirist to substitute self-questioning for dialogue, presenting the curious appearance of a man talking to himself: "What though the sacred issue of my soul / I here expose to idiots' control?" Marston asks himself in *The Scourge of Villainy*. "What though I bare to lewd Opinion / Lay ope to vulgar profanation / My very Genius [?]" (pp. 64–65). Rhetorical self-questioning, substituting for the dangerous dialectic, expresses the satirist's manly resistance to "lewd Opinion" (characteristically, that phrase simultaneously sexualizes and demonizes the foreign psyche). The satirist's view that hybridized, interactive discourse is hermaphroditic and hence unmanly is similarly evident in some remarks in the *Discoveries* of Ben Jonson (who, despite his lifelong self-association with Horace, proved more at home in a tough Juvenalian satiric context). In *Discoveries*, Jonson first urges a return to "composition manly," which avoids "effeminate phrase" (VIII, 585 & 588, lines 797, 699).[108] Then, using (like Marston) the connective androgynous symbol of Hermes negatively (and substituting the Roman name for the Greek), Jonson complains that now, "Mercury . . . is the President of Language" (VIII, 621, 1883–84).

Finally, the satirical character sketch, derived from classical writers like Juvenal and Martial and popular among late-sixteenth-century English satirists, gave consummate linguistic form to the satirist's view of himself as a concrete entity, guarding his maleness against the threatening encroachments of the feminine or feminized Other. The character sketch fixed its subject, sometimes idealizing, sometimes ridiculing, but always objectifying the living being that it discursively framed.[109] Such sketches commonly constructed the image of an effeminate male or aggressive female, which the author viewed from the detached perspective of an observer, thus avoiding dangerous dialectical contact with the gender transgressor. Jonson's epigram "On Sir Voluptuous Beast" assumes this scornful and detached stance (and also represents the misogynistic conflation of eros with effeminacy, through the "draining" of classical myth). Jonson scornfully observes

> While Beast instructs his fair and innocent wife,
> In the past pleasures of his sensual life,
> Telling the motions of each petticoat,
> And how his Ganymede mov'd, and how his goat.
>
> (8.34.1–4)

When, partly in response to the banning of published satire in 1599, drama became the English satirists' central vehicle, the satirical resistance to the threat of dialectical engagement was problematized. Satire's self-contained masculine ethic pulls against dramatic dialogue's "feminizing" inclusiveness; the comic satirists battled stage dialogue's flow toward equalized identities in various ways. One way was humors comedy's tactic of adapting the character sketch to an onstage speech, delivered by a privileged masculine wit prior to the entrance of an effeminate or virago-like character. The preliminary character sketch fixed and defined the gender transgressor in the audience's imagination prior to the appearance of the transgressive character, invalidating any claims to subjective autonomy he/she might later make. Thus Clerimont in Jonson's *Epicoene* "puts down" the effeminate Amorous La-Foole prior to La-Foole's appearance:

> He is one of the Braveries, though he be none o' the Wits. . . . He does give plays, and suppers, and invites his guests to 'em, aloud, out of his windore, as they ride by in coaches. . . . He is never without a spare banquet, or sweet-meats in his chamber, for their women to alight at. (1.3.29–41)

Dramatic satirists also used spoken or written authorial prologues as a means of defusing the dangerous multivocality inherent in the dramatic form. Most famous are Jonson's prologues (to *Poetaster*, *Volpone*, *Epicoene*, and *The Alchemist*, among other plays); however, prologues were widely used by other comic satirists like Marston (witness the extensive introductory material in Marston's *Malcontent*, as well as the prologues to the anonymous satiric *Parnassus Plays*). The prologue performed for the playwright the same function that the introductory "character" speech performed for the male wits in humors comedy: it secured the authority of the male satirical voice against the competing, feminizing claims of the dialectically involved characters. The tendency of satirical playwrights (most notably Jonson) to promote printed versions of their plays, which could include lengthy authorial dedications and introductions, demonstrates, as did Aristophanes' revised and printed *Clouds*, this impulse to wrest individual control away from a threatening dialogic medium. The printed product suggests its author's privileged distance from theater, a dangerous, active forum that "exists . . . in the face-to-face encounter between speaker and listener, in the community of discourse" (to borrow Roy Liuzza's definition of medieval oral tradition).[109] Printed plays constituted a flight from spoken dialogue; by means of them the Renaissance satirist registered a "removal from the scene" that "investe[d] him with *auctoritas*."[111]

Analysis of the anonymous early-seventeenth-century pamphlets *Hic-Mulier* ("The Man-Woman") and *Haec-Vir* ("The Woman-

Man") reveals an intriguing competition between satirical verbal self-sufficiency and androgynizing dialectic.[112] Both pamphlets appeared in 1620; the first, *Hic-Mulier*, delivers a Juvenalian declamation against transvestite women:

> Since the days of Adam women were never so masculine. . . . You have taken the monstrousness of your deformity in apparel, exchanging the modest attire of the comely hood, cawl, coif, handsome dress or kerchief, to the cloudy ruffianly broad-brimm'd hat, and wanton feather . . . the glory of a fair large hair, to the shame of most ruffianly short locks.

The passage shows the satirical tendency to project licentious sexuality on the most innocent objects (the "wanton feather") and to conflate licentiousness with transgressive hermaphrodism. Further, the author displays customary satirical defensiveness in his demand for the reappearance of visible gender distinctions through the enforcement of sumptuary laws, appropriately rendered militant and gendered male: "Let therefore the powerful statute of apparel but lift up his battle-axe, and crush the offenders in pieces." The word "monster" or "monstrousness" appears six times in the author's description of these "new Hermaphrodites"; at one point he calls the men-women "Mearemaids, or rather Meare-Monsters." His language demonstrates the satirical tendency to subvert the symbols that customarily attend mythic androgyny—half-human beasts, the sea—by scornfully tying them to specific contemporary social ills. These androgynes are not (despite the curious vehemence of the author's attack on them) potent, but empty; they are "neither men, nor women, but just good for nothing." Finally, the writer's expository style, imposing a single-author view on the object of scrutiny, guards against the destabilizing presence of alternative perspectives that might allow the man-woman some agency and power.

In contrast, *Haec-Vir*, which appeared in print soon after *Hic-Mulier*, restores this androgyne to dignity by dialectical means, answering the *Hic-Mulier*'s author's expository diatribe with "a brief Dialogue between *Haec-Vir* the Womanish-Man and *Hic-Mulier* the Man-Woman" (which begins with both characters comically mistaking each other for members of their own sex). While *Haec-Vir* ostensibly reaffirms the gender boundaries prescribed by *Hic-Mulier*, as the man-woman agrees to return to womanliness when the woman-man returns to maleness, the destabilizing properties of its dialectical form subvert this surface agreement, investing the female androgyne with a dangerously volatile creative power. *Haec-Vir*'s female speaker derives mythic potency by associating her costume choices with seasonal change (thus refuting *Hic-Mulier*'s accusations of her unnaturalness): "For what is the world, but a very shop or ware-house of change? Sometimes Winter, sometimes Summer; day and night . . . there is nothing but change. . . . Nature to every thing hath given a singular delight in change. . . . shall only woman . . . be only deprived of this benefit?" After these lines, the woman's sudden attack on the effeminate man's "ruffs," "earrings," and "fans and feathers," as well as her final shrewd reversal, as she claims that women have "preserved (though to [their] own shames) those manly things [men] have forsaken," seems less like authentic conversion to *Hic-Mulier*'s conservative position than a feminine fast-step: a demonstration of Nature's "singular delight in change" and hence a validation of the woman's earlier argument. Thus dialogue, countering satirical exposition, facilitates an argument for the healthy naturalness of a growing culture, and—with some qualifications—links the image of natural cultural change to the fluid androgyne.

Haec-Vir's partial reclamation of the androgyne's potency exists in uneasy balance with its own satiric scorn for the effeminate courtiers who have "abandoned masculinity" through transvestite attire. In a sense this single document, with its inclusion of antithetical viewpoints and the shift it accomplishes from the declamatory to the dialectical mode, condenses and rehearses the Renaissance's long-winded literary and stage confrontation between the satiric and the mythic androgyne.

This confrontation was, however, most fully conducted and elaborated on stage, through the competing genres of Shakespearean and Jonsonian comedy. The classic critical distinction between the Shakespearean and the Jonsonian comic form can, in fact, be said to hinge on these playwrights' antithetical uses of the all-important androgyne. While both Shakespeare and Jonson occasionally experimented with each other's comic perspective and devices, including each other's androgynous types, each playwright was fundamentally drawn to a separate vision of androgyny embodying and representing a distinct classical ethos. Shakespeare's transvestite heroines and feminized male lovers recontextualized the beast-androgyne myths, invoking the mythic beast-androgyne's symbolism of transcendence in a way that challenged contemporary notions of fixed gender distinctions and sexual separateness. Conversely, Jonson's aggressive females and effeminate male social-climbers reiterated classical satirical recoil from the feminine, and from the threat posed by eros to self-sufficient masculine identity.

We may recall that the classical androgyny debate first erupted on an Athenian stage in 405 B.C., by way of Aristophanes' attacks in *The Frogs* on Euripides and eros. It should not be surprising that two thousand years later, as the androgyny dispute was energetically revived and reinterpreted in Elizabethan England, the battle eventually found expression in a second *poetomachia* between the Renaissance theatrical masters. By 1600, the conflicting aims of Shakespearean mythic and Jonsonian satiric androgyny had begun to be registered in a dramatic face-off far more elaborate and extended than *The Frogs*: a staged argument over comic style that formed a crucial part of the late-Elizabethan Theater Wars. It is to an examination of the specific ground of Shakespeare's and Jonson's eventual stage quarrel, the antithetical manifestations of beast-androgyny in their comic works, that we now will turn.

2

Mazes, Water, Dolphins, Beasts:
The Shakespearean Androgyne's
Defiance of Closure

Th'imperious seas breeds monsters. . . .

—*Cymbeline*

For Shakespeare as for the Greeks, the androgyne was a powerful symbol of human synergy. Along with Shakespeare's more obvious "stagings" of androgyny—his numerous cross-dressed female characters, who constitute for their audiences visible images of mythic hermaphrodism—the language and plots of Shakespearean comedy work in various ways to body forth the androgynous principle, or the abstract spirit of potent human connectedness.[1] In nearly all of its stage manifestations, Shakespearean androgyny is, like the love Diotima defines in Plato's *Symposium*, neither self nor Other, but an intermediary force linking the two—a wave oscillating between self and Other, linking the separated entities in powerful relational identity. Shakespearean androgyny is movement, potency, fertility, promise, possibility, and pregnancy; it is, as is eros, the impulse to bond and to procreate.

The transvestite female characters—such as Portia, Viola, Rosalind, and Imogen—who power so many of Shakespeare's comic plots are, of course, central media for the expression of the androgynous principle. Their ability both to catalyze romantic relationships and to baffle conventional gender distinctions by synthesizing seemingly oppositional human attributes has been the appropriate focus of numerous critics.[2] But exclusive attention to the transvestites distracts us from the other dramatic means through which mythic androgyny is asserted in Shakespeare. Specifically, Shakespearean comedy promotes erotic identity-in-relationship through a cluster of visual and verbal images, syntactical devices, dialogic modes, and specific invocations of androgyny myths, all of which combine with plot in ways that unsettle our notions of the characters' and our isolated, stably gendered identities, urging instead an experiential sense of transsexual connectedness. The androgynous principle is essentially unreasonable, defying logic and the rational categories with which we customarily order our lives and ourselves. Its medium is the irrational, often emotional sense of communal identity—again, eros—that Shakespeare provokes through these various dramatic means.

A crucial method by which the comedies dissolve distinctions between gendered selves is what Richard Altick calls "iterative imagery":[3] repeated invocations of key images associated with self-loss, or with the confounding of private identity through relatedness. Building on Lyly's theatrical adaptation of Greek mythic androgyny in *Gallathea*, Shakespeare's comic dialogue further elaborates the Greeks' association between water, the beast or beast-human, and androgyny, complicating the mythic network of symbols with additional images suggesting hermaphroditic connection. In Shakespearean comedy, characters impelled by a yearning to bond with others (what Plato's Aristophanes calls "our desire to be complete") frequently associate their erotic experience with the action of drowning, sailing, or being in some way invaded or surrounded by water; they see themselves as horses or asses, but are unsure whether they ride or are ridden; they experience themselves or others as monsters; in addition, they consciously undertake risk or "hazard" (*The Merchant of Venice* 1.1.151, *All's Well that Ends Well* 2.1.183), and they think they dream or are lost in a maze. Dream, in which the identities of dreamer and dreamed blend and merge, is an appropriate additional metaphor for androgynous erotic engagement. As Thelma Greenfield writes, the dream metaphor "befits the triumphant dazzle of Ovidian metamorphoses" in both Lylyan and Shakespearean theater.[4] Shakespeare also "dazzles" characters and audience by enactments of, or reference to, self-loss in a maze, as when Puck leads the bewildered lovers of *A Midsummer Night's Dream* "Up and down, up and down" through the Athenian wood (3.2.396), or when *The Tempest*'s lost characters "tread" a "maze" (3.3.2), or when Petruchio, arriving in Padua, claims to have "thrust [him]self into this maze, / Happily to wive and thrive as best [he] may" (*The Taming of the Shrew* 1.2.55–56). The suggestion of self-confounding loss conveyed by Petruchio's reference to "maze" recurs later in *Shrew*, where, in the Veronese countryside, Petruchio so baffles Kate with his "hurly" of bizarre behavior (4.1.203) that she "sits as one new risen from a dream" (4.1.186).

The connection between maze (or hurly) and dream becomes clearer if we recall that at the center of the maze in classical myth resides the half-human Minotaur, offspring of the sexual encounter between Pasiphae and the bull.[5] Likewise, at the heart of Shakespeare's amorous characters' mazy, dreamlike bafflement is the beast encounter: the erotically conjoined human identity—what Iago calls "the beast with two backs" (*Othello* 1.1.116–17)—that the comedy requires them to acknowledge as new self. These images—of water, dreams, mazes, horses that change place with their riders, and monsters that are half one thing and half another—seem habitually connected in Shakespeare's imagination.[6] They recur, shuffled and reshuffled, in various associative patterns, emerging repeatedly in support of the erotic bonding action of the comic plots.

In Shakespeare, as in the old Greek romances, a marriage quest or a family reunion is frequently begun by water-crossing; in *The Comedy of Errors*, *The Merchant of Venice*, *Twelfth Night*, *Cymbeline*, *Pericles*, *The Winter's Tale*, and *The Tempest*, for example, protagonists undergo an ocean journey as a crucial (though often unwitting) step toward marriage. A sea voyage signifies the protagonist's openness to risk and availability for erotic transformation: his or her willingness to be penetrated by new experiences and ultimately by an alterior personality. The plot action of sea voyage and romantic encounter is underwritten by verbal reiterations of water images that relate the processes of dissolution and flow to the invasion of private identity by the yearned-for Other. The bonding implied by these metaphors is potentially heterosexual and marital, but may not initially express itself as such; like the *Symposium*'s description of an energy binding "all to all," the Shakespearean androgynous principle points to a universal connective force. Shakespeare defines various forms of human kinship—of "kindness" in the word's earliest sense—as wellsprings of personal identity, liminal steps to the ultimate developmental stage realized in marital relationship.[7] The potential for androgynous sexual interaction is indicated simply by a character's originary involvement in any relationship from which he or she derives a primary sense of self. Thus, in *As You Like It*, Rosalind's androgyny is prefigured by her bond with her cousin Celia, described by Celia in quasi-erotic terms that culminate in the image of Juno's drifting swans:

> We still have slept together,
> Rose at an instant, learn'd, play'd, eat together,

And wheresoe'er we went, like Juno's swans,
Still we went coupled and inseparable.

(AYLI 1.3.73–76)

Similarly, Hermia's recollection of her and Helena's "ancient love" in
A Midsummer Night's Dream, though it lacks specific reference to
the coalescent image of flowing water, uses language that recalls the
erotic picture of pond-dwelling Hermaphroditus (recall Aneau's
emblem in chapter 1): Hermia thinks of herself and Helena as "an union
in partition, / Two lovely berries moulded on one stem; / So with two
seeming bodies, but one heart" (3.2.210–12). Both the relationship's
originary hold on Hermia's imagination and the erotic suggestiveness
of its description suggest her availability for ultimate sexual union
with Lysander, which requires application of the "Hermes" connective ability her name signifies to an "Aphroditic" relationship. Like
Hermia, the Shakespearean androgynous or erotically inclined character is always already related: related in origin and related in destiny.
As in the classical androgyny myths, water provides an appropriate
symbolic medium for the expression of this creature's connective sense
of self and erotic potential.

In *The Comedy of Errors*, Antipholus of Syracuse's androgynous
openness, like Rosalind's, Celia's, Hermia's, and Helena's, is revealed
in his location of selfhood in relational identity with a lost brother
and mother, an attitude that he frames in terms of water flow and the
absence of private boundaries.

I to the world am like a drop of water,
That in the ocean seeks another drop,
Who, falling there to find his fellow forth
(Unseen, inquisitive), confounds himself
So I, to find a mother and a brother,
In quest of them (unhappy), ah, lose myself.

(1.2.35–40)

Similarly, Viola's availability for eventual union with Orsino in
Twelfth Night is adumbrated by her initial yearning for her lost twin,
Antonio, expressed, like Antipholus's complaint, with reference to
moving water. Her response to the news that Antonio may have survived shipwreck, "Tempests are kind and salt waves fresh in love"
(TN 3.4.384), enforces the idea of human kinship and ties it symbolically to the action of sea-change, representing the androgynous
principle of reunion traced by *Twelfth Night* as a whole.

The longing for lost kin is, in fact, a central transformative motivation for numerous Shakespearean comic characters, including Pericles, *The Winter's Tale*'s Leontes, and Imogen's exiled brothers in *Cymbeline* (whose androgynous transformational power is suggested by Posthumus's observation, "[T]heir . . . nobleness could have turned a distaff to a lance" [5.4.33–34]). For nearly all of these characters, however, the yearning for reunion with brothers, children, or siblings is a liminal condition, preliminary to and suggestive of their androgynous availability for procreative sexual connection. In Shakespearean comedy as in classical myth, the most intimate and powerful relational identity suggested by the fluid androgyne is the spiritual and sexual bond between lovers.

This bond is expressed in *The Comedy of Errors*, wherein Adriana's likening of herself and her husband's conjugal unity to a body of water recalls (like Hermia's description of herself and Helena) Salmacis's plea to her lover and the origin of Hermaphroditus in the crystal pool. Calling (the supposed) Antipholus of Ephesus "estranged from [him]self," Adriana explains,

> Thyself I call it, being strange to me,
> That, undividable incorporate,
> Am better than thy dear self's better part.
> Ah, do not tear away thyself from me;
> For know, my love, as easy mayst thou fall
> A drop of water in the breaking gulf,
> And take unmingled thence that drop again
> Without addition or diminishing,
> As take from me thyself and not me too.
>
> (2.2.120–29)

Similarly, Rosalind's description of her love for Orlando in *As You Like It* invokes the imagery of water to defy notions of measured self-containment. She tells Celia that her "affection hath an unknown bottom, like the bay of Portugal" (4.1.207–8); and of Celia's playful reluctance to tell her news of Orlando, Rosalind says, "One inch of delay more is a South-sea of discovery" (3.2.196–97). Florizel's vision of Perdita in *The Winter's Tale*, born of his enchanted attachment to her, recalls Gayle Whittier's description of the fluid androgyne's "body . . . in motion . . . replacing stability with progressive activity": Florizel wishes Perdita "a wave o' th'sea, that [she] might ever do / Nothing but [dance]; move still, still so, / And own no other function" (4.4.141–43). Portia's "eye shall be the stream / And wat'ry death bed" for

Bassanio in *The Merchant of Venice*; Portia's "stream" image further expresses the hermaphroditic, self-confounding bonding impulse framed in her earlier pledge to Bassanio: "One half of me is yours, the other half yours—/ Mine own, I would say; but if mine, then yours, / And so all yours" (3.2.16–18). In *Much Ado about Nothing*, Don Pedro describes Claudio's love for Hero as both "flood" and the "bridge" that will span the flood (1.1.316), conflating in one paradoxical image the suggestion of ruptured (flooded) private identity and the imminent reparation of the gap that now separates the lovers. In *A Midsummer Night's Dream*, the "wat'ry eye" of the moon (3.1.198), "governess of floods" (2.1.103), presides over the play's erotic action. The symbolism of fluid interchange suits *Dream*'s lovers' continual trading of the roles of pursuer and pursued, which (like the interaction between the *Symposium*'s Socrates and Alcibiades) involves symbolic gender switches as well: "[T]he story shall be chang'd: / Apollo flies, and Daphne holds the chase," Helena tells Demetrius (2.1.230–31). In *Twelfth Night*, Sebastian responds to Olivia's love suit with language that conflates the images of flowing water and dream, auguring the impending transformation of their separate selves into a conjugal whole:

> How runs the stream?
> Or am I mad, or else this is a dream.
> Let fancy still my sense in Lethe steep;
> If it be thus to dream, still let me sleep!
>
> (4.1.60–63)

Analogous lines occur in *The Comedy of Errors*, where Antipholus of Syracuse frames his attraction to Luciana in language that conflates images of sea-voyaging and dream: "Am I . . . Sleeping or waking? . . . I'll . . . persever so, / And in this mist at all adventures go" (2.2.-212–16). Kate's energetic presence reminds Petruchio of "the swelling Adriatic seas" (*Shrew* 1.2.74). And so forth. We see a comic conflation of the images of water, dream-transformation, and hermaphrodism in the induction to *The Taming of the Shrew*, when the derelict Christopher Sly, having had his head bathed "in warm distilled waters" (line 48), awakens to a new "wife"—the cross-dressed boy servant with whom the joking lord has provided him—and imagines impending erotic experience with (him)/her in terms of dream. "Am I a lord, and have I such a lady? / Or do I dream? Or have I dream'd till now?" Sly wonders (lines 68–69). Significantly, in departing from the Sly plot with Sly asleep and the joke unresolved, *Shrew* leaves him deep within the action of erotic dream these lines describe, elevating the induction's "sly" suggestion of hermaphroditic encounter from practical joke to mythic suggestion of joined conjugal identities—the central subject of the play proper. Bottom's recollection of his erotic dream which "hath no bottom" (*AMND* 4.1.216), reminiscent of Rosalind's bottomless affection for Orlando, also conflates dream and water images to express the unbounded energies of eros.

Tears and rain are also symbolic indicators of the union of separated selves, or of the yearning for such union. Referring to Miranda's engagement to Ferdinand, Prospero tells Alonso that he has lost his daughter "In this last tempest" (*Tempest* 5.1.153). The tears that accompany Imogen's reunion with Cymbeline and Posthumus are "holy water" (*Cymbeline* 5.5.269); the severed families and lovers of *The Winter's Tale* "[wade] in tears" at their mutual rediscovery in the play's last act (5.5.46). The Countess Rossillion perceives Helena's love for the absent Bertram through Helena's "salt tears" (1.3.171ff.); the countess's phrase conflates the action of weeping with the symbolism of sea-change. In all of these plots, the opening of private selves, necessary for the recognition of an expanded identity-in-relationship with another, is precipitated, facilitated, and symbolically represented by the dissolving action of water, in the form of rain, sea, or floods of tears. Again, the watery medium is the necessary element for the conjoined erotic identity toward which Shakespeare's comic plots flow: an identity that is "androgynous" in that it overrides the distinctions between its gendered participants.

Since androgyny is essentially connective—literally a "medium" —androgyny and androgynizing water are frequently linked to some form of in-betweenness. Transvestite characters imagine themselves as half female and half male, as when Rosalind vows to encase her inner "woman's fear" in a "swashing," "mannish" exterior (*AYLI* 1.3.119–21). Others perceive them as half boys, half men: Viola seems to be "in standing water, between boy and man" (*TN* 11.5.159), and the male-disguised Portia is a "young . . . body" with an "old . . . head" (*MV* 4.1.163–64). Images of dolphins, understood in the Renaissance as amphibious, "halfway" creatures that survived in both water and air, are also commonly linked with erotic action, duplicating the symbolism of sexual jointure resident in visually hermaphroditic characters such as Rosalind, Viola, and Portia. Erotically charged characters are either like dolphins or—in another beast-human image—they ride them. Of the king's cure by Helena in *All's*

Well that Ends Well, Lord Lafew comments, "[Y]our dolphin is not lustier" (2.3.25). The half-human water creature and the dolphin merge in Oberon's reference to an enchanting mermaid seated on a dolphin, whose song he has heard (*AMSND* 2.1.150–51). *Twelfth Night*'s Sebastian, comically fated for marriage with Olivia, survives a shipwreck riding "on the dolphin's back" (1.2.15). That Shakespeare habitually thought of dolphins in erotic terms is perhaps most clearly suggested by Cleopatra's description of Antony in *Antony and Cleopatra*: "His delights / were dolphin-like, they showed his back above / The element they liv'd in" (5.2.88–90).

No discussion of Shakespearean dolphins would be complete without a glance at *Henry V*'s "Prince Dolphin" (2.4.29), despite the fact that he does not fit the erotic paradigm. In fact, the Dolphin's fatuous speech of praise for his "mistress" horse (3.7.44), a "Pegasus" (l. 14) whose trotting sound is "more musical than the pipe of Hermes" (l. 17), parodies the tropes that Shakespeare more sympathetically assigns to his genuine lovers, for whom horses and "Hermias" signify human love. Unlike these amorous characters, the Dolphin proves fatuously obsessed with an real animal. Further, the French Dolphin's contention that his horse can gallop through fire and air (4.2.4), like his boast regarding his own imminent battlefield achievements (3.7.80–81), is merely ironic in light of the ensuing French defeat, which reveals that the horse was really just a horse, and the Dolphin just a big fish.

Henry V, however, does contain a mythic response to the mundane Dolphin, in the person of Henry himself. *Henry V*'s comic denouement is facilitated by Henry's invocation of the horse-emblem of marital unity, which he applies to himself and the French princess Katherine: he would "leap into a wife" as he would "vau[l]t into [his] saddle" [5.2.139, 137]). Through Henry, who completes England's assimilation of France with his own conquest of Katherine, Shakespeare demonstrates the broad communal function of eros (and also mythically justifies England's developing ethos of imperialism). In *1 Henry IV*, the most comic of Shakespeare's histories, Prince Hal is a Dionysus: accompanied by a sack-soused Falstaff/Silenus and inspired by the grape, Hal shows fertile imaginative power and an androgynous ability to represent various English voices and genders, including those of Hotspur and Hotspur's wife. In *1 Henry IV*'s long tavern scene (2.4), Hal first demonstrates his erotic ability to bind distinct experiential realms through his play with Falstaff, as the two trade back and forth the identities of prince and king.[8] Further, Hal's mockery of Hotspur's anti-erotic preference of horse to wife in this scene adumbrates the contrast between Hal/Henry and the powerless Dolphin realized in *Henry V*. Unlike Hotspur, who rejects his Kate for a horse—declaring "[W]hen I am a'horseback I will swear I love thee infinitely" (2.3.101–2)—and unlike the Dolphin, who prefers horse to human mistress, King Henry responds appropriately to both horse and woman. Henry not only invests *his* Kate with erotic beast symbolism but includes marriage and procreation in his vision of nationalistic expansion. "Shall not thou and I . . . compound a boy, half French, half English, that shall go to Constantinople and take the Turk by the beard?" Henry asks Katherine (5.2.206–9); Queen Isabel's subsequent lines represent the "incorporate league" of France and England itself as a love match (5.2.359–66).[9] Henry's ethos of creative communality has temporarily displaced Hotspur's and the Dolphin's stubborn individualism, achieving a temporary comic moment in the bloody history cycle. In his final scene, Henry thus proves mythically amphibious. His political power derives from his ability to imagine communal wholeness in erotic terms, and thus to negotiate and produce in various arenas of experience, including the romantic (and in this arena his lack of facility with conventional love discourse argues his genuine verbal power).

Unlike the history plays, Shakespearean comedy (and some tragedy) uses erotic beast symbolism primarily to define the conjugal realm, treating marital selfhood rather than national identity as a generative center. In the comedies the mythic dolphin's representation of the androgynous assimilation of unlike halves into an erotic whole is analogously registered in references to other "halfway" beasts. The "Pegasus," the Paduan inn in *The Taming of the Shrew* (4.4.5), presents another image of a beast that resides in two elements, this time earth and air (as Prince Dolphin's steed fails to do). A version of the mythic sexualized beast-human appears in the name of the Venetian inn to which Desdemona and Othello elope, "the Saggitary" (*Othello* 1.3.115), and of the Syracusans' lodging house in *The Comedy of Errors*, "the Centaur" (1.2.9). In this same play, Antipholus of Syracuse conflates the metaphor of the watery commingling of erotic identities with the image of the half-human mermaid, beseeching Luciana,

> O, train me not, sweet mermaid, with thy note,
> To drown me in thy [sister's] flood of tears.
> Sing, siren, for thyself, and I will dote;
> Spread o'er the silver waves thy golden hairs,
> And as a [bed] I'll take [them], and there lie,

And in that glorious supposition think
He gains by death that hath such means to die. . . .

(3.2.39–51)

Lovers appear, to others or to themselves, quasi-animalistic; in *Love's Labour's Lost* Katherine calls Boyet "gentle beast" when he offers to kiss her (2.1.222), and in *Much Ado about Nothing* Benedick describes the amorous Claudio as a "calf" born of a sexual encounter between a "strange bull" that, like "Bull Jove, . . . leapt [Claudio's] father's cow" (5.4.50, 48–49). The reference to beastly erotic pairing also emerges in *As You Like It*, where Jaques conflates water and animal imagery in his description of the various romantic couples in Arden (particularly Audrey and Touchstone): "There is sure another flood toward, and these couples are coming to the ark. Here comes a pair of very strange beasts" (*AYLI* 5.4.35–37).

Like Lyly, Shakespeare also frequently uses various declensions of the word "monster" to describe the condition of characters impelled by androgynous yearning for erotic completion. In her transvestite garb the lonely, love-struck Viola is, in her own terms, a "poor monster" (*TN* 2.2.34). *All's Well*'s Helena is "monstrous desperate" to be joined with Bertram (2.1.183–84); both Bertram's initial resistance to her and the fatedness of their eventual union is (paradoxically) suggested by the king's lines to him, "I wonder, sir, [sith] wives are monsters to you, . . . / Yet you desire to marry" (5.3.155–57). In *The Merchant of Venice*, Portia's doting description of Bassanio's courtship blends the erotic imagery of ocean and monstrousness, recalling both classical myth and Lyly's more recent *Gallathea*:

> Now he goes,
> With no less presence, but with much more love,
> Than young Alcides, when he did redeem
> The virgin tribute paid by howling Troy
> To the sea-monster. . . .

(*MV* 3.2.53–57)

And in *The Taming of the Shrew*, Petruchio's impending married state is heralded by his monstrous appearance on his wedding day: wearing a bizarre gallimaufry of garments, accompanied by a ragamuffin servant, and striding a cross-dressed horse—a stallion with a "woman's crupper of velure" (3.2.60–61)—Petruchio presents a hermaphroditic horse/human apparition that Biondello describes as "a monster, a very monster in apparel" (3.2.69–70). Petruchio's monstrous androgyny is suggested not only by his partially transvestite wedding garb, but by other characters' feminizing references to his Kate-like qualities (his servant Curtis calls him "more shrew than she" [4.1.85–86]). Similar gender confusion occurs in *A Midsummer Night's Dream* when, in the Athenian wood, Helena's syntactically unclear sentence confers erotic monstrousness simultaneously on herself and the fleeing Demetrius: "no marvel though Demetrius / Do, as a monster, fly my presence thus" (2.2.96–97). Monstrousness and gender-baffling are again linked later in *Dream* when Bottom, anxious to play the woman's part in Peter Quince's play, gives an example of the "monstrous little voice" with which he will impersonate Thisbe: "'Thisne! Thisne!'" (1.2.52–53). As "feminine" male, Bottom, like Viola, Petruchio, and both Helenas, represents monstrousness as a kind of double personhood (the idea is reiterated by Hermia when, upon waking outside the Athenian wood, she seems to see the previous night's confusion "with parted eye, / When every thing seems double" [5.1.189–90]).

Bottom, in fact, is the chief means by which eros and "double" monstrousness are linked in *Dream*. Like the ass in Apuleius's second-century *Metamorphoses* (whose influence on *A Midsummer Night's Dream* has been noted), the "translated" Bottom is erotically claimed by a woman ("My mistress with a monster is in love," says Puck [3.2.6]). His transformation to an ass is comically celebrated with an apparently consummated "marriage" to Titania (see 3.1.197–201). Moreover, despite William Carroll's contention that Bottom is given an ass *head* merely,[10] not only the graphic eroticism of the Apuleian source but Shakespeare's play itself slyly suggests otherwise, in a way that adds to the events' sexual charge. The rehumanized Bottom's amazed recollection of his "dream"—"Methought I was, and methought I had—but man is but [a patch'd] fool, if he will offer to say what methought I had" (4.1.208–11)—gains erotic significance when we consider that from classical times the ass, as Jan Kott reports, "was credited with the strongest sexual potency and . . . the longest and hardest phallus."[11] But Shakespeare, while thus subtly maintaining the eroticism of Apuleius's tale, departs significantly from the Roman author in that he clearly bestows only partial bestiality on his transformed character (Apuleius's narrator, we recall, was a complete ass). Like that of the other lovers in *Dream* and elsewhere in Shakespeare, Bottom's monstrousness is inextricably tied to his halfway condition, itself a symbolic register of the joining of separate parts that is the erotic process. In one sense, Bottom's desire to play a role in "Ercles' [Hercules'] vein" (1.2.40) has been realized in his comic interlude with Titania. Like Hercules' transvestism, Bottom's head of an ass signifies his ability to depart from an earlier-known identity and embrace a new selfhood defined by erotic experience with an absolutely different type of person. Thus on several symbolic levels, the half-human Bottom's sexual encounter with Titania assists *Dream*'s general progress toward the creation of hermaphroditic conjugal beings (ultimately, the play will unite or reunite four previously estranged couples). In Shakespearean comedy, halfway monsters symbolize the androgynous erotic unity to which they aspire. Like the intrinsically androgynous humans described in Plato's *Symposium*, Rosalind, Viola, Antonio, Petruchio, Helena, Demetrius, Bottom, and others are pregnant with the possibility of relationship. Their monstrousness both adumbrates and represents their longed-for synthesis.

But despite its relatively constant general valence, Shakespearean comic monstrousness is a volatile metaphor. The androgynous monster consistently represents sexual relatedness, but Shakespeare employs its image in various ways to stress different truths about that relatedness.

One of the crucial aspects of androgynous relationship in both classical myth and comedy is its baffling, often frustrating presence-in-absence. Since eros demands continuous pursuit—demands, paradoxically, to be both practiced and chased— the longed-for coalescence of opposites it regularly offers just as regularly disappears. Shakespeare sometimes expresses love's elusive character by means of plot endings that defer erotic experience, as in *Love's Labor's Lost, Twelfth Night,* and (more comically) *Shrew*'s Christopher Sly plot, where Sly's "lady" avoids his embrace and where Sly himself (like Aristophanes before *Symposium*'s clinching argument) nods off just prior to Petruchio's entrance (1.1.248ff.).[12] Importantly, however, Shakespeare's beast/androgyny tropes do not present eros as *endless* sexual deferral: the horse/rider emblem includes no carrot on a stick. Instead, Shakespeare's play with androgynous images suggests that the experience of achieved eros—of marital partnership, of emotional connection, or of sexual fulfillment—is, to quote the *Symposium*'s Diotima, "always being renewed and in other respects passing away" (207E). Erotic experience is, in other words, a cyclical process involving frustrating search, affectionate embrace, painful self-loss, joyful fulfillment, and states in between, all of which are realized in dynamic activity. Our participation in eros thus involves our ongoing movement *toward* complete relatedness, a condition that is always available but never for long. In Diotima's words, "[A]nything [Need] finds his way to always slips away, and for this reason Love is never completely without resources, nor is he ever rich" (*Symposium* 204A).

A Midsummer Night's Dream's final scenes, which carefully announce and then withhold stories and performances embodying the jointure of opposites, are richly suggestive of the *Symposium*'s conclusions regarding the elusiveness of erotic symbiosis. The dramatic offerings offered to *Dream*'s newlywed couples include a version of potent Hercules' "battle with the Centaurs" sung by an unsexed "Athenian eunuch," but "We'll none of that," says Theseus, nor of the staged "riot of the tipsy Bacchanals," intriguing though these entertainments sound (5.1.44–48). The "Merry and tragical" play we do see (5.1.57) is indeed an instance of union-in-opposition, recalling Socrates' argument at the *Symposium*'s end commending the tragic dramatist who could also write comedy (and, to us, recalling Francis Meres's famous compliment to Shakespeare).[13] But significantly, like the lost conclusion to Socrates' argument, the mechanicals' play's epilogue—"Bottom's Dream," promised in 4.1 (lines 215–16)—is denied us (5.1.355), just as the story of the dream has earlier been withheld from Bottom's friends (4.2.34). The missing "monsters" of *Dream*'s last scenes—the deferred Hercules, centaurs, and eunuch, and the untold tale of "translated" Bottom (3.1.119)—bear witness in their absence to the frustrating "disappearing acts" that eros necessarily performs.

Another of the problematic valences of Shakespeare's erotic beast imagery is the paradoxical comic embrace of the cuckold's risk. Over and over in the comedies, male androgyny is registered in the image of the willing cuckold. In other words, male acceptance of the risk of female sexual betrayal emerges as a necessary aspect of the erotic openness that conjugal identity requires. A characteristic feature of Shakespearean tragedy is its male protagonists' inability to come to terms with the identity of the cuckold: both Hamlet and Othello withdraw completely from erotic relationship in response to the very idea of uncontrolled female sexuality.[14] Comedy requires of its male heroes an antithetical attitude. For comedy to achieve its erotic outcomes—for lovers' identities truly to merge in open, free-flowing erotic relationship—the male subject must give up his intent to control the female body, including its reproductive capability. Thus Shakespearean comedy rejects a satirical mind-set framed twenty-two hundred years before (if not earlier): the paranoid proprietary attitude toward female sexuality. The control that this defensive mind-set characteristically exerts over satiric expression is evident in the following passage from Semonides:

> For where
> there is a woman in the house, no one can ask
> a friend to come and stay with him, and still feel safe.
> Even the wife who appears to be the best-behaved
> turns out to be the one who lets herself go wrong.
> Her husband gawps and doesn't notice; neighbors do,
> and smile to see how still another man gets fooled.
> ("An Essay on Women")

Semonides' lines interpret female sexual infidelity as a threat to homosocially derived masculine status; like Othello, who fears becoming the "fixed figure" of "scorn" as a result of Desdemona's alleged adultery (4.2.54), the satiric speaker dreads the cuckold's loss of his own untarnished image in the eyes of male peers. Unlike the satirist or tragic hero, the Shakespearean comic character must and can forgo his hold on this self-image, as well as his control of that image's biological reproduction through woman. In place of proprietary paranoia, the hero accepts simple participation in erotic activity without obsessive regard to himself. Thus in Shakespeare, the embrace of eros requires the displacement of masculine ego. The erotic celebrant does not seek to impose his own identity on the world; instead, he submits personal identity to an invasive, overriding erotic power. The Shakespearean metaphor for the comic male's necessary sacrifice of ego to eros is his theoretical acceptance of the cuckold's horn.

Mythic comic plot action thus works to overcome the male lover's resistance to an erotic beast that simultaneously represents conjoined erotic identity and the cuckold's risk. *Much Ado*'s Benedick, for example, expresses his initial resistance to marriage in language that merges the image of the cuckold and the erotic bull (as well as the horse):

> The savage bull may [bear the yoke], but if ever the sensible Benedick bear it, pluck off the bull's horns, and set them in my forehead, and let me be vildly painted, and in such great letters as they write "Here is a good horse to hire," let them signify under my sign, "Here you may see Benedick the married man." (1.1.262–68)

The aspect of the cuckold is intimately tied in Benedick's imagination to various manifestations of the mythic beast-hermaphrodite, as this and other passages show; notably, he later frames his fear that Beatrice will somehow steal his masculine identity in terms that re-present the image of transvestite Hercules: "She would have made Hercules have turn'd spit, yea, and have cleft his club to make the fire too" (2.1.252–53). The cleft club, like the cleft horns of the cuckold, suggests the replacement of the phallus by the "cleft" female genitalia, a frightening image that Benedick simultaneously invents and repudiates. But the comic plot overturns Benedick's initial refusal to play the role of feminized Hercules, since his friends' plot to join him to Beatrice—described by Don Pedro as "one of Hercules' labors" (2.1.365)—succeeds. Paradoxically, Benedick's crucial decision late in the play to challenge the slanderous Claudio on Beatrice's behalf—to accept, like Hercules, a female taskmaster, and to act as her surrogate—is presented as Benedick's achievement of genuine manhood. The challenge "is a man's office," Beatrice insists (4.1.266); her claim is borne out by the ensuing action, when a coldly dignified Benedick confronts the rude "fashion-mongering boys," Claudio and Don Pedro (5.1.94ff.). *Much Ado about Nothing* thus radically proposes that the embrace of androgyny is not just the defining task of a lover, but the defining task of a man. In introducing and then inverting Benedick's misogynistic recoil from horn-beasts and Hercules, *Much Ado* dramatizes the comic male protagonist's necessary grasp of the cleft club, which finally represents not castration (as Benedick initially fears) but creative conjugal identity. The cleft club and the horned cuckold simultaneously represent the mature male's conjointure with the female, involving both his acceptance of his inability to control her physical being and his willingness to embrace her deepest commitments as his own. Correspondingly, the mature Shakespearean female accepts the risk of cucqueanery, or male adultery, in pursuit of the larger goal of marital unity. Beatrice may be the only Renaissance heroine who imagines *herself* as horned cuckold, defending her initial brazen resistance to marriage on the grounds that "God sends a curst cow short horns—but to a cow too curst he sends none" (2.1.22–24). The mutuality of risk within eros is underscored by Beatrice's temporary appropriation of the horned cuckold's image and is validated by her final agreement to marry despite the fact that "Men were deceivers ever" (2.3.63).

Other comic characters re-present *Much Ado*'s lovers' peculiarly Elizabethan version of the classical horned/hooved/Herculean erotic beast. In *As You Like It*, Touchstone's decision to marry Audrey is accompanied by his brave approval of the "horn-beasts"—men—he sees in Arden: "Courage!" he tells himself; "As horns are odious, they are necessary." He adds, "So is the forehead of a married man more honorable than the bare brow of a bachelor" (*AYLI* 3.3.50–53, 60–61). The comedies posit an absolute identity between marriage and the cuckold's risk, as does Touchstone in the above lines. In *Love's Labor's Lost*, Boyet's words to the deer- (and dear-) hunting Rosaline identify cuckoldry as an inevitable consequence of marriage: "My lady goes to kill horns, but if thou marry, / Hang me by the neck if horns that year miscarry" (4.1.111–12). And *All's Well that Ends Well*'s Clown describes cuckoldry as an experience unifying all married males: "[Y]oung Charbon the puritan and Old Poysam the papist, howsome'er their hearts are sever'd in religion, their heads are both one: they may jowl horns together like any deer i' th' herd" (1.3.51–55). However, so far from shunning the cuckold's identity or even categorizing it as the special risk of a specific married population, *As You Like It*, *Love's Labor's*, and *All's Well* present and even glorify cuckoldry as an inevitable aspect of manhood—of conjugal manhood, which, in these plays as in *Much Ado*, is the only truly appropriate masculine identity.[15] Thus the foresters' song in *As You Like It*'s fourth act ennobles the cuckold beast, turning his horns into a symbol of the erotic procreative life force:

> Take thou no scorn to wear the horn,
> It was a crest ere thou wast born,
> Thy father's father wore it,
> And thy father bore it.
> The horn, the horn, the lusty horn
> Is not a thing to laugh to scorn.
>
> (4.2.13–18)

The lines parallel Benedick's joking acknowledgment at *Much Ado*'s close that "There is no staff more reverent than one tipp'd with horn" (5.4.123–24).

Thus agreement to wear the "reverent" cuckold's horn allows the lover access to the divinity intrinsic to eros. *Much Ado* conflates the image of the horned cuckold with that of the potent bull Zeus in Claudio's lines to Benedick regarding Benedick's imminent marriage:

> Tush, fear not, man, we'll tip thy horns with gold,
> And all Europe shall rejoice at thee,

> As once Europa did at lusty Jove,
> When he would play the noble beast in love.
>
> (5.4.44–47)

Similarly, some lines in *The Merry Wives of Windsor* paradoxically merge the absurd image of the cuckold with references to potent Zeus and to the powerful stag Actaeon, another transformed erotic beast from classical myth (see 3.2.42–43 and 5.5.1–15). In *Merry Wives* as a whole Shakespeare presents an uncharacteristically satirical vision of the androgynous beast encounter, reducing or "draining" these mythic symbols in a manner more typical of Renaissance humors comedy than of mythic theater. Indeed, in a later chapter I will discuss *Merry Wives* as a curious (and unrepeated) experiment with the developing humors genre. However, the very juxtaposition that *Merry Wives* creates between the images of horned Zeus, powerful Actaeon, and the cuckold, however satirical, suggests, as do Claudio's lines in *Much Ado*, the proximity of these mythic figures in Shakespeare's imagination. Shakespeare's associations between the cuckold, bull Zeus, and potent Actaeon characteristically achieve another synthesis of unlike opposites in the service of eros: another demonstration of the androgynous unifying principle, with its paradoxical conferral of human immortality.

The cuckoldry obsession is not, I would argue, fundamentally misogynistic, although the plays' near-obsessive concern with possible *female* sexual betrayal tempts us to see it this way. The male cuckoldry anxiety emerges legitimately and appropriately from Shakespeare's position as a male playwright, who naturally identifies most closely with the marital anxieties of his male characters.[16] Shakespeare, in fact, takes pains to expose the frequent illogicality and groundlessness of this habitual male terror, playing his anxious Benedicks off against resoundingly virtuous Heros, Beatrices, Rosalinds, and Imogens, whose sexual fidelity defies the pervasive male suspicion of women. But male fear of betrayal, like irrational eros, is nonetheless validated by the comedies as an inescapable psychological component of the conjugal beast. Man's claim to his legitimate androgynous, or marital, identity thus requires him to proceed hand-in-hand with this inescapable human fear.

Along with the willingness to risk betrayal, the Shakespearean beast is used to suggest the necessity of sharing gratification and power in androgynous marriage. Equally significant among the subvalences of the beast-human metaphor is the symbolism of shared or alternating positions and powers within the love relationship (again, a theme suggested by the structure of the *Symposium*'s androgyne, which comically propels itself through alternating use of its eight arms and legs). As in numerous instances of classical myth, Shakespeare invokes metaphors of horses and riders for this purpose, and to express other aspects of sexual relatedness. Riders and horses are used as images of sexual encounter, as in both Ovid's and Apuleius's *Metamorphoses*; to suggest the reasoned control that a contractual partnership exerts on sexual energy, as in Plato's *Phaedrus*; or to impart a sense of the interchangeability of power roles within a healthy, progressive erotic relationship, as in the *Symposium*.

Jeanne Addison Roberts has demonstrated the habitual association that Shakespeare's plays forge between wives and horses. Men throughout the comedies describe their relationships with women in terms of human dominance of, or attempts to dominate, unruly mares. Roberts writes, however, that some Shakespearean comedy criticizes this patriarchal formulation, arguing that *The Taming of the Shrew* specifically rejects "the emblem of female horse and male rider as a proper emblem for marriage."[17] Suggesting the connection between the Latin *equus* and the word "equal," Roberts suggests that "the marital goal of Kate and Petruchio will be, not to ride each other but to ride side by side, in control of their horses"[18]—in other words, to cooperate in controlling their mutual carnal energies, imparting a kind of dual or androgynous character to the Phaedran charioteer. Roberts, in fact, argues that suggestions of marriage as hermaphrodism gradually replace suggestions of marriage as human-beast relationship in *Shrew*, and that this metaphorical shift suggests Kate's and Petruchio's achievement of a mature and dignified sexual partnership.

I would suggest, however, that the imagery of horse and rider in *Shrew* and other comedies is, as in Greek mythology, intimately involved with the image of hermaphrodism in complex ways that are not fully explained by Roberts's reading of *Shrew*. Roberts suggests an evolutionary process by which more sophisticated human emblems of marriage replace the grosser, inappropriate animal images. But in fact, *Shrew* and other Shakespearean comedies replicate, complicate, and ceaselessly reshuffle the full set of mythic relational symbols, which includes, but does not end with, the androgyne. The horse-rider emblem, along with other half-beast figures, is one of these symbols. Thus, rather than introducing and ultimately rejecting the horse-rider image, Shakespeare exploits it, like the mermaid and dolphin images, to represent the shifting power dynamics within marriage, as well as the occasional, inescapable ridiculousness—the *un*-dignified moments—of a healthy erotic relationship. Thus the hermaphrodite accompanies but does not replace the horse-rider and other beast-human symbols: *Shrew*'s final metaphor for Kate's and Petruchio's wedded unity is, after all, the falcon and falconer image they dramatically enact in the play's last scene. Instead of abandoning erotic animals for hermaphrodites, Shakespeare's language, representing the shifting image patterns of Ovid, Plato, Apuleius, Euripides, and the Orphic Hymns, oscillates *between* metaphors of horse/rider, other erotic beasts, and hermaphrodism; the images, like the oscillation itself, express both the intense physical vitality of eros and the circulation of energy within the sexual relationship.

Thus characters who imagine erotic relationship in terms of horse-rider (or ass-rider) connections characteristically generate confusion regarding the identity of the hooved beast, or of the controlling agent in the beast-human partnership. For one thing, women can invert the patriarchal formula, characterizing men as horses. Beatrice calls Claudio and Don Pedro "hobby-horses," and her friend Margaret regenders *both* the animal images Petruchio assigns Kate, calling for "a hawk, a horse, or a husband" (*MAAN* 3.1.73, 3.4.55); also, *The Merchant of Venice*'s Portia describes her Neapolitan suitor as "a colt indeed, for he doth nothing but talk of his horse" (1.2.40–41). Further, amorous males can represent other amorous or married men or even themselves as horses, asses, or both. Although the tragic protagonist's ultimate resistance to androgynous conjugal identity has been noted, *Othello* provides us with a clear example of Shakespeare's imaginative correspondence between male horses and erotic encounter: Iago's description of Othello and Desdemona as "the beast with two backs" is linked with the image of Othello as powerful stallion, or "Barbary horse" (1.1.116–17, 111–12). A comic version of Iago's image emerges in Benedick's fantasy of his married self as "a good horse to hire" (*MAAN* 1.1.266). In *A Midsummer Night's Dream*, Puck says, "The man shall have his mare" (3.2.463), but it is the male Bottom who is most conspicuously rendered a hooved beast in that play, and it is Bottom who rightly concludes, "Man is but an ass" (4.2.206). In *The Comedy of Errors*, as in *A Midsummer Night's Dream*, the married male is the beast; Syracusan Dromio's newfound "wife" exerts on him "such claims as you would lay to your horse, and she would have me as a beast" (3.2.84–86). Both Bottom's appetite for hay and his erotic experiences are prefigured by Dromio's additional complaint, "she rides me, and I long for grass" (2.2.200). And Dromio's association between personal bestiality, marriage, and his loss of private, bounded identity is expressed in his observation, "I am an ass, I am a woman's man, and besides myself" (3.2.77–78).

At times, syntactical confusion or a rapidly altering use of the horse image destabilizes the gendering of the image entirely. This ungendering occurs in *Love's Labor's Lost*, when Moth tells Don Armado, "[Y]our love [is] perhaps a hackney" (3.1.32). Moth's metaphor seems simultaneously to refer to the don's passion for Jaquenetta and to Jaquenetta herself. Gendered identities are further confounded later in this passage when a male emissary appropriates the role of the horse, carrying the don's love message to Jaquenetta, a process that Moth describes as "a horse to be embassador for an ass" (lines 51–52). Finally, Moth imagines a doubled erotic hooved messenger beast, telling the don, "[Y]ou must send the ass upon the horse, for he is very slow gaited" (lines 54–55). Moth's comic image inextricably confounds the gendered identities of lover, beloved, and love "embassador"; significantly, in making the doubled equine beast the erotic messenger, the image assigns the monstrous ass-horse the Hermetic, erotically connective role that Shakespeare elsewhere bestows on the transvestite heroine (Viola is the clearest example, although the cross-dressed Julia, like Viola, delivers love letters [*TGV* 4.4.90ff.]). In Shakespearean comedy as a whole, the horse and the androgyne share the common symbolic burden of erotic conductivity.

This erotic "in between" force can manifest itself in verbal exchanges wherein the symbolic value of the horse is rapidly and repeatedly transformed by the dialogic participants. In *Love's Labor's Lost*, Katherine quickly appropriates and makes complimentary Berowne's slighting reference to her "equine" wit:

> PER. Your wit's too hot, it speeds too fast,
> 'twill tire.
>
> KATH. Not till it leave the rider in the mire.
>
> (2.1.119–20)

Dramatizing the process it describes, Katherine's line also anticipates events in the later *Shrew*, where, in a gender reversal, Petruchio's wit engineers Kate's dumping by her horse (4.1.73ff.). Like the earlier Katherine, however, *Shrew*'s Kate proves generally able to assert intermittent control of the horse image through dialogic interplay with Petruchio. In fact, beginning with their initial meeting, dialogue allows

Kate and Petruchio the means continually to pass back and forth the metaphorical ass/horse role in their relationship:

> KATE.   Asses are made to bear, and so are you.
>
> PET.   Women are made to bear, and so are you.
>
> KATE.   No such jade as you, if me you mean.
>
> (2.1.199–201)

This trading of ass/horse insults echoes in Beatrice's and Benedick's repartee in *Much Ado about Nothing*:

> BEAT.   If he have wit enough to keep himself
>   warm, let him bear it for a difference
>   between himself and his horse.
>   . . . .
>
> BEN.   I would my horse had the speed of your
>   tongue.
>   . . . . . .
>
> BEAT.   You always end with a jade's trick. . . .
>
> (1.1.68–70, 140–41, 144)

These shifting interpretations of the horse's symbolism are facilitated by dialogue, the appropriate verbal medium for the expression and formation of the androgynous relation. In Shakespeare, the effect of rapid-fire, punning interchanges like these is (for audiences as well as characters involved in the transformative dialectical process) a condition of dazzlement, analogous and appropriate to the confusing hurly or maze, or the watery dissolution of previously separated personalities into an androgynous whole. Interactive dialogue stages the process of identity recombination necessary to eros, verbally interweaving its creative participants; it is an auditory "image" that re-presents the vision of Plato's split androgyne-halves, who try "weaving themselves together" (*Symposium* 191B). In making stichomythic dialectical exchange the medium for changing manifestations of the erotic horse symbol, Shakespeare compounds the intrinsic symbolism of dialogue, layering and reinforcing the various images suggestive of interactive, androgynous, relational erotic identity.

In *Shrew*, the circulatory exchange of symbolic horse identities begun by Kate's and Petruchio's initial dialogue is furthered by the servant Grumio's report of Kate's fall into the mud on the way to Petruchio's house: "[H]er horse fell, and she under her horse . . . he left her with the horse upon her" (4.1.73–75). From her symbolic imaging as Petruchio's "horse . . . ox . . . ass . . . anything" in the scene immediately preceding (3.2.232), Kate has become the rider, and then the woman paradoxically ridden by the horse (and we recall Petruchio's own close identification with his horse on his way to his and Kate's wedding).

It could, of course, be argued that the unstable(d) horse symbol in both *Much Ado* and *Shrew* suggests the problem to be overcome: that Beatrice's transformation to lover and Kate's to obedient wife are not complete until they accept the subject position of horses with Benedick and Petruchio as benevolent riders, and thus fix the moral emblem. But the plot of *Much Ado* argues otherwise: it is, in fact, Benedick whose moral growth is evidenced by his willingness to accept Beatrice's guidance, expressed through his agreement to confront his erstwhile friend Claudio on the slandered Hero's (and Beatrice's) behalf. And in the subsequent scene where Benedick challenges Claudio, it is Claudio, not Beatrice, who appears horselike to Benedick: "[Y]our wit ambles well," Benedick sarcastically tells him. Rather than locating woman's properly submissive identity in the symbol of the controlled horse, *Much Ado*'s action seems to validate the shifting valences and genders that the horse image variously assumes in the play. Nor does *The Taming of the Shrew* really support the image of the woman as male-dominated horse (in this, though not in all particulars, Roberts and I agree). The synergistic verbal and physical interplay that characterizes Kate's and Petruchio's relationship throughout *Shrew*, as well as the center stage dominance that Kate demonstrates in the play's final scene, suggests that the volatile symbol of the moving horse and rider cannot *be* so stabilized: that its resistance to stasis, like that of the fluid androgyne, is in fact the tenor of the metaphor. Of all Shakespeare's comedies, *The Taming of the Shrew* most fully exploits the value of the interchangeable horse and rider as a symbol of mobile marital energy. But the horse-rider symbol's androgynous suggestion of alternating power exchange between gendered selves periodically emerges alongside analogous erotic symbols throughout the comedies, as we have seen.

William Carroll has asserted that Shakespeare's Ovidianism dictates a "way to marriage, to achieved eros . . . through the monstrous":

that in Shakespeare "love can only . . . be consummated . . . after some trial of the monstrous has been survived, some transformational stage passed through."[19] His assessment runs in tandem with Roberts's perception of the liminality of animal images in *Shrew*. To both Carroll and Roberts, the Ovidian transformations suggested by the horse and other bestial images are necessary degradations that must finally be left behind; e.g., the lovers in *Shrew* must "move through a whole zoo of animal metaphors before they achieve the dignity of a human marriage."[20] I would suggest, however, that the "monstrous" Ovidian animality that Carroll and Roberts perceptively discern in Shakespeare is not (as they argue) a mere preliminary stage or ordeal to prepare lovers for conjugality, but rather the symbolic equivalent of that final stage of erotic fulfillment, as well as the stages in between. The Shakespearean comic beast-monster is analogous to the Platonic androgyne, the "beast with two backs" figuring heterosexual unity, of the kind visually emblematized by Pietro Pomponazzi's sixteenth-century medal. On the Renaissance and particularly the Shakespearean stage, that androgyne realizes the tremendous comic potential implicit in its (and other) beast/human images. Like the mythic dolphin, who breathes water and air, and Pegasus, who treads ground and sky, the stage androgyne performs in both "masculine" and "feminine" behavioral realms, demonstrating a heterogenous talent for the ceaseless negotiation between self and Other that is marriage. The androgynous Shakespearean comic character enacts the skill of which the "mixed" beast is the symbol: the temporary adoption within eros of its Other's psychological position and the resultant inhabiting of that Other's emotional experience. Thus this beast-human, of which the transvestite heroine is the central (though not the exclusive) example, is able in Shakespeare not only to signify transsexual erotic unity, but to function dramatically to bring that unity into being.

The androgynous beast, then, figured and supported by animal imagery as well as transvestite stage incarnations, operates to connect isolated selves, bridging their separated worlds. The androgyne, like Hermes, is a traveling agent, a visitor to exiles, and a forger of erotic relationship through the medium of shared communication. Impelled (at least eventually) by eros, Petruchio shuttles between Verona and Padua. Similarly, Rosalind moves between the court and Arden; her connective role is suggested by her chosen pseudonym "Ganymede" (one of the cupbearers who move back and forth between the Olympian gods). Portia oscillates between Belmont and Venice, Julia between Verona and Milan, Antipholus of Syracuse between Syracuse and Ephesus, and Imogen between London and Wales. Viola is most clearly a Hermes figure, acting as "post" or message-boy between Orsino and Olivia (2.1.284). The fluid, interactive mobility of these erotic agents, exercised most powerfully through their engaging conversation, draws the frustrated, marginalized, and solipsistic individuals whom they visit into the mainstream world, reinvolving them in human relationship. *The Taming of the Shrew*'s Kate, *The Merchant of Venice*'s Antonio, *As You Like It*'s mournful Orlando, *Cymbeline*'s exiled princes, and *Twelfth Night*'s Orsino and Olivia are a few of the initially marginalized, self-obsessed, or simply lonely characters whom the Hermetically inspired androgyne returns to the "full stream of the world" (*AYLI* 3.2.420).

Numerous language and plot devices dramatize the androgyne's Hermetic or connective function, as these "monsters" operate both to symbolize and restore expansive, relational human selfhood. In *Twelfth Night* and *The Comedy of Errors*, the twinning of separated protagonists, like Antipholus's description of himself and his brother as two drops of water, provides an image of the essential sharedness of human identity, reinforcing the androgynous suggestion of the plays as a whole.[21] Whenever she appears, the transvestite female character, the primary expressive medium for Shakespearean androgyny, gives dramatic form to the interpenetration and reunification expressed in the above plays by the imagery of twinning and water. Like bodies of water, which separate families and lovers but paradoxically (since they can be traversed) also connect them, the transvestite character's male garb temporarily separates her from physical relationship with her beloved, but also provides the space for the conversational encounters that begin psychologically to connect them. Symbolic or actual costume in Shakespearean comedy indicates and facilitates psychic transformation, as when Bassanio entreats Gratiano to "put on / [his] boldest suit of mirth" (*MV* 2.2.201–2). Frequently, clothes contain a romantic or sexual charge: to *Cymbeline*'s Imogen, the "mean'st garment / that ever hath but clipt [Posthumus's] body, / is dear[er]" than Cloten in his entirety (2.3.133–34), and Jessica's temporary male disguise in *Merchant* is to Lorenzo a "lovely garnish" (2.6.45). While satire distrusts "effeminate" transvestite garb, Shakespearean mythic comedy invests it with deep erotic significance. Male disguise, conferring a symbolic double-genderedness, is thus essential to the initiation of the new relational identity that the transvestite's cross-dressed body prefigures.

The Shakespearean transvestite thus simultaneously discloses permeable gender barriers and facilitates their crossing by herself and others, allowing men and women to meet in new, erotic, double-gendered relational identities. Nerissa's shocked response to her mistress Portia's suggestion that the two of them cross-dress—"Why, shall we turn to men?"—elicits from Portia a joking response that discloses the deep symbolic correspondence between transvestite garb and erotic marital relationship: "Fie, what a question's that, / If thou wert near a lewd interpreter!" (*MV* 3.4.78–80). Portia (who is, of course, the lewd interpreter) exploits the bawdy Elizabethan valence of "turning to men" (having sex) and conflates it with her own transvestite image, suggesting the erotic significance of her temporary male role. In posing as a lawyer to save her husband's friend Antonio, Portia is in fact "turning to" him: metaphorically assuming Bassanio's identity in order to express and validate their sexual and spiritual bond. We recall that in *Much Ado about Nothing*, Benedick achieves manhood by performing as Beatrice's surrogate in the defense of her friend. *The Merchant of Venice* realizes an analogous paradox, as Portia expresses wifeliness through acting on her husband's behalf, discharging Bassanio's moral obligation to Antonio.

The expression of the hermaphroditic conjugal bond by transvestite characters like Portia has the effect of opening sealed, rigidly gendered spaces between male and female characters. Shakespeare uses transvestite and otherwise androgynous females both to illuminate legitimate "masculine" qualities in their characters—that is, to allow them contexts for fuller, gender-free being—and to provide the same space of possibility for male characters caught in rigid "masculine" roles. That is, female androgynous "monstrousness" becomes a catalyst for male androgyny, which leads to friendship, sharing, and romantic fulfillment (as in *Twelfth Night*, where Viola's male costume, which renders her a "poor monster" [2.2.32], allows Orsino to befriend and know her in a way he cannot know the undisguised Olivia). Female transvestism tends to provoke responsive male androgyny by allowing female characters the chance to practice self-sacrificial service—a necessary marital behavior—as when the disguised Julia and Viola (however unhappily) deliver their beloveds' billet-doux to other women, and Portia the lawyer redeems her husband's friend. Unconventionally, these women serve actively, while their men perform the passive "feminine" roles of hoping and waiting. Thus androgyny allows both sexes to inhabit realms of experience that are properly human but culturally gender-specific. These male and female characters' movements across socially constructed gender barriers into an open human zone make possible their formation of new, friendship-based sexual identities in marriage.

For example, the male-disguised Portia, defeating Shylock in the Venetian court, demonstrates her actual possession of the "male" qualities of courage, authority, and verbal combativeness, while it allows Bassanio, a mere spectator in this scene, the "feminine" experience of helplessness and passivity (see 4.2). Portia's experiment in "maleness" is completed by her ultimate revelation to Bassanio that "Portia was the doctor" (5.1.269): an admission that, besides resolving the comical dispute about the whereabouts of her ring, enforces Bassanio's attention to her ability to play a "male" role better than he. This shared understanding of the fictive nature of certain socially inscribed gender distinctions, born of Portia's and Bassanio's mutual experience of role reversal, is a necessary precondition for Shakespearean marriage; it is an interior character change that survives the lovers' inevitable outward, formal return to traditional sex roles. But it also represents the hermaphroditic condition *of* marriage, where a couple becomes a double-sexed unit. (Portia and Bassanio are, in fact, already married when Portia dons male disguise.)

Rosalind's androgyny in *As You Like It* provides an analogous experience for herself and Orlando. Her assumption of male disguise begins immediately, as does Portia's, to explode gender categories by illuminating stereotypically male behavior as fictive role-play, performable by either sex. "We'll have a swashing and a martial outside, / As many other mannish cowards have / That do outface it with their semblances," Rosalind tells Celia (1.3.120–22), echoing Portia's vow to Nerissa that, garbed as a man, she'll "speak of frays / Like a fine bragging youth, and tell quaint lies" (3.4.68–69). Real male behavior in *As You Like It* is at times amusingly "feminine": pining for Rosalind, Orlando behaves like the "effeminate" and "moonish youth" who Rosalind herself claims to be (3.2.410). Viewed together, the behavior of these androgynous love-monsters elides conventional gender distinctions and demonstrates the lovers' mutual possession of both "masculine" and "feminine" characteristics. Rosalind's transvestism and her and Orlando's words and actions combine to disclose a shared hermaphroditic condition that prefigures and justifies their eventual marriage.

Shakespearean comedies that do not employ the cross-dressing motif frequently generate a sense of human androgyny through dissolving the distinctions between male and female behavioral characteristics. In *Much Ado about Nothing*, Beatrice's feminine vengefulness matches Claudio's masculine outrage at Hero, as Beatrice expresses the violent wish to "eat [Claudio's] heart in the market-place" (4.1.306–7). Beatrice's beastliness is born of hatred, not love; still, it functions to illustrate a correspondence between male and female emotion. Similarly, the metaphor of human desire as beastliness, which William Carroll has carefully traced in A Midsummer Night's Dream exists side-by-side with language and stage action that conflate the behavior of both male and female lovers. Gender swapping is the order (or disorder) of the play: recall Helena's regendering of classical erotic-god-beast in her warning to Demetrius, "Run when you will; the story shall be chang'd / Apollo flies, and Daphne holds the chase" (2.1.230–31). The expansion-through-confusion of mythic gender roles is Dream's informing principle. In Homer's Odyssey, Circe and desire change men to swine; in Dream, eros transforms both men and women to beasts. Not only Demetrius and Lysander but all four of the lovers are virtually interchangeable, variously pursuing one another through the wood and all breaking out in violent argument in 3.2. Their androgynous likeness parallels that of Titania and Oberon, co-supreme rulers whose powers seem equal, as well as that of Theseus and Hippolyta, the soldier duke and the Amazon warrior he "woo'd . . . with [his] sword" (1.1.16). Finally, the hermaphrodism of the plays' lovers is reflected in that of the wood's fairies, who, as Carolyn Heilbrun says of The Tempest's Ariel, "sur[pass] any sexual delineation."[22]

Characters, cross-dressed and otherwise, who are primary conductors of erotic energy frequently use or provoke language that confounds gender distinctions in various ways. Thus these Hermetic characters' very stage presence results in the continual destabilization of fixed gender categories, for their fellow characters and for the audience as well. For example, the powerfully masculine Petruchio describes his verbal powers as "mother wit" (TS 2.1.263). (A more detailed anatomization of the androgynous verbal faculty is given by Love's Labor's Lost's Holofernes, who says that speech is both "begot in the ventricle of memory" and "nourished in the womb of [pia mater]" [4.2.68–69].) Rosalind uses the pronoun "his" to describe alleged feminine "offenses" to Orlando (AYLI 3.2.349): the "evils . . . laid to the charge of women" are "like one another . . . every one fault seeming monstrous till his fellow-fault [comes] to match it" (3.2.352–56). On one level, Rosalind's use of "his" and the male adjective "fellow" to describe the charges against women thrusts these charges back on the misogynistic male who originated them. But on another, mythic level, the passage's verbal double-gendering works with the familiar reference to the "monstrous" to baffle gender distinctions, duplicating Rosalind's own androgynous embodiment of the connective erotic principle. Rosalind's androgynous conversation provides (as she promises) the cure for Orlando's love longing; the description of her role as female physician, like Portia's as doctor of laws and Helena's as the paradoxical "Doctor She" in *All's Well* (2.1.79), presents yet another linguistic reminder of the erotically constituted double-gendered entity.

The image of the viola-da-gamba that Viola's name invokes functions similarly to suggest the harmonious combination of male and female. Early modern drama commonly linked the viola with femininity; for example, Moll Cutpurse plays the viola in Dekker's *Roaring Girl*; Jonson's *Poetaster*, *Volpone*, and *Cynthia's Revels* all feature viola-playing women, and his *Every Man out of His Humor* features a female character named "Sa*violina*" (my emphasis). The viola-da-gamba's shape and the way that it was played (resting between parted knees) resulted in its common Renaissance literary usage as a bawdy metaphor for the female genitalia; thus for an Elizabethan audience Viola's name would have reinforced a sense of her female sexuality. But the image of the viola is inseparable from the suggestion of the bow with which it is played, adding a phallic significance to the fundamentally feminine reference, much like the ambiguous bawdiness evoked by Orsino's reference to Cesario's "small pipe" (throat, or immature penis), which "Is as the maiden's organ" (*TN* 1.4.32–33). Thus Viola's name, like her cross-dressed body, suggests a relational identity in which the sexes may harmoniously converge.

In addition to the verbal confusions resulting from comic characters' regendering of abstract qualities and mythic symbols, and from gender-riddling names and titles such as "Viola" and "Doctor She," the comedies confound gender through their erotic characters' dialectical conversation. As in the trade-off of beast insults in *Shrew* and *Much Ado* previously described, dialogue between Shakespearean lovers frequently functions further to "dazzle" and obliterate their own and the audience's rational sense of gendered human identity, and to replace it with a condition of emotional unity. Petruchio's and Kate's androgynous conjugality is well expressed by the scene late in *Shrew* when, glancing skyward on the Paduan road, they mutually confuse the mythically masculine sun with the feminine moon:

PET.   I say it is the moon.

KATH.   I know it is the moon.

PET.   Nay then you lie; it is the blessed sun.

KATH.   Then God be blest, it [is] the blessed sun. . . . .

(4.5.16–18)

Some dialogue in *Love's Labor's Lost* offers a more explicit androgynous "reading" of the cosmos, as Boyet playfully rejects the sexist gendering of the sun as male. To Moth's recitation of a line of poetry, "'Once to behold with your sun-beamed eyes,'" Boyet responds, "[The women] will not answer to that epithet; / You were best call it 'daughter-beamed eyes'" (5.2.169, 171–72). This dialectical language of gender unsettlement is a verbal constant in the presence of erotic comic characters. We see this, again, in *Shrew*, when Kate's and Petruchio's sun-moon dialogue is immediately followed by their assumed confusion over the sexual identity of their fellow traveler, old Vincentio (4.5.27–49), and in *As You Like It*, when Touchstone tells Celia and Rosalind to "swear by your beards that I am a knave," and they do (1.2.71–74). All of these dialogic elisions of standard male-female distinctions unite with the visual spectacle of the transvestite female to challenge the theater audience's isolation of characters and of themselves in stable, oppositional gender categories.

Not surprisingly, the comedies' location of androgynous synergy in the unstable medium of dialectical exchange imparts a contrary valence to static speech modes that resist imaginative verbal sharing. Shakespearean comedy, in fact, demonstrates and mocks the misogynistic, androgyny-resistant psychic positions and accompanying verbal modes of classical and Renaissance satirists and antitheatricalists. Shakespeare's comedy also confronts and repudiates the limiting, non-dialectical discourse of the Petrarchan lover, which it ingeniously links to the solipsistic thought and language of the scholastic and the satirist.

This mythic commentary on satiric verbal modes is most clearly illustrated in *As You Like It*, and that play's specific confrontation with Jonsonian technique in the Theater Wars of 1599–1601 will be examined in detail in a later chapter. However, commentary on the limitations of what might be called "non-androgynous discourse" is evident in other Shakespearean comedies as well. Characteristically in Shakespeare, resistance to the androgynous principle of erotic conjointure is registered in a comic character's refusal to participate in interactive, transformative conversation with a member of the opposite sex, or with anyone at all. The plays' comic outcomes necessitate either the transformation of this character's verbal mode so that he involves himself in interactive language, thus assuming an expanded androgynous being; or the repudiation of the (usually male) resistant character and the refractory genderedness his speech expresses.

Thus the androgyne's central function as erotic agent is to initiate dialogue that "opens" such closed characters, moving them toward "imaginative displacement, adoption of unfamiliar psychic hypotheses, experiments with untried states of feeling" (to recall Jonas Barish's phrase). In so doing, the androgyne engages himself/herself and the dialectical participant in a process of mutual transformation through psychic discovery of unfamiliar erotic territory. The dialectical encounter begun by *Shrew*'s Petruchio facilitates Kate's experiential "bedazzle[ment]" (4.5.46) such that, loosening her rational grasp of what she personally "knows" to be true ("I know it is the sun that shines so bright" [4.5.5]), she progresses into the irrational experience of shared playfulness with Petruchio ("I know it is the moon" [4.5.16]). Arguably, Petruchio himself is emotionally altered, his "shrewishness" quelled, by his dialectical connection with a now-willing playmate. Although Kate's and Petruchio's relationship is far from socially equal, the play's final scenes demonstrate their emotional and imaginative parity, born of the dialectical "bedazzlement" and psychic connection that Petruchio's conversation initiates.

Other erotic/androgynous agents in Shakespeare begin similar processes of shared psychic transformation through dialogue. In *As You Like It*, Rosalind/Ganymede's conversation exposes both Orlando and Phebe to startling alternative visions of themselves. "[M]y uncle . . . taught me how to know a man in love; . . . you [are] not," she tells Orlando, blasting what their ensuing dialogue will reveal to be his fundamentally false Petrarchan pose. "[M]istress, know yourself . . . ./ you are not for all markets" (3.5.57, 60), she warns Phebe, offering a similar challenge to the conventional romantic speech patterns that trap Phebe in the role of disdainful mistress and Silvius in that of doting lover. Rosalind is a master of the art of interruption. With wholesome rudeness, she advances verbally to destroy all would-be lovers' sterile romantic postures, urging upon them the liberating alternative of progressive erotic connection.[23] Rosalind herself is erotically transformed by the dialogic processes she initiates, which enable her to move from speechless adoration of Orlando into interactive friendship with him.

In *Twelfth Night*, Viola similarly transforms both Olivia's and Orsino's stylized, solipsistic mournfulness and her own through shattering her listeners' static interpretations of themselves with "unfamiliar psychic hypotheses," advanced through conversation. "If I do not usurp myself, I am [the lady of the house]," Olivia greets Viola (1.5.186). Viola counters with a rude paradox: "[Y]ou do usurp yourself; for what is yours to bestow is not yours to reserve" (lines 187–89). Her statement borrows and then inverts Olivia's own phrase to propose to her an unfamiliar, baffling vision of identity that is not privately owned, but erotically shared. And like Olivia's, Viola's own movement into erotic relationship is accomplished through the conversational mode of speech and being that she adopts with both Olivia and Orsino: a mode that, by its very nature, continually introduces to both verbal participants unfamiliar or oppositional perspectives on the self and the self's relationship to others.

Thus dialogue in Shakespeare imitates the manner of the modern therapeutic relationship, which "underscores the intersubjective nature of reality. . . . alert[ing] the participants to discrepant definitions of the situation stemming from different personal histories," in the words of the authors of the recent sociological work, *Habits of the Heart*.[24] But the Shakespearean conversational process, while it may invoke the rational categories of definition and historical account, does not actually transform its speakers by rational means. It transforms through baffling the participants' "reasonable" notions of their psychological separateness. In place of these notions, Shakespeare's comic dialogue provides an interactive *experience* of psychic cooperation that weaves its verbal players together, creating, through affirming, their subrational connectedness.

Those who initially or consistently resist this conversational experience inhabit definable and analogous psychological categories. Academic misogyny, love melancholy, and satiric scorn, as noted, are intermittently associated in Shakespeare's comedies, and are presented as rigid postures of withdrawal from the moving world of interactive conversational engagement. Rosalind, for example, speaks of a fictive Petrarchan suitor's retirement from "the full stream of the world" into "a nook merely monastic" (*AYLI* 3.3.420–21). Her language links the isolating tendencies of the love-struck Orlando, who wanders alone and pins bad poetry on trees (3.2), with those of the satirical

Jaques, who withdraws from the final wedding celebration to an "abandon'd cave" at the play's end (5.4.196). The link between Orlando's love-longing and Jaques's satirical melancholy will be further explored in chapter 5; here it is sufficient to note that by means of these characters' connection, Shakespeare clarifies the distinction between androgynous conversational participation and any form of removal from feminine society. Isolationism, whether erotically or satirically motivated, is intrinsically opposed to the androgynous principle Rosalind represents and performs; androgyny demands expression in the kind of participatory discourse she facilitates.

Love's Labor's Lost presents an early example of the Shakespearean connection between characteristically male patterns of withdrawal (such as satirical or academic detachment) and Petrarchan isolationism. In this play the Navarran lords' misogynistic scholarly project represents, like the behavior of Rosalind's fictional suitor, a "monastic" flight from the feminine: through a three-year retreat from the society of women into books, the men plan to secure their rational male grasp, or control, of the world (1.1). As Berowne knows, the men's withdrawal into reason will constitute a flight from the experiential sense of heterogenous human connectedness, or "common sense" (*LLL* 1.1.57). Appropriately, the legal terms of this academic existence include the proscription of conversation between male and female: "'If any man be seen to talk with a woman within the term of three years, he shall endure . . . public shame'" (*LLL* 1.1.129–31). The men's isolating project, of course, is immediately disrupted by the arrival of the talkative Frenchwomen, which transforms their academic ardor into amorous energy. But the men's ultimate failure progressively to connect with the women is intimately tied to their initial academic motivation and its accompanying resistance to verbal interaction with females. Rosaline, Katherine, the French Princess, and the "androgynous" Hermetic emissaries Moth and Boyet are at home in the dialogic conversational mode that, in Shakespeare, creates erotic connection, but, despite their amorous desire, the Navarrans are not. They consistently withdraw, stymied, after short stichomythic encounters with the women (see, for example, 2.1.180–214 and 5.2.179–241), proving more at home in all-male conversation: in 4.3 they collectively decide to woo the women; when they have difficulty talking to them in 5.2, *"They converse apart"* (l. 238f.). Ultimately, these men indulge their romantic passion, not through active conversational involvement with the objects of their fancy, but through isolated musing and the writing of love poetry—in other words, through communion with self-generated Petrarchan images of ideal beauty, rather than with real women.

The secondary plot involving Don Armado recapitulates the first plot's mockery of academic/Petrarchan withdrawal, demonstrating the isolated male's propensity, like the Marstonian satirist, to engage *himself* in a kind of false dialogue. The don supplies his own conversation: "Who came? the king. Why did he come? to see. Why did he see? to overcome," etc., (*LLL* 4.1.71–72). Don Armado's pedantic verbal self-involvement is essentially analogous to his romantic idealization of Jaquenetta, which he, in the style of the Navarran lords, expresses through written love poetry rather than through immediate physical contact and conversation. Through Armado and the Navarrans, *Love's Labor's Lost* demonstrates that in Shakespeare, to quote W. Thomas MacCary, "love of the narcissistic type leads almost inevitably to philosophical speculation,"[25] and that the reverse also occurs. The stage direction, "*Enter* Berowne, *with a paper in his hand, alone*" (4.3), like Orlando's solitary entrance "[*with a paper*]" in *As You Like It*'s third act (scene 2), sets up a visual emblem of the isolated discursive position of this play's would-be lovers, and links the Petrarchan mode (the paper, the ensuing scene reveals, is a love poem) with the academic misogyny of the play's first scene. Through Berowne, in fact, Shakespeare presents a configuration that was to become habitual for him: the merged images of the isolated romantic idealist and the equally isolated satirical commentator. Berowne's speech in 3.1 curiously melds the discursive modes of love-longing and satirical misogyny. One of his similes—"What! I love, I sue, I seek a wife / A woman, that is like a German [clock], / Still a-repairing, ever out of frame" (lines 189–91)—in fact anticipates Captain Otter's satirical portrait of his nagging wife in Jonson's *Epicoene:* "She takes herself asunder still when she goes to bed . . . and about next day noon is put together again, like a great German clock" (V, 4.2.97–99). Like Captain Otter's catalog of his wife's flaws, Berowne's solitary romantic-satiric musings, which objectify rather than engage their object, are fundamentally anti-erotic. But while *Epicoene*'s women justify male scorn (as a later chapter will demonstrate), the female charmers of *Love's Labor's Lost* do not. Jonson's *Epicoene* gives men the last word, but *Love's Labor's* bestows its final voice on the women, who, in repudiating the Navarrans, reject these men's separatist verbal modes and the anti-androgynous mind-sets from which those modes emerge.

The verbal mode of the Shakespearean separatist, or anti-androgyne, is an attempt to control and reify discourse; hence Shakespeare's Petrarchan lovers and other isolationists commit themselves, not to people, but to paper. The tactic brings to mind both the classical and the Elizabethan satirists' impulse to set their writings (even dramatic writings) in print, and the satirical playwrights' attempts further to control their characters through character sketches and their works' interpretation through explanatory prologues. Prologues and epilogues in Shakespearean comedy are relatively rare (at least in comparison to the number written by Jonson and Marston); where they occur, they differ significantly from those of the satirists in that they present the actors rather than the playwrights as the agents responsible for the plays' achievements.[26] Thus in Shakespearean comedy, unlike in humors satire, the "poet and the player" do not go "to cuffs in the question" of the play's meaning (*Hamlet* 2.2.353–54). Leaving the play in the hands of the actors, as well as refusing to consign its volatility to the reified folio form, is for Shakespeare a way of further validating the open-ended, circulatory relationship represented both by his androgynous heroes and their native dialogic medium.

This open-ended mode of theatrical production imitates similar androgynizing processes within the plays. Shakespeare pits the set speeches, pensive soliloquies and written messages of his *anti*-androgynes against the more powerful dialogic mode of his erotic characters, demonstrating that authentic human creative power is located, not in contemplative introspection, but in heterogenous relationship, and released in synergistic conversation. Orsino's love letters, for example, are no contest for the witty verbal repartee that Viola provides Olivia. It is the latter, not the former, that arouses Olivia's erotic interest. And in *The Merchant of Venice*, even before Portia delivers the devastating legal reading that will save Antonio's life, her conversational style has crucially altered the deadly atmosphere of the all-male Venetian court, transforming it from an arena in which confrontational speeches express rigid, unchanging moral positions to a forum of synergistic conversational exchange:

> POR. I am informed thoroughly of the cause.
> Which is the merchant here? and which the Jew?
>
> DUKE. Antonio and old Shylock, both stand forth.

POR.   Is your name Shylock?

SHY.   Shylock is my name.

POR.   Of a strange nature is the suit you follow,
Yet in such rule that the Venetian law
Cannot impugn you as you do proceed.—
You stand within this danger, do you not?

ANT.   Ay, so he says.

POR.   Do you confess the bond?

ANT.   I do.

POR.   Then must the Jew be merciful.

SHY.   On what compulsion must I? Tell me that.

POR.   The quality of mercy is not strained. . . .

(4.1.173–84)

A comparison of the rapid-fire question-and-answer dialogue that Portia here initiates with the longer, set speeches of the men prior to her entrance will reveal the principle of verbal interaction that Portia/ Balthazar, as androgyne, represents. In the tragedies, male protagonists self-destructively withdraw from this "feminized" conversational engagement into introspective soliloquy, but in the comedies the androgynous dialectic restores male characters to relationship and life. Thus Posthumus's reconciliation with Imogen at *Cymbeline*'s conclusion is achieved through a progressive conversational exchange between nine male and female characters, including the cross-dressed Imogen. This healthy and androgynous conversational interaction subverts and replaces the misogynistic ethic framed in Posthumus's earlier soliloquy, in which, suspecting Imogen of adultery, he maligns not only all females but any "feminized" portion of himself.

Posthumus's soliloquy is worth investigating, for in its form and in its causes it illustrates Shakespeare's view of the danger of satiric, introspective recoil from androgynous male-female conversation. Posthumus's set speech, in fact, presents a distorted version of the androgynous ideal, in which all human evil in men *or* women is characterized as "the woman's part":

> Could I find out
> The woman's part in me—for there's no motion
> That tends to vice in man, but I affirm
> It is the woman's; flattering, hers; deceiving, hers;
> Lust and rank thoughts, hers, hers, revenges, hers;
> Ambitions, covetings, change of prides, disdain,
> Nice longing, slanders, mutability,
> All faults that name, nay, that hell knows,
> Why, hers, in part or all, but rather, all;
> For even to vice
> They are not constant, but are changing still. . . .
>
> (2.5.19–30)

Appropriately, Posthumus concludes his antiwoman tirade with a vow to turn satirist: "I'll write against them, / Detest them, curse them" (lines 32–33). Posthumus's false conviction of Imogen's guilt and his misogynistic stance result from his failure to communicate with Imogen regarding Iachimo's accusation against her (like Othello and *Much Ado*'s Claudio, he has simply accepted a male friend's story about his bride). The soliloquy, acted by this male character alone on stage, is thus the appropriate visual symbol and verbal form for the expression of his consequent despair, delivered in language that iron-ically demonizes the quality of androgynous "mutability" and falsely projects the characteristic of changeableness entirely onto the female. *Cymbeline* as a whole rejects Posthumus's nightmarish formulation of androgyny, revealing the types of immoral "mutability" that he here indicts to be the man's part (Iachimo's and Posthumus's own) at least as much as the woman's, but ultimately reclaiming Posthumus for the legitimate androgynous wholeness of marriage with Imogen, expressed, finally, in interactive conversation.

In Shakespearean comedy (and in tragedy as well), men who talk to themselves are generally in moral and psychological trouble. Their solipsistic discursive modes express a closed, satirical resistance to androgynous community that, happily, is thwarted by the overall design of their comic worlds. Shakespeare's mocking inclusion of the anti-androgynous principle within his mythic drama suggests the esca-lating conflict between mythic and satiric perspectives on androgyny that characterized English Renaissance society as a whole, though it also suggests Shakespeare's curious interest in the competing satirical mode. The early modern cultural confrontation between androgy-nous and anti-androgynous principles was a key component of the various dramatic rivalries played out in the London "poets' war" between 1599 and 1601; Shakespeare's part in the "war," as my first chapter argues, centered on this issue. In later chapters, I will discuss both Shakespeare's brief experimentation with the anti-androgynous satiric comic mode in *The Merry Wives of Windsor* and his ultimate repudiation of this mode in *As You Like It*. First, however, it will be necessary to examine the primary dramatic challenge to Shakespeare's mythic androgynous principle as it took shape in the classically inspired satiric comedies of Ben Jonson.

3

Jonson, Satire, and the Empty Hermaphrodite

Melanion is our ideal;
his loathing makes us free.
Our dearest aim is the gemlike flame
of his misogyny.
                    —Aristophanes, *Lysistrata*

In Ben Jonson's satire we find the most fully realized and philosophically justified representation of the Renaissance anti-androgynous ethic, a principle derived from and supported by a combined tradition of Semonidean and Juvenalian disgust, Aristophanic ridicule, scholastic isolationism, and (paradoxically) Puritan antitheatricalism.[1] Like Shakespeare, Jonson responded to past and contemporary constructions of androgyny with spirited comic invention, elaborating and complicating his models for the developing medium of the stage. This chapter will explore Jonson's complex representation of the anti-androgynous moral perspectives and some of the literary modes of both classical satirists and Renaissance critics of social transvestism. In the process, the chapter will point to Jonson's specific rebuttal of the principles of mythic androgyny and some of its popular forms. Specifically, I will discuss the reified and guarded construction of masculinity that informs Jonson's resistance to erotic "feminization" and will demonstrate the relationship of this construction to Jonsonian satire's reduction or "draining" of classical, Lylyan, and Shakespearean mythic androgyny symbols so that, as in the works of Aristophanes, Martial, and fellow satirists like Marston, the signifiers of transcendent human synergy become particularized, local embodiments of contemporary social illness. For Jonson, as for the classical satirists (I will argue), moral resistance to a hermaphrodism characterized as deviance accounts for key features of literary and dramatic style. Finally, I will discuss Jonson's *Epicoene* as a comic reclamation of satiric male identity from the feminizing encroachments of marriage, the sexualized female, and the playhouse.

With a few significant exceptions, to be discussed in the next chapter, Jonson uses androgynous figures to reinscribe notions of absolute gender difference and to criticize those who try to transgress or elide gender barriers. Jonsonian satire rehearses the values of both the classical satirists and the Elizabethan antitheatricalists in that it presents all gender-transgressive attempts as not only inappropriate but ultimately ineffectual. That is, Jonson describes a moral universe in which men are men and women are not, and in which the attempts of members of either sex to play opposite-sex roles are thus merely imitative. Like Martial's lesbian Bassa, whose "portentous lust imitates man," Jonson's androgynous characters are incapable of the authentic hermaphroditic transformations that Shakespeare's mythic lovers undergo. Jonson's satiric construction of male personhood as stoically detached, rationally guarded, and psychologically complete militates against myth's androgynous ethic, which argues our human incompleteness without transformative erotic relationship. In Jonson's moral universe, where real men stand on their own, such androgynous transformation is neither warranted nor even possible. Thus, to quote Mary Beth Rose, Jonsonian androgyny "is merely a sham."[2]

What Jonsonian satire inveighs against, then, is not a genuine androgynizing process, in which separated "male" and "female" elements recombine into a synergistic whole. Since the satiric definition of identity as private and self-contained rejects genuine hermaphrodism as a possibility, the "androgynous" action satire criticizes is simply imitation itself. In Jonson, the performance of other-sex behavior is, by definition, affectation—again, a sham.

Jonson's concept of the gendered self as fixed, properly immobile, and falsely obscured by any imitations of the opposite sex differs fundamentally from the Shakespearean vision of the protean self committed, like Antipholus of Syracuse, to the possibility of being "create[d] . . . new" by love. Thomas Greene has demonstrated that the vision of human identity generated by Jonson's poetry, drama, and prose depends on images of concrete objects and geometrical forms— a far cry from Shakespeare's images of sea-wrack and ocean voyaging.[3] Jonson, in fact, reifies the self, presenting it as a stably situated thing: a "cedar," a "fine well-timbered gallant" (V, *Volpone* 4.5.123– 24), a "Pillar" (VIII, 176, 15). This Jonsonian description of the grounded, solid self recalls Archilochus's stated preference for "a man short and squarely set upon his legs . . . not to be shaken from the place he plants his feet" (no. 7). Both the Greek and the English satirist articulate a model of identity antithetical to Shakespeare's vision of the self as fluid and relational, defined by its pull toward a necessary convergence with other-gendered and other-sexed minds and bodies. For Jonson, the individual self is defined by its stand *against* the feminizing pull of the Other, whose claims to relational identity with the subject self are—paradoxically—both empty and threatening.

This conflicted notion of the self as whole and stable but also continually threatened is evident in this famous passage from Jonson's *Discoveries*:

> I have considered, our whole life is like a play: wherein every man, forgetful of himself, is in travail with expression of another. Nay, we so insist on imitating others, as we cannot (when it is necessary) return to our selves. . . . (VIII, 597, 1093–96)

The above lines represent the self as a prior, integral, firmly *placed* entity, and further suggest that this grounded self is male. Jonson here implies what he elaborates more fully elsewhere: the classic satirical vision of masculinity as an absolute quality, and femininity as the absence of this quality. Women have no intrinsic "virtue" in the word's original Latin sense of "manliness." Jonson's work relies on this originary meaning, linking solid and active virtue to the idea of maleness (the "only moral survivor" in *The Devil Is an Ass* is, for example, named "Eustace Manly," as Ronald Huebert has pointed out).[4] Thus, the destabilizing threat to the integral identity is simply the corrosive feminine pull toward associative selfhood, which both is and can effect the erasure of maleness. One of Jonson's nondramatic writings best articulates this misogynistic paradigm of human identity: in his poem "That Women Are But Men's Shadows," Jonson avers that "men at weakest, [women] are strongest, / But grant us perfect, they're not known" (VIII, 104, 9–10).

This Jonsonian gender model has important implications for the assignment of gender roles in his humors satire. Specifically, it allows Jonsonian men a binary option: men may define themselves as manly or androgynous according to their resistance to or acquiescence in feminizing relational identity. The avenues for Jonsonian female behavior, however, are threefold. First, women may demonstrate their femaleness through the exercise of passive virtues such as silence, obedience,

chastity, and the presentation of a beautiful appearance. The validation of feminine silence as the appropriate obverse of masculine speaking is registered in this verse from *Epicoene*:

> Silence in woman, is like speech in man,
>   Deny't who can.
> . . . .
>   Nor, is't a tale,
> That female vice should be a virtue male,
> Or masculine vice, a female virtue be. . . .
>
> (V, 2.3.123–28)

The verse's penultimate line suggests women's second alternative, a
converse of the first: they may enact "female vice" by inappropriately
aping masculine qualities, such as spirited speaking, marital dominance, sexual aggressiveness and/or promiscuity, and the presentation
(willing or unwilling) of a rugged (or "autumnal") appearance (V, *Epicoene* 1.1.85). Thirdly (and more rarely), some exceptional women
may augment their passive feminine virtues with certain masculine
qualities that Jonson deems appropriate and commendable for either
sex, such as judiciousness and real (as opposed to feigned) learnedness; however, even these virtues remain resolutely gendered male.
Thus Jonson's poem to Lucy, countess of Bedford, commends her both
for her possession of "each softest virtue" and her one male attribute,
a "learned, and manly soul" (VIII, 52, 11 and 13).

Like Lucy, the virtuous female characters in Jonson's poems and
plays demonstrate femininity through "soft" behaviors, like quiet
obedience. *Bartholomew Fair*'s Grace Wellborn is reserved and only
modestly clever, as though Jonson recoiled from giving her the robust
energy of that play's male wits, and *Volpone*'s Celia's pliancy and helplessness in the face of her husband's abuse and Volpone's rape attempt
render her a near-static emblem of feminine goodness. Celia's virtue
is evident in several forms of inaction: her acquiescence in her husband
Corvino's attempt to prostitute her to Volpone reaches a passive
extreme, but she ultimately refuses to cooperate when Volpone tries
to seduce her (though she is saved from rape only by Bonario's timely
rescue) (V, *Volpone* 3.7). Ultimately, the Venetian magistrates send
Celia "Home, to her father" (5.12.144): resituating her in the daughter's (rather than the wife's) role, the men preserve her honor by remov-
ing her from the arena of male sexual predation (she is not, of course,
divorced; the play holds out no possibility of a more fortunate future

marriage). Thus Celia emerges as an emblem of the nonsexualized woman, virtuous in her various postures of chaste inaction.

However, Jonson at times links female purity and innocence with complete obedience to men's domineering sexual instructions, as in the epigram where "Sir Voluptuous Beast"

> instructs his fair and innocent wife
> In the past pleasures of his sensual life
> Telling the motions of each petticoat,
> And how his Ganymede moved, and how his goat,
> And now, her (hourly) her own cucquean makes
> In varied shapes, which for his lust she takes. . . .
>
> (VIII, 34, 1–6)

Here the woman is paradoxically degraded through de-feminizing erotic performance, which makes her the sexual interloper in her own marriage, while her "soft" compliance yet expresses her feminine innocence. The poem clearly criticizes Sir Beast's treatment of her, but the poem's satiric target is neither Beast's lust nor his sexual dominance but the effeminate theatricality he brings to erotic activity, which requires her to play the part (among other parts) of a "Ganymede," or sexualized boy. Volpone's aggression toward Celia demonstrates a like paradoxical effeminacy, as he sexually tempts her to "act Ovid's tales, / Thou, like Europa now, and I like Jove" (3.7.221–22); in both epigram and play scene, the "voluptuous" excess inheres in the character's feminized impulse toward shape-changing[5] rather than in his rapacious energy, which for Jonson is definitively masculine. Sexual dominance is a "virtue male," to which the virtuous feminine response is either passive resistance—refusing sexual action—or obedient acquiescence: agreeing to be acted upon. For Jonson as for most earlier satirists, initiatory sexuality itself seemed unfeminine: a female vice, or failure to *be* female in Jonsonian terms. But these terms derive from the earliest frames of satirical reference, as where Semonides' essay praises the good woman who "takes no delight . . . when the conversation's about sex."

Thus Jonsonian satire, like most classical satire, relegates erotic aggression—in pursuit, not of symbiosis, but of sexual dominance—to the masculine domain. A man compromises and hence feminizes his own aggression when he inflames it by playacting: by imagining his erotic object and himself as things other than what they are ("Thou, like Europa now, and I like Jove"). Such effeminization can be registered in erotic relationship with boys imagined as women, like Sir

Beast's former "Ganymede" or like Dauphine's catamite or "engle" in *Epicoene* (V, 1.1.25), whose presence suggests Dauphine's unmanly and self-lamented "diffidence" with real women (4.1.53–54, 68).[6] To educate Dauphine, his friend Truewit describes appropriate (i.e., definitive) male sexual behavior in terms of aggression and conquest (in fact, in terms of rape):

> A man should not doubt to overcome any woman. Think he can vanquish 'em, and he shall: for though they deny, their desire is to be tempted. . . . Ostend, you saw, was taken at last. . . . If they take [kisses], they'll take more—though they strive, they would be overcome. (V, 4.1.72–83)

When men initiate and dominate sexual relations, real women submit or flee. Thus, conversely, satire genders proper female sexual attitudes as responsive, in one way or another, to initiatory male desire. Aristophanic comedy, which ranges between comic and satiric poles, is exceptional in that it allows its female heroes a great deal of sexual enthusiasm, most notably in the comic *Lysistrata*, where the women are clearly erotically impelled. But even in Aristophanes, female sexual desire is properly *responsive* to male aggression—which is, in Truewit's terms, "an acceptable violence" (V, *Epicoene* 4.1.85)— rather than aggressive in its own right.[7] In satire, aggressive female sexuality is reserved for "Bassas": monstrous women whose "portentous lust imitates man," to recall Martial's phrase once more. Women's "masculine" lust may target (most monstrously) other women, as does Bassa's, but it is more frequently heterosexual. Juvenal's sixth satire presents the classic satiric dichotomy between feminine chastity, which recoils simultaneously from bold masculine endeavor and sexual pursuit, and antithetically "masculine" female sexual aggression, which reveals itself in inappropriate courage:

> Consideration of danger,
> If a woman is honest, chills her heart
> with foreboding,
> She shakes at the knees, hardly can stand,
> so great is her terror.
> But your bold ones have great nerve for
> their shameful adventure.
> . . . .
> . . . if it's a lover she follows, her stomach is
> made of cast iron.

> She would puke on her spouse, but now she feeds
> with the sailors,
> Wanders all over the ship, has fun in hauling
> the hand ropes.
>
> (6:95–102)

Like Juvenal (whose sixth satire, "Against Women," is integral to the structure and values of Jonson's *Epicoene)*, Jonson presents excessively sexualized women as interlopers in a male moral landscape, and hence threats to male power—indeed, to male sexual identity. Jonson's hermaphroditic female characters represent the classical satirical construction of aggressive initiatory sexuality, and maintain its thematic connection to other illicit incursions into male territory, such as the realms of scholarship and literary production. Feminine scholarship is suspect because it is sexualized. Women study the classics, not to acquire knowledge of timeless truths available to reasoning minds, but to feed their rapacious physical desires for sexual mastery and titillating change. These female hermaphrodites use what they learn to entrap men, as is illustrated in the curriculum of *Epicoene*'s female "Collegiates" (V, 1.1.75). Like the twentieth-century coed seeking her "MRS. degree," these women study seductive arts, discussing "the mysteries of writing letters" and finding a "rich gown" for "a great day; a new one for the next; a richer for the third," as well as how to hire "embroiderers, jewellers, [at]tire-women, sempsters, feathermen," and "perfumers" (V, 2.2.103–9).[8] Similarly, *Volpone*'s Lady Wouldbe, who "would be" as intellectually and sexually powerful as a man, reads and discusses love poetry and Pythagoras (whose theory of the transmigration of souls from men to animals is ironically associated with the sexual threat she represents). Her intrusive volubility and false learnedness are linked with her explicit sexual interest in Volpone: "Come, in faith, I must / Visit you more, a days; and make you well: / Laugh, and be lusty" (V, 3.4.113–15). The female characters in *Cynthia's Revels* are likewise engaged in the "study" of seductive entrapment through the appropriation of sexual freedoms that are properly male. *Cynthia's Revels* creates a nightmarish equivalence between feminine sexual control and castration in the words of the lady Philautia, who wishes "that I might send for any man I list, and have his head cut off, when I have done with him; or made an eunuch, if he denied me" (IV, 4.1.166–68). The association Jonson habitually forges between feminine lust and unlawful, castrating entry into the male world of learning and letters—

his characterization of both transgressions as a species of female her-maphrodism—is also evident in his thinly veiled attack on Lady Cecilia Bulstrode, a poet who had publicly criticized him. An epigram of Jonson's describes Bulstrode as "The Court Pucelle" (whore) who "with Tribade lust" can "force a Muse, / And in an epicoene fury can write news" (VIII, 222, 7–8). As Rosalind Miles writes, these lines figuratively charge Bulstrode with "a lesbian rape (the muse of poetry being a female, and therefore properly accessible only to masculine advances)."[9]

Finally, Jonson (again like Juvenal) further divorces this threat-ening false scholarship/verbosity/sexual aggression from genuine female personhood by accusing the gender criminals of willful steril-ity. Like the sexually obsessed female who "pays the abortionist" in Juvenal's sixth satire (line 597), the female collegiates in *Epicoene* use "excellent receipts" (drugs) to prevent conception (V, 4.3.57), as does "Fine Madame Would-Be" of Jonson's epigram, who finds "both loss of time and loss of sport / In a great belly" (VIII, 46, 10–11).

Thus the Jonsonian female androgyne is characterized by social uselessness (since, in the interests of maintaining an active sex life, she avoids pregnancy) and various forms of aggressiveness that render her an intruder in the masculine domains of scholarship, volubility, literary creativity, and initiatory sexuality. The sexualized female is, paradoxically, masculine, and hence a threat to male sexuality, con-strued as dominance or detachment (detachment being another form of control over the irrational sexual instinct). *Bartholomew Fair's* tough, mannish Ursula, the pig-woman, proves to be an interesting figure to analyze in light of this Jonsonian satiric ethic. Ursula is unusual among Jonson's females: her authentic creative ability, man-ifested in her dialogically inspired wit, makes her partially reminis-cent of Shakespeare's androgynous heroines, as my next chapter will demonstrate. But even Ursula is radically compromised as a female figure by her obvious unattractiveness to the male wit-heroes Quarlous and Winwife, who regard her with fascinated horror and perceive in her the potential obliteration of their own masculine iden-tities. Quarlous observes that "he that would venture for't . . . might sink into her, and be drown'd a week, ere any friend he had, could find where he were" (VI, 2.5.95–97).[10]

This typically Jonsonian fear of self-loss[11] through contact with the grossly sexualized female—a female whose very availability and sexual energy render her, paradoxically, manlike—represents the dual recoil from eroticism and transvestism registered not just in classical satire, but in Puritan antitheatrical tracts and pamphlets like *Haec-Vir* (recall William Prynne's association of female mannishness with "Whorishness," and Anthony Munday's simultaneous resistance to the cross-dressed boy actors and the "harlots" adrift in the theater audience). Jonson's defensive-aggressive attitude towards emotional feminization represents the militant posture of the antitheatricalists and opponents of social transvestism, who championed "The Overthrow of Stage Plays" (John Rainolds's title)[12] and urged "the powerful Statute of apparel" to "lift up his Battle-Axe" (to recall *Hic-Mulier*). From Jonson's satirical standpoint, as from some Renaissance Puritans' perspective, men needed to respond aggressively to the perils of social androgyny. Jonson's insistence on vigorous struggle against these perils is, in Alexander Leggatt's words, "consistent with his idea that . . . virtue must expect to be exercised in combat . . . and must be defined by its own efforts against adversity."[13] For Jonson, masculine sexual identity might be protected and affirmed through physical dominance of the female—through "overcom[ing]" the woman, to recall Truewit's phrase, much as stage plays might be "overthrown"—but masculine sexual identity could also be nullified by emotional or psychological identification *with* the female. Thus Jonsonian satire, like classical satirical writings and antitheatrical pamphlets, is marked by a scornful resistance to emotional or psychic connection with women, which it presents as androgynization (that is, as feminization of the male).

Hence the Jonsonian fear of masculine self-loss asserts itself in the reduction of symbols that, in Lylyan and Shakespearean mythic comedy, validate androgynous transsexual synthesis. Jonsonian satire (like all satire) repudiates eros, the divine procreative force that—for the Greeks, the Renaissance Neoplatonists, and mythic playwrights like Lyly and Shakespeare—was vitally linked to androgyny. For Jonson, eros was simply a sham: an illusion of transsexual connectedness born of a fatuous submission to unmanly sentiment. Thus the Lylyan/Shakespearean metaphors of watery dissolution, dream, maze, violas, alchemy, magical transvestism, and beast-monsters appear, inverted, in Jonson's comedies, invested with negative valences. Jonson uses these symbols, along with specific hermaphrodite myths, to suggest illicit departures from authentic identities: "imitating others," so that "we cannot return to ourselves," to recall the lines from *Discoveries*.

The Jonsonian vision of grounded male identity is clearly at odds with the Shakespearean vision of the protean self, available for transformative interaction with another. Thus in Jonson's work, metaphors of watery transformation are used to indicate the total dissolution of an integrated personality—not the awakening of the authentic, double-gendered relational entity, but a reduction of the prior, individual self to nothingness. Typically, it is some form of "feminizing" erotic compulsion that threatens this reduction. Again we may cite Quarlous's bawdy response to the portly, commanding Ursula: "[H]e that would venture for't . . . might sink into her, and be drown'd a week, ere any friend he had, could find where he were." Significantly, Quarlous's comic assessment of Ursula's dangers recoils from her power to "drown" a man's identity through monstrous sexual dominance; conversely, Quarlous locates salvific, restorative power in a presumably male friend.

The formula and imagery recur throughout Jonson's satiric work. Witty, cynical, and detached men remained separate and whole through their self-sufficient resistance to romantic involvement, evident either in their stoic withdrawal from all social ties (*Every Man Out of His Humour*'s Macilente/Asper is a case in point here), or their preference for balanced, reasoned relationships with other men (relationships that are masculinized by their competitive nature, as I will later demonstrate). Conversely, dim-witted, fatuous, and emotional effeminates—like "Sir *Amorous* La-Foole" (my emphasis)—lose all claims to masculinity through their dissolute involvement in a sea of chaotic feminine behaviors and associations. Such vain social preoccupations and attachments cause these characters' integrity figuratively to dissolve. Thus a courtier's face is described as "over-flowing" (IV, CR 2.3.46), a changeable man as "more inconstant than the sea" (III, *The Case Is Altered*, 5.1.16), and a clothing-obsessed man as "melt[ing] away [him]self / In flashing bravery" (fine clothing) (III, *Every Man in His Humour* 1.1.76–77). The chattering of foppish courtiers and "Collegiate" ladies in *Epicoene* is a "sea break[ing] in upon Morose," threatening to "o'erwhelm" him: "It beats already at my shores," he complains (V, 3.6.2–4). Volpone's integrity (such as it is) is threatened by Lady Wouldbe's "flood of words! a very torrent!" (V, *Volpone*, 3.4.64). A humor itself is an enervating liquid that "flow[s] continually / In some one part," "wanting power to control itself" (III, *EMO* induction, lines 100–101, 97). Thus in *Every Man in His Humour*'s folio version, Cash describes Kitely's obsessive and potentially contagious desire for his wife in terms of uncontrollable flood and drowning:

> Where should this flood of passion
> (trow) take head? ha?
> Best, dream no longer of this running humour,

> For fear I sink! the violence of the stream
> Already hath transported me so far,
> That I can feel no ground at all!
>
> (III, 3.3.140–44)[14]

The above lines present a definitive contrast to Shakespeare's characteristic use of water (and dream) imagery. Antipholus of Syracuse, we recall, makes a similar connection between his erotic yearning for Luciana and the subsuming action of water; yet *The Comedy of Errors* validates Antipholus's self-loss as a necessary phase in his and Luciana's coalescence into a new, conjugal self. In characteristic Jonsonian fashion, *Every Man In*'s plot antithetically prescribes masculine resistance to the destructive pull of emotional "flood." The determined stand against the passion tide represents the standard Jonsonian defensive posture, which always safeguards, or prescribes a return to, the preexistent male identity Jonson defines in *Discoveries*.

Jonson's negative use of the metaphors of dream and maze similarly validate the male resistance to self-loss, in contrast to the positive erotic/androgynous valence given by Shakespeare to these metaphors. In Jonson's "Epistle to a Friend, to Persuade him to the Wars," Jonson links the defining masculine activity of military endeavor with resistance to sleep: "Wake, friend, from forth thy lethargy," Jonson begins, going on to describe "sleepy life" as a grave for "Man's buried honour" (VIII, 162, lines 1, 7). The maze, which in Shakespearean comedy signifies the necessary bafflement preparatory to marital involvement—the preparation for the erotic beast encounter—is seen by Jonson as the self-alienating trap of the world. In the *Underwood*, Jonson presents the world as a "maze of custom, error, strife" that threatens the individual consciousness (VIII, 116, 60). The illicit scams of *The Alchemist*'s projectors are a version of this "dark labyrinth" (V, 3.3.308). A tricky lawyer described in *Cynthia's Revels* has a "labyrinthine face" as deceptive as the courtier's "over-flowing" one (IV, 2.3.31). Analogously, in the 1601 version of *Every Man in His Humour*, old Lorenzo's supposition of his son's dissoluteness is registered in a vision of mazy, pointless wandering:

> his course is so irregular,
> So loose affected, and depriv'd of grace,
> And he himself withal so far fallen off
> From his first place, that scarce no note remains
> To tell men's judgements where he lately stood. . . .
>
> (III, 1.4.44–48)

The passage reiterates the distinction in *Discoveries* between the self-destructive effects of wandering and the original groundedness of masculine being. Again, Jonson presents the self as firmly *placed*. Because of a man's natural groundedness, maze-wandering brings not self-expansion, as in Shakespeare, but the loss of all identity. And for the Jonsonian satiric male, the loss of private identity is not a precondition for the acquisition of relational identity; it is, instead, a surrender to emptiness.

The association between self-emptying and hermaphrodism derives, again, from the characteristic satiric vision of masculine self-loss as an invalid submission to female sexual control. The link between Jonsonian "empty" hermaphrodism and feminine sexual coercion is sometimes reinforced through Jonson's use of musical and alchemical metaphors. As I argued in my second chapter, Shakespeare uses the image of the viola, with its genital symbolism of instrument and bow, to suggest the harmonious erotic convergence of male and female bodies. The image of the viola is also sexual in Jonson, but, like the imagery of water, maze, and dream, the Jonsonian viola poses the symbolic threat of destructive feminization. Jonson links the viol with the threateningly sexualized, domineering females with whom his fops and court-climbers associate. *Every Man Out of His Humour*'s Saviolina is one such, as is *Poetaster*'s Cytheris, who "baits" men "with a viol" (IV, 4.3.59–60), and *The Alchemist*'s Dol Common, with whom Face jokes about her "viol" (V, 2.3.245). Dol's illicit and threatening sexuality, implicit in the image of the viol or viola-da-gamba, is also linked to the false alchemical art of Subtle, Face's and Dol's confederate. Alchemy, associated in the Renaissance (and specifically in Lyly's *Gallathea*) with the mystical symbol of the hermaphrodite, is *The Alchemist*'s central emblem of specious transformation. And significantly, Subtle's description of the alchemical combination of unlike elements explicitly links his bogus art to invalid (because impossible) androgynous synthesis:

> Of that ayrie,
> And oily water, mercury is engendered;
> Sulphur o' the fat, and earthy part: the one
> (Which is the last) supplying the place of male,
> The other of the female, in all metals.
> Some do believe hermaphrodeity,
> That both do act. . . .
>
> (V, 2.3.159–64)

Believing in real "hermaphrodeity" is, for Jonson, gullibility equivalent to believing in this alchemical process. Here as elsewhere, Jonson uses mythic signifiers of transsexual erotic connectedness to indicate bogus transformations: the encroachments of sexual passion on the reasoning male self.

Two Jonsonian masques, *Mercury Vindicated from the Alchemists at Court* and *Lovers Made Men*, significantly elaborate the Jonsonian reduction of the connective symbols of Hermes/Mercury (whom Jonson elsewhere calls "the cheater" [VIII, 10; 7, 22]) and the alchemical process. The distinct aims and conventions of the masque render these entertainments a source of radically different commentary on gender relations than that offered by Jonson's comedies; in general, the masques resist the satiric perspective on gender, and their inclusion is thus not appropriate for this discussion. The above-cited masques, however, are instructive (as are some of Jonson's nonsatiric poems) for their conspicuous reiteration of Jonson's characteristic resistance to the dangerous androgynous principle. The title *Mercury Vindicated from the Alchemists at Court* suggests, on the surface, that the court is the healthy cultural center at which the dramatic exposure of the alchemists, the bogus transformers, can occur. However, the title more subtly indicates the court as the corrupt site of the alchemists' invalid experiments. Thus the masque's repudiation of their false art (accomplished, significantly, by the identification of the sun—not Mercury—as the true source of social order) constitutes a sly repudiation of the effeminate court environment, even as it ostensibly praises this world and its president, James I (the sun). In *Lovers Made Men*, as the title indicates, romantic passion initially distances the protagonists from true masculinity. Significantly, it is Mercury—again, in myth, the bringer of connective erotic relationship—who tempts the men into romantic self-loss. Escaping Mercury's dangerous influence, the men ultimately free themselves from passion and, in so doing, recover true manhood. Like Jonson's satirical work, both of these masques use mythic symbols in order to invert these symbols' valence of authentic human synergy. The masques reinforce the anti-androgynous, antiromantic, anticonnective action characteristic of satire, locating human dignity in the figure of the rational, self-sufficient male.

In contrast to the masques, the humors plays are centrally concerned to stage *failed* masculine self-sufficiency. The failures of manhood appear most conspicuously through the deployment of a key metaphor signifying theatrical effeminization: male obsession with fashionable clothing or adornment. Transvestite garb in Shakespeare-an comedy is generally worn by women, both to indicate and facilitate the necessary erotic expansion of the wearers into double-gendered, relational identity. In Jonson's satire, contrastingly, excessive adornment is a feature of male androgyny, and—like all androgynous characteristics—it signifies a dearth or reduction of proper selfhood. The presentation of clothing-obsessed males in Jonson's humors drama embodies the attitude expressed in the *Discoveries* that "Too much pickedness [trimness, adornment] is not manly" (VIII, 607, 1422) and that fine clothing masks mental "deformity" (line 1432).

The feminized male's literal investment in his clothing is everywhere evident in Jonson's comedies. (Jonson's chronic penury, well documented in his numerous poetic pleas to patrons for financial backing, was doubtless related to the expense these elaborately costumed characters must have entailed.)[15] *Epicoene*'s Amorous La-Foole identifies key points in his life through memories of what he was wearing on those occasions: "I had as fair a gold jerkin on that day, as any was worn . . . at Cadiz, none disprais'd; and I came over in it hither, show'd myself to my friends" (V, 1.4.61–64). Men like La-Foole "wear purer linen" than either women or "the french hermaphrodite," according to one of the collegiates (V, *Epicoene* 4.6.30–31). The gallants in *Cynthia's Revels* are "made all of clothes" (IV, 3.4.23). Fungoso calls *Every Man Out*'s Fastidious Brisk "a very fine suit of clothes" (III, 2.3.124); an epigram in *Underwood* calls modern men "tailors' blocks, / Cover'd with tissue" (VIII, 216, 99–100); Horace refers to *Poetaster*'s Crispinus as "your silkiness" (IV, 3.1.248); and so on. Like the gaudily clad gallant in *Haec-Vir* whom Hic-Mulier initially mistakes for a woman, these men are feminized through the visible analogy between themselves and the female characters on stage.

More importantly, however, Jonson's parallel presentation of women as characteristically clothing-obsessed helps create a sense of the *psychological* analogies between the plays' courtiers and their women, and thus to accentuate the effeminates' monstrous departure from true maleness. As *The Case Is Altered*'s virtuous Onion observes, "[A]pparel makes a man forget himself" (III, 5.6.47–48). It does so by enforcing a psychic as well as a physical association between the man and his female associates, who demonstrate an identical sartorial obsession. In *Eastward Ho*, Girtred, like the typical male fop, associates her*self* with her fine clothing: "I will be a lady . . . . to dye rich scarlet black, pretty; to line a Grogaram gown" (IV, 1.2.17–20). In *Cynthia's Revels*, the court ladies' entire conversation concerns sex and clothes (see, for example, 2.4). The complaint of these women (like that of *Epicoene*'s aggrieved collegiate) that the men outdo them in adornment—"we cannot have a new peculiar court-tire, but these retainers will have it" (IV, *CR*, 2.4.77–78)—reinforces our sense of the feminized Jonsonian male's invalid melding with the maze or sea of the world. Immersed in the vain, feminized court environment, the humorous male becomes, like *Every Man Out*'s Fastidious Brisk, both "masculine and feminine," and hence neuter (III, 2.6.7). In sharing feminine obsessions, this male internalizes the vanity that, in satire, *is* femaleness (as Horace tells the silk-clad Crispinus, "You have much of the mother in you" [IV, *Poetaster* 3.1.185]). He thus empties himself of male qualities.

The men who most successfully safeguard their masculinity are those who hold themselves apart from the feminized maze of both high and low London society, particularly from close physical and psychological association with women. In *The Alchemist*, for example, Face is finally masculinized by his ultimate repudiation of Dol Common (5.4) and also of Dame Pliant, in whom he had initially expressed sexual interest (4.3.85). *Every Man Out*'s Macilente affirms his self-sufficient maleness largely through resisting his attraction to Deliro's wife, Fallace, as well as through exposing and banishing the plays' humors characters so that he finally stands alone, with "soul at peace" (III, 5.11.54). *Epicoene*'s master wits, though compromised by their involvement with the plays' collegiates, maintain a measure of masculine integrity by affirming a primary competitive relationship with each other. As such, all these male characters contrast markedly with the effeminates, who are reprehensible not just for their grandiose attire but for their uncontrolled attraction to and psychological sympathy with women (qualities distinct from the masculine desire for sexual overmastery that Truewit expresses in *Epicoene* 4.1, and that women are criticized for mirroring). The effeminate La-Foole, as noted, is called "Amorous" La-Foole; his name suggests his fatuous preoccupation with women. In Clerimont's mocking description, La-Foole goes "to watch when ladies are gone to the China houses, or to the Exchange, that he may meet 'em by chance. . . . He is never without a spare banquet, or sweet-meats in his chamber, for their women to alight at, and come up to" (1.3.36–41). *The Merry Wives of Windsor*, Shakespeare's uncharacteristic experiment in the "Jonsonian" humors mode, similarly links amorous behavior to androgyny through Falstaff's description of "these lisping hawthorn buds that come like women in men's apparel" to say "I love thee"

(3.2.71–73). Similarly, *Every Man In*'s Kitely and *Every Man Out*'s Deliro and Puntarvolo are feminized by their obsession with their wives (a characteristic duplicated in *Merry Wives*'s Master Ford). Mythic comic heroes are lovers; satiric comic heroes, in contrast, are those who expose the affections of the lovers as vanities, as do Truewit, Brainworm, and Macilente (respectively) in the above Jonsonian plays. "If you love your wife, or rather, dote on her . . . ," a sentence of Truewit's begins, demonstrating typical Jonsonian doubt regarding the possibility of healthy affections between the sexes (V, *Epicoene*, 2.2.91). Jonsonian "doting" is not Shakespearean love. Destructive rather than expansive, it "feeds upon" the lover and makes him "Cupid's gull" (III, *CIA* 4.5.10, 15). Dependency of any kind is gendered female, since both good and bad women in the Jonsonian universe acquire selfhood in relation to their men. In the mythic universe, it is also appropriate for men to acquire selves through male-female relationship; in the satiric universe, men who try to do this prove deficient in moral identity (which, for men, must be self-structured). Thus a common Jonsonian metaphor for men who display undue, "effeminate" interest in women or who rely on others for psychic sustenance is "parasite." The word is invoked often as an image of insufficient masculinity, as in a poem where Jonson has his Muse inspire him to write "things manly, and not smelling parasite" (VIII, 48, 14). The Jonsonian courtiers' attachments to women, to women's world, and to each other's effete company are, then, parasitical. Such pseudo-erotic relations are, in the words of *Cynthia's Revels*'s wise Crites, "monstrous affections" (IV, 5.4.290); in other words, they are affectations. Relational identity threatens Jonsonian integrity. Thus Jonson's satires present amorous desire as a humor: a corrosive, disabling force. Jonson embraces the self-destructive viewpoint of Sidney's Musidorus in *Arcadia*, the enemy of love who reductively construes Pyrocles' erotic transformation as degeneration into effeminacy. Invoking the satirist's nightmare of Hercules in love, Mucidorus warns that "this effeminate love of a woman doth so womanize a man that (if he yield to it) it will not only make him an Amazon, but a launder, a distaff-spinner, or whatsoever vile occupation their idle heads can imagine, and their weak hands perform."[16]

Unlike Sidney's *Arcadia*, which rejects Mucidorus's misogyny and validates Pyrocles' passion, Jonson's specific references to the myths of erotic transformation manifest the satirical reduction of romantic love to parasitism or doting. Like the classical satirists and like his satiric contemporaries, Jonson treats such myths ironically, using the beast-encounter characters and symbols as signifiers of invalid contemporary blurrings of gender, or false eros. Renaissance satiric playwrights generally enjoyed mocking the Ovidian myths of erotic transformation, as a scene from the anonymous *Return from Parnassus* demonstrates. A furiously composing poet inadvertently reduces the symbols of divine eros to ridiculous animal images as he writes,

> Nay silver Cynthia, do not trouble me:
> Straight will I thy Endymion's story write,
> To which thou halest me on [both] day and night.
> You light skirt stars, this is your wonted guise,
> By gloomy night perk out your doubtful heads:
> But when Don Phoebus shows his flashing snout,
> You are sky puppies straight, your light is out.
>
> (Part II, 2.1.458–65)[17]

Jonson, too, makes Ovid a specific target, associating him with the most vulgar entertainments. In *The Alchemist*, Face tricks the sensualist Epicure Mammon into romantic enthusiasm over a tryst with prostitute Dol by urging him to "Rain [on her] as many showers, as Jove did drops / Unto his Dane [Danae]" (V, 4.1.26–27). In *Epicoene*, Ovid is used reductively to justify the obsession of the henpecked "hermaphrodite" Captain Otter with "[his] bull, and [his] bear, as well as [his] horse"—his animal-shaped drinking mugs (V, 3.3.118–19). Clerimont's recounting of Ovidian erotic beast myths such as that of Pasiphae and the bull provokes Otter's response, "I will have these stories painted i' the bear-garden, *ex Ovidi metamorphosii*" (lines 130–32). The human-beast image implicitly suggests his unnatural, gender-blurred relationship with the domineering Mrs. Otter, and confirms his status as otter or "*animal amphibium*," an androgynous beast of two natures (1.4.26). (Thus *Epicoene* also overturns the magical valence given by Shakespeare to amphibious dolphins.) Ovid is again treated satirically in *Volpone*'s seduction scene, when Volpone inflames his illicit ardor by proposing that he and Celia

> act Ovid's tales,
> Thou, like Europa now, and I like Jove,
> Then I like Mars, and thou like Erycine,
> So, of the rest, till we have quite run through
> And weary'd all the fables of the gods. . . .
>
> (3.7.221–25)

We may also recall the "Voluptuous Beast" epigram's mockery of the Ganymede myth from Ovid, as erotic Ganymede becomes a degraded role played by poor Mrs. Beast to satisfy her husband's lust. That Shakespeare was more indulgent than Jonson toward the kind of erotic play that "On Sir Voluptuous Beast" condemns is suggested by the close of *Twelfth Night*, in which Orsino, having discovered that "Cesario" is the woman Viola, immediately expresses the desire to "see [her] in [her] woman's weeds" (5.1.273). Orsino's subsequent lines, delivered to a boy actor whom the audience knew was male, have a sly double significance that recalls Jonson's epigram:

> Cesario, come—
> For so you shall be while you are a man;
> But when in other habits you are seen,
> Orsino's mistress, and his fancy's queen.
>
> (lines 385–88)

Here Shakespeare, like Lyly, sympathetically merges the mythic motifs of Ovidian erotic transformation with a built-in trope of Elizabethan theatrical convention, male transvestism. In Jonson's work, however, Ovidian transformation myths are ironically linked to what Jonson clearly views as depraved sexual theater. A similar effect occurs in Jonson's plays' references to specific mythic figures associated with erotic convergence, as in Lady Wouldbe's hilarious reference to her husband's supposed paramour (who is actually a man) as a "land-siren" (V, *Volpone*, 4.2.47).

Lady Wouldbe's mistake is instructive in the context of Jonsonian unravelings or reductions of Lylyan/Shakespearean erotic androgyny motifs. Her jealousy is caused by her assumption that Sir Politic Wouldbe's friend Peregrine, a traveler lately arrived from the sea, is a young woman in drag ("your hermaphrodite," she derisively calls him [line 48]). To an audience familiar with mythic comic plots like that of *Twelfth Night*, her error would seem natural, and might even have been shared by the audience, to whom a young male actor playing a man could not have looked very different from a young male actor playing a woman playing a man. Lady Wouldbe's mistake thus constitutes a specific satiric response to mythic comedy's reliance on transvestism as a symbol of erotic possibility. Significantly, Peregrine turns out *not* to be a magical female surprise like Rosalind or Viola. Thus *Volpone*, centrally concerned to present figures of "empty" hermaphrodism (such as the eunuch, Castrone, and the hermaphrodite

Androgyno, to whom sex is "stale" [V, 1.2.55]), reveals stage transvestism as another false erotic promise: a theatrical sham.

Cynthia's Revels provides yet another satirical response to mythic stage transvestism. Its plot involves the effeminate, clothing-obsessed courtiers Asotus and Amorphus, who become "mutually enamor'd" with each other's appearance when they meet by the Fountain of Self-Love (IV, 1.4.59). Their romantic inclination toward each other really indicates their vain self-obsession, since each presents the image of the fashionably dressed gentleman to which they mutually aspire. "[Y]our sweet disposition . . . hath made you another myself in mine eye, and struck me enamor'd on your beauties," Amorphus tells Asotus (lines 136–37). Wise Crites, observing the action from a privileged marginal stage position, skeptically remarks, "'Heart, they'll change doublets anon" (line 170). The scene seems satirically to invert the action and meaning of Lyly's *Gallathea*, in a way analogous to Aristophanes' reductions of erotic beast/hermaphrodite mysteries (in *The Clouds*, for example, Aristophanes [as himself] describes a mythic beast-sacrifice tragedy as "an ancient play" in which the playwright "quite sensibly fed [an] old bitch to a sea monster" [p. 64]). Like Aristophanes, Jonson turns theater against itself, here presenting erotic transvestism as a playhouse illusion in which fatuous self-indulgence is masked as authentic human connection.

Asotus's and Amorphus's vain sentimentality also parallels Marston's parody of romantic comedy in the 1599 comedy *Histrio-Mastix* (not to be confused with William Prynne's later prose work of the same name). In Marston's play, an actor's effeminate sentimentality hinders his recitation of lines from a Shakespeare-like reunion scene: "'My son, thou art a lost child,'" an actor begins, adding, "(This is a passion, note you the passion?) / . . . 'O prodigal child, and child prodigal,'" he continues, and then breaks down: "Read the rest, sirs, I cannot read for tears" (1.1).[18] Like Marston, Jonson mocks mythic-romantic scenes dramatizing relational identity, turning the methods of mythic drama on their heads to do so. Tears, which in Shakespeare's plays are "holy water" (*Cymbeline* 5.5.269) sanctifying miraculously restored relationships, are in humors comedy merely founts of self-love: ludicrous indicators of missing masculinity.

The satiric inversion of mythic drama also involves the reductive treatment of the potent beast metaphors, which Jonson divests of their Lylyan/Shakespearean relational valences. Amorphus's name in the above scene does not indicate his availability for reshaping into an expanded synergistic identity, but his reprehensible self-loss. Similarly,

Asotus's nominal link with the ass suggests, not his willingness to be a fool for love, but his bestial nature. Like the stars who become "sky puppies" in the *Parnassus* poet's bad verse, divine Ovidian beasts are reduced to emblems of human degradation in Jonson's plays. In a way antithetical to myth and reminiscent of Roman satire, Jonsonian animal and monster images describe gender-transgressive human deformities.[19] Thus the dictatorial wife Chloë in *Poetaster* describes her marital tyranny in terms of horse riding (recalling the satiric emblem pictured in my first chapter): "'Sbodie, give husbands the head a little more, and they'll be nothing but head shortly" (IV, 2.1.77–78). Chloë's monstrous animalism is most obviously reproduced in *Epicoene*, whose termagant wives have names like "Lady Centaur" and "Mrs. Otter." An epigram of Jonson's calls "most of women . . . the common monster" (VIII, 195, 24), while *The Alchemist*'s Subtle refers to his and Face's lust-controlled customers as "all the monsters" (V, 4.3.46). Like Shakespeare, Jonson uses images of monstrousness and animalism to indicate a halfway condition between maleness and femaleness (most notably in the case of *Epicoene*'s hermaphrodites). But whereas the halfway condition of Shakespearean beast-monsters is the source of their power, halfwayness in Jonson indicates a power vacuum: a loss of sexual personhood. As Jonson says in *Discoveries*, "Contraries are not mixed" (VIII, 563, 10). (Recall the Athenian women's condemnation of the transvestite Mnesilochus in Aristophanes' *Thesmophoriasuzae*: "What contradictions his life shows! . . . Do you pretend to be a man?") Rather than unleashing a synergistic energy, Jonsonian male and female contraries cancel each other out. Thus the feminized Jonsonian male is not empowered, in the mythic manner of Dionysus, Odysseus, Antipholus, Petruchio, or Orlando. Instead, he loses maleness entirely.

This observation brings us back to this chapter's starting point: the justification of Jonson's satiric posture of militant masculine aggression. As my first chapter argued, satire derives from an ethos of attack that is, at bottom, a will to defend the isolated male authorial consciousness from the encroachments of the feminized Other. Satire genders female the acceptance of penetration and usurpation, and genders male the act of usurpation; if the male fails to usurp he will be usurped, and feminized. In Jonson's humors comedy, physically dominant sexuality is one means of defense against the feminizing threat of emotional connection with the Other; other means include withdrawal into exclusively male society and ridicule of women or effeminate men. Thus the *viri boni*, or virtuous male wits, in Jonson's plays are generally distinguished from effeminate males (as was Jonson himself) both by a cavalier sexuality and by general competitiveness in various arenas (including the sexual), as well as by their preference for male over female company and their detached mockery of women and effeminates.[20] Conversely, effeminate, androgynous men are marked by their *pretense* to sexual conquest, as well as by their enjoyment of women's company and by the psychological proximity to the female imagination indicated by this enjoyment and by their feminine behaviors. Such men's effeminacy is registered in their lack of *genuine* aggressive behavior, evident both in the paucity of their real sexual victories and their unwillingness to participate in other masculine physical contests, like dueling. A line in Jonson's "On the Town's Honest Man," a sarcastic attack on his erstwhile collaborator Inigo Jones, suggests the priority of combativeness in Jonson's masculine value system. Jonson remarks contemptuously that "it" (the neuter Inigo-monster) "will see its sister naked, ere a sword" (VIII, 74, 22). Analogously, the effeminate Amorous La-Foole's first dramatized characteristic in *Epicoene* is his nonconfrontationality. "It should be extremely against my will, sir, if I contested with any man," he tells Clerimont (V, 1.4.19–20). *Every Man in His Humour*'s Captain Bobadill is also revealed as deficient in manliness when he crumbles in the face of a physical challenge from Downright (who suspects him of stealing). Downright's subsequent beating and disarming of Bobadill, involving the symbolic removal of the captain's phallus through the appropriation of his sword, completes the exposure of Bobadill's reprehensible effeminacy, inseparable from his reluctance to fight (III, 4.7). The physical cowardice of *Epicoene*'s La-Foole and Jack Daw is, like Bobadill's, explicitly dramatized, as Truewit engineers these fops' willing submission to nose-tweaking and butt-kicking at the hands (and feet) of the play's wits in preference to a duel with each other (V, 4.5). There are no real stakes in the combat Truewit proposes between Daw and La-Foole: their cowardice lies in their unwillingness to fight for the mere sake of fighting! *Epicoene* links the fops' deficiency of physical valor with their inability to conquer sexually, as the wits later expose the falseness of La-Foole's and Daw's claims to have slept with Epicoene (V, 5.4).

These exposure scenes demonstrate that, unlike Shakespeare, who powers his comic plots through the medium of androgynous (usually) female heroes, Jonson bestows controlling comic power on groups of detached male wits, whose practical jokes perform a "stripping" function, exposing other characters' androgyny as vain affectations, or "humors." (Again, the qualified but important exception of Ursula will be later discussed.) *Poetaster's* Horace and Virgil, *Epicoene's* Dauphine, Truewit, and Clerimont, *Bartholomew Fair's* Quarlous and Winwife, the folio *Every Man in His Humour's* Downright, Brainworm and young Knowell, *The Alchemist's* Face and Love-Wit, *Volpone's* Peregrine, the Merchants, and even, to a certain extent, Mosca and Volpone, as well as *Every Man Out of His Humour's* Macilente and (with some qualifications) Carlo Buffone—all fall into the category of controlling wits. While these male characters are not all virtuous (especially those in the last two plays cited), they all at times occupy dominant stage positions that enable them to initiate and monitor comic action. By so placing them, Jonson both enforces audience sympathy for them and scorn for the objects of their scorn, and renders them authorial figures within the dramas, licensing their mockery of the androgynes.

The best of these wits are characterized by a physical, verbal, and imaginative competitiveness that demonstrates their aggressive masculinity. For Jonson, real men are generally willing to fight for something, like *Volpone's* Bonario, who leaps out from behind the arras to defend Celia from Volpone (V, 3.7), and like *Epicoene's* Truewit, who interrupts Morose's "If I had . . . vitiated your mother; ravished your sisters . . ." with "I would kill you, sir, I would kill you, if you had" (V, 2.2.50–53). Physical combat is, as Truewit says, a "manly . . . right" (V, *Epicoene* 4.5.73–74). Jonson does frequently ridicule compulsive quarrelsomeness (such as that exhibited by *The Alchemist's* Kastril and *Bartholomew Fair's* Zeal-of-the-Land Busy), and in the *Underwood* he identifies "true Valour" as

> the Law
> Of daring not to do a wrong . . .
> . . . to sleight it, being done to you!
> . . . .
> To bend, to break, provoke, or suffer it!
>
> (VIII, 233, 14–18)

However, the *Underwood* lines and the mockery of Kastril and Busy seem simply ironic when we view them next to Jonson's celebrated vindictiveness in the Theater Wars (to be discussed in my final chapter) and his propensity to strike at—even to create—various enemies at the slightest provocation (recall, for example, his nasty epigram "To the Court Pucelle"). That Jonson at times criticizes violence, yet validates the fighting instinct of his play's wits, may mean one of two things (and perhaps both): first, that Jonson felt that he had internalized the principle of discriminatory violence, and that as a result the quarrels he picked, or picked for his analogues within his plays, had intrinsic justification; second, that Jonson was occasionally capable of mocking both himself and his Juvenalian context of satirical anger. Whatever the explanation for the contradiction, it is clear that Jonsonian satire associates creative power with the aggressive confrontationality of its male wits. Their competitive streaks confirm their measurable emotional distance from one another. For Jonson, quarreling manifests necessary psychological distinctions between men. It is quite literally "differing": enacting difference. Unlike the effeminate courtier, the self-sufficient Jonsonian male is psychologically distinguishable from the other males in his environment, as well as from spouse or mistress (if such indeed exist). The intense individualism dictated by the satiric model of identity allows him, at best, psychological alliance (rather than convergence) with other men. Hence, male contest is "an acceptable violence" (recalling Truewit's phrase): an allowable and even necessary satiric context for the demonstration of what Eve Sedgwick calls "homosocial bonding."[21]

The context of contest is not merely physical, but verbal and imaginative. Truewit, Dauphine, and Clerimont power *Epicoene*'s comic plots with competing schemes to dupe and humiliate both Dauphine's uncle Morose and the effeminate social climbers Sir Amorous La-Foole and Jack Daw; Dauphine's successful master-plot, by which he secures his inheritance by tricking Morose into "marrying" a boy, wins "the better half of the garland" from his friends (V, 5.4.225). In *Bartholomew Fair*, Winwife's and Quarlous's masculinity resides largely in their own "quarlous"ness and desire to "win"; part of the plot involves their contest for the hand of Grace Wellborn, and they also compete verbally with Ursula (VI, 2.5). *The Alchemist*'s Face is certainly as knavish as the confederates, Subtle and Dol Common, with whom he dupes gullible customers, but Face is redeemed through his ability to triumph over Dol and Subtle in a contest of wits—specifically, by his successful appropriation of all their money and his acquisition of a wealthy widow for his master, Love-Wit, a virtual sexual victory (V, 5.5). Face evades punishment by presenting Love-Wit with Dame Pliant, whom he had earlier intended for himself (4.3.85); his bestowal of this "pliant" female prize on his master merges sexual contest with other forms of male aggression. Confrontationality in the forms of sexual contest, fighting, and other competition may at times be presented as excessive in Jonson's work; my point is not that it is always shown to be appropriate, but that it is always gendered *male*. When it is excessive, as in the character of the ridiculously quarrelsome Kastril, it is an excess of maleness. The violent characters in Jonson's plays may be wrong, but they are never androgynous, as are termagants such as *Epicoene*'s Mrs. Otter, who is masculinized largely by references to her habit of beating her husband (V, 4.2). Thus the exercise of native, authentic confrontationality helps distinguish Jonson's male wits from the various effeminate characters they mock—like Jack Daw and Amorous La-Foole, who will give each other "any satisfaction . . . but fighting" (V, *Epicoene* 4.5.75).

Like the impulse for dominance registered through sexual conquest, the impulse for dominance realized through fighting is an essential indicator of virility because it constitutes nontheatrical, physical proof of the same. Like Onion, the middle-class hero of *The Case Is Altered*, who "*breaks his head*" in a bout with foils (III, 2.7.104), the physically brave or "tall" man demonstrates interior valor, or "play[s] an honest part" (*CIA* 2.7.143–44). In the satirical system, maleness is an irreducible inner quality producing aggressive action, while femininity is airy nothingness. (The false etymology *mollis aer*, or "gentle air," for the Latin *mulier* [woman], was, in fact, a popular mistake in the Renaissance; Shakespeare reproduces it in *Cymbeline*, though he gives the phrase a positive valence [5.5.447–48].[22] Conversely, the Elizabethan slang word "stones" [testicles] suggests the common vision of masculine hardness.) Male aggression (that is, aggression performed by males) is authentic in that it proceeds from real qualities within the self. Female aggression is, conversely, inauthentic because it does not originate in intrinsic, justifying maleness. (Women's intrinsic qualities are, we recall, not active but passive "soft virtues.") Thus conspicuously active female behaviors are *imitations* of masculinity, or theatrical effects.

Jonson's presentation of theatrical imitation itself as both bestial (apish) *and* feminine follows logically from this construction of masculinity and femininity as legitimate enactment and false imitation. Since the active exercise of intrinsic virtue is what men do, the theatrical imitation of active virtue is what women do. (As the verse from *Epicoene*, quoted initially, suggests, the female enactment of behaviors that are virtuous in men is "female vice.") Thus feigning—*any* behavior that does not proceed from qualities legitimately located in the subject—is perceived as characteristically feminine, or (for a man) effeminate.

Jonson, however, is careful to distinguish between the inauthentic theatrical imitativeness demonstrated by simpering effeminates and aggressive women and the legitimate, manly imitation that actually assimilates virtuous quality into the imitating subject's own self. In *Discoveries*, Jonson describes legitimate imitation in his list of the true poet's qualities:

> To make one excellent man above the rest, and so to follow him, till he grow very he: or, so like him, as the copy may be mistaken for the principal. Not as a creature that swallows what it takes in crude, raw, or indigested; but that feeds with an appetite, and hath a stomach to concoct, divide, and turn all into nourishment. (VIII, 638, 2466–75)

These lines, like many others in Jonson, associate authentic imitation with personal assimilation of virtuous qualities, through a digestive metaphor that suggests the actual addition of the virtues imitated to the imitating subject's own being. The virtues imitated, in other words, are not assumed or theatrically performed, but actually synthesized into the imitator's own psychological anatomy.[23] This metaphor of the acquisition of virtue as physical expansion parallels other Jonsonian images of virtue as geometrical or architectural form. The deceased Henry Morison's nobility is thus revealed in the perfect "short measures" and "sphere" of his humanity (VIII, 244–45, 74, 52), and Philip Sidney's in the "proportion" of his house at Penshurst ("To Penshurst," VIII, 96, 99). Both species of metaphor accomplish the reification of abstract qualities into physical things.

The crucial difference between these Jonsonian metaphors of virtuous *synthesis* and mythic metaphors suggesting human *synergy* is just this reification. In *Discoveries* Jonson describes a private, personal acquisition of virtuous qualities also held by others, so that the individual subject incorporates "language and . . . truth" to grow personally in "weight" (VIII, 131, 7–12). No longer a mere imitator, he rationally assimilates knowledge and becomes a product of the lessons learned. Mythic synergy, on the other hand, emphasizes irrational process rather than rational product. According to the mythic model, through temporarily inhabiting the role of another the "imitator" experiences an ineffable synergistic communication with another being. That communicative interaction, variously imaged in mythic literature and drama as flowing water, beast-human relationship, maze-wandering, dreaming, and so on, is not capable of entrapment in particularized forms. It exists both in androgynous erotic activity and verbal relationship between its participants, whose identity now derives from that relationship. Here also transformative imitation as presented in myth differs vitally from that prescribed by Jonson. For Jonson, the synthesizing of knowledge that contributes to the growth of the private personality is not erotic or sexualized. It has strictly to do with the imitation/assimilation of masculine virtue through the exercise of reason. A man, in other words, becomes increasingly manly —not androgynized—by the imitation of other good men, a process accomplished primarily by the cognitive assimilation of their noble writings (which are works of rational philosophy, not the sensual love poetry read by women and fops). For Jonson, man's authentic growth through *intellectual* imitation stands in strict contrast to man's androgynized degeneration through *theatrical* imitation, or through the dangerous sexual encroachments of aggressive females who theatrically imitate *him*.

The ironies intrinsic to Jonson's use of the theatrical medium, whose very functioning in Renaissance England depended on the performative skills of cross-dressed males, to present this anti-androgynous stance have been noted by several contemporary scholars. Jonas Barish writes, "[W]ithin [Jonson's] plays or outside them, in structure or in moralizing comment, we find a distrust of theatricality, particularly as it manifests itself in acting, miming, or changing, and a corresponding bias in favor of the 'real'—the undisguised, unacted, and unchanging."[24] And Ronald Huebert wonders more specifically "how Jonson felt in a world where Celia and Lady Politic Wouldbe and Dol Common and Grace Wellborn weren't 'real' women . . . but young men in drag?" He adds that Jonson probably "felt far more comfortable when he left the tiring-house at Blackfriars and entered the Apollo Room . . . where men could be trusted to be men."[25] Doubtless Jonson's frequent use of boys' acting companies such as the children of Paul's, which rendered the performance of both male and female roles literal child's play, defused the moral problem a great deal,[26] but evidence "within the plays or outside them," to use Barish's phrase, suggests that Jonson's antipathy toward imitative gender transgression resonated in his tense relationship with the theater itself, and was, as I have partially demonstrated, structurally crucial to his plays' design.

Besides incorporating occasional plot devices that mocked the mythic-comic transvestite convention, Jonson safeguarded his plays' moral messages through rhetorical techniques that distanced the moral "poetry" of his works from threatening theatrical "spectacle," which appealed illegitimately to audience emotion. Like other satirical playwrights, Jonson gave his witty male characters the power to "fix" interpretations of his voluble effeminates and aggressive females through set character descriptions delivered in advance of the entrances of these "hermaphrodites" (recall Clerimont's initiatory fourteen-line description of Amorous La-Foole: "He is one of the Braveries, though he be none o' the Wits. . . ." [1.3.27–41]). And like Aristophanes long before him, Jonson employed publication as a device to secure his interpretive authority over the plays, padding the folio versions with lengthy prefatory material clarifying his authorial messages. *Volpone, Poetaster, Every Man Out, Every Man In,* and numerous other Jonsonian comedies were formally or informally addressed to readers, indicating Jonson's preferred evasion of the dangerous multivocality of actual theater. In the 1601 *Poetaster,* Jonson exercises the shrewd ploy of publishing additional dialogue (not included in the performed play), in which he as author speaks to fictive adversaries, whom he vanquishes resoundingly with a rational defense of his satire. The printed additional dialogue suggests Jonson's felt need to exert literary control over the dangerous dialectic, whose androgynous power to destabilize set ideological positions endangered Jonson's model of resolute manliness.

Within the plays, Jonson tends to use rapid-fire, interactive dialogue in a way antithetical to its use in Shakespearean mythic comedy. In Shakespeare, as my last chapter argued, dialogue allows and represents a creative synergy, weaving separated speakers together in a cooperative and communicative relational identity. But Jonson "drains" the potent symbolism of Shakespearean mythic dialectic in much the same way he empties other mythic androgyny symbols of their erotic valence. In Jonsonian satire, dialectic is indeed androgynizing, but invalidly so: it is generally used to demonstrate an inappropriate likeness between its participants, whose particular, solid, gendered individuation (if it existed) would register itself in controlled, self-sufficient speaking patterns. Thus Asotus and Amorphus of *Cynthia's Revel*'s unwittingly dramatize their effeminate collapse into like images of vanity through dialogue, which obliterates the distinctions that should exist between them:

AMO. Your ribband too does most gracefully, in troth.

ASO. 'Tis the most gentle, and receiv'd wear now, sir.

AMO. Believe me, sir (I speak it not to humour you), I
have not seen a young gentleman (generally) put
on his clothes with more judgement.

ASO. O, 'tis your pleasure to say so, sir.

AMO. No, as I am virtuous (being altogether un-travel'd)
it strikes me into wonder.

ASO. I do propose to travel, sir, at spring.

AMO. I think I shall affect you, sir. This last speech of
yours hath begun to make you dear to me.

(IV, 1.4.118–28)

And so on. The degeneration of these characters' maleness is evident
in the conflation of their clothing-obsessed psyches, dramatized in this
scene not only by their (presumably) near-identical costumes, but by
fatuous dialogue that confirms their likeness. These foppish effeminates collapse into each other, and thus into vanity; dialogue obliterates the distinctions which, according to the Jonsonian model of
legitimate male selfhood, should be visibly and verbally apparent.
"[I]s there any difference between you?" Crites shrewdly asks Asotus
prior to the pair's conversation. "No," Asotus responds (1.4.52–53).
The interchange recalls an analogous exchange in the earlier *Every
Man Out*, where after a similarly silly conversation between the
courtlings Shift and Fastidious Brisk, a character asks Shift, "What
was the difference between that gallant that's gone, and you, sir?"
"No difference," Shift replies (III, 3.6.100–1022). The surface query
is, of course, "Were you two arguing?" An affirmative response to
this might redeem these characters' dissolving masculinity. But the
question's underlying suggestion and the negative responses given
indicate a deeper comic horror dramatized by the courtlings' vain dialogue: their loss of all manly individuality, in a blur of feminized moral
formlessness.

The corrosive androgynizing power of dialectic is most clearly evident in *Epicoene*, where the courtiers' conversation blends with that

of the female collegiates, providing an auditory image of the groups' invalid androgynous likeness. In Jonsonian comedy, it is declamatory speaking ability, not skill at wiseacre repartee, that generally indicates self-sufficient masculine wholeness. For example, *Poetaster*'s Caesar, Virgil, and Horace (the last a figure of Jonson) demonstrate their rational self-control through lengthy, polished set speeches (see, for example, IV, 4.7.37–53, and 5.1–2). Dialogue, in contrast, is deployed by Jonson to indicate the unhealthy collapse of all relevant distinctions between the speakers, including and especially gender distinctions.

As apers of other-sex behavior, the effeminate males and the androgynous women of *Epicoene* demonstrate a Jonsonian paradox. Mrs. Otter's violence, for example, is real violence, but her authentic exercise of this masculine behavior renders her a false female. Yet it does not make her male: a male virtue is, after all, a female vice, or deficiency, in the terms of the play. Her male behavior can only be feigned (however authentic the blows may feel to Captain Otter). Thus, imitating maleness and obscuring femaleness, Mrs. Otter loses all gender, and paradoxically becomes what she, as a woman, is anyway: nothing. Her monstrousness is simply her theatricality: her pretense to be something (specifically, to be a man). In satiric construction, femininity is the absence of maleness, and hermaphrodism is a different *kind* of absence of maleness; it is the emptiness of the *pretense* to masculine being.

The converse is true of *Epicoene*'s effeminate courtiers. Their theatrical femininity involves a departure from the authentic masculine virtue that they should properly exercise. Rather than a masking of the unreal, it is a flight from the real into the intrinsic emptiness of femininity. While the "male" behavior of Mrs. Otter, Lady Centaur, and the female collegiates hides feminine absence, the "female" behavior of Amorous La-Foole and Jack Daw enacts abandonment of masculine presence. These men's effeminate practices—notably their obsession with theatrical costume and their "amorous" psychological congress with vain women—are, like Mrs. Otter's violence, real theatrical effects, but effeminacy's theatrical status only compounds its *un*reality: it is the imitation of vanity, or nothing times two.

Of course, the female androgynous equation of nothing imitating something (0×1) and the male androgynous equation of nothing imitating nothing (0×0) have identical results: a zero product. Both versions of hermaphrodite are nothing—mere emptiness. The single difference for the male hermaphrodites is that, as biological men, they might have been real.

Epicoene's final scene realizes this possibility. This scene, with its dramatic revelation to both characters *and* audience of the boy inhabiting Lady Epicoene's disguise, is designed, not to accentuate the play's collapse into androgynous emptiness, but genuinely to reclaim the stage androgyne's irreducibly male body from the feminizing threat of marriage, the sexualized female, and the playhouse itself. While the "stripping" action of Jonsonian satire reveals the nothingness underlying the feminized male's pretensions, Epicoene's final stripping exposes the solid masculine generative presence on which the satiric drama is based, and from which it proceeds. The last-minute "reduction" of the female character Epicoene to the boy actor playing her role is actually not a reduction at all, but a restoration of genuine, nontheatrical male identity from the feminized environment Morose's collegiate-infested home has become,[27] as well as from the marital threat. The "monstrous hazards . . . [of] a wife" presented in *Epicoene* (2.2.41-42) contrast radically with the Shakespearean theme of marital "hazard" as erotic opportunity (e.g., *Merchant of Venice* 1.1.51), just as the Juvenalian image of "goblin matrimony" with which Truewit frightens Morose (*Epicoene* 2.2.32) stands in contradistinction to Hymen, the wedding god who blesses *As You Like It*'s final scene. Thus, appropriately, the restorative stripping move that makes Morose's wife disappear ("*He takes off Epicoene's peruke*" [V, 5.4.204]) is performed by Dauphine, Boy/Epicoene's male friend, in a winning gesture that simultaneously saves Morose from the threat marriage poses to his identity and affirms the competitive male bonding pattern authorized by the play. In defeating both Morose's scheme to disinherit him and his friends' rival jokes, Dauphine paradoxically confirms his contestatory masculine bond with the men, which is the healthy Jonsonian alternative to feminizing conjugal relationship. Likewise, Dauphine rescues the boy playing Epicoene from the horrifying, Swiftian threat posed by the play's sexually rapacious women, which the boy describes in the play's first scene:

> The gentlewomen play with me, and throw me on the bed; and carry me in to my lady; and she kisses me with her oil'd face; and puts a peruke on my head; and asks me an' I will wear her gown; and I say, no; and then she hits me a blow o' the ear, and calls me innocent, and lets me go. (1.1.13–18)

These "masculine" females, whose androgyny is registered in their domineering sexuality and their aggressive volubility, are, appropriately, rendered speechless by the final restorative stripping of this boy. The play's last words are given to Truewit, who chastises both hermaphroditic species' vain pretensions in a final, thirty-line demonstration of male declamatory self-possession (lines 224–53).

Thus *Epicoene*'s concluding action deploys a complex variety of Jonsonian satirical weapons to recall the real male body from the androgynizing threat posed by the feminized theatrical world. In city or humors satire, "misogyny is a structural principle," Mary Beth Rose writes.[28] *Epicoene* bears out Rose's claim, demonstrating a defensive recoil from a perilous invalid hermaphrodism. In a sense, Jonson's sudden, shocking replacement of mistress Epicoene with the body of the boy who plays her is an act of theatrical bad faith: a transgression of the implicit contract between playwrights and audience regarding trust in the "truth" of theatrical illusion. In a deeper sense, however, Jonson's explosion of the theatrically sacred transvestite completes the structural misogyny of his play. The departure from theatrical convention is, in Jonsonian moral terms, a profoundly generous act that protects male characters and audience members from a far greater cheat: the false promise of relational identity extended by the illusory mythic androgyne.

4

Experimental Androgynes: Falstaff, Ursula, and *The New Inn*

he looks like a mid-wife in man's apparel, the . . . fat fool . . .
in his over-familiar playing face.

—Jonson, *Poetaster*

[M]y womb swells. . . .

—Jonson, "The Poet to the Painter"

Shakespearean romantic comedy and Jonsonian humors comedy are
crucially invested in the countervailing principles of mythic and satiric
androgyny. Nevertheless, as I indicated in my first chapter, Shakespeare's
and Jonson's respective involvements in the staging of transcendent and
"freakish" hermaphrodism did not preclude their occasional experimentation with each other's comic methods, including comic androgynous types. A comparative analysis of the evolving Renaissance stage
androgyne in each man's work reveals, in fact, a concentrated attention on the other's dramatic achievements. Their mutual fascination
was recorded in a staged argument that began in the late 1590s and
continued on Jonson's part long after Shakespeare's retirement from
the London theater world in 1613 (Jonson was, ironically, a masterful theatrical conversationalist, despite the implicit resistance to dialogue evident in much of his work). The most active and heated
moment in the two playwrights' intertheatrical engagement was the
particular phase of the 1599–1601 *poetomachia*, or Theater Wars,
during which Jonson and Shakespeare confronted each other through
metadramatic plays commenting on the respective merits of mythic
comedy and humors satire. As my next chapter will argue, this stage
debate necessarily centered—as do the perspectives of myth and satire
generally—on the use of the androgyne symbol. However, both before

and after this key moment in their artistic relationship, each play-wright "tried out" the other's opposing androgyne within his own dramatic context, with intriguing results.

Shakespeare's experiment with the satirical androgyne occurred in the first half of his dramatic career. This chapter will provide a reading of *The Merry Wives of Windsor* as Shakespeare's single authentic experiment in the developing humors genre: an uncharacteristic and problematic Shakespearean use of the anti-androgynous satiric context. *The Merry Wives of Windsor* shares certain key features with humors comedy, and is (I think) entitled to be called one; still, as I will ultimately argue, the play's satirical format is radically compromised by Shakespeare's apparently irresistible impulse to give comic control to women. The technique demonstrates Shakespeare's ultimate imaginative distance from the satirical mind-set—his unwillingness or inability to incorporate a "structural principle" of misogyny (recalling Mary Beth Rose's phrase) even into his only English city comedy. In *Merry Wives*, Shakespeare reduces the rich "Silenus" Falstaff of the Henry plays to an impotent humors character, whose stage transvestism associates him with sexual failure rather than creative power. But significantly, Shakespeare followed *Merry Wives*'s presentation of this ludicrous "Jonsonian" transvestite with two of his boldest validations of mythic hermaphrodism, *As You Like It* and *Twelfth Night*. Further, not only did these last-mentioned plays return decisively to Shakespeare's customary mythic mode, they recontextualized the figure of the satirical wit—which, in the doubled personhood of Mistresses Ford and Page, constituted *Merry Wives*'s controlling spirit—so as to comment on that figure's social uselessness (as did other turn-of-the century Shakespearean works). From this point forward, Shakespearean comedy generally repudiated the anti-androgynous principle, and the satiric mind-set from which it derived.

Unlike the "Jonsonian" Falstaff of Shakespeare's *Merry Wives*, the Jonsonian versions of the "Shakespearean" androgyne emerged relatively late in Jonson's career, after *Every Man In*, *Every Man Out*, *Volpone*, *The Alchemist*, and *Epicoene* had fully developed his anti-androgynous principle. Just as *Merry Wives* combines elements of mythic comedy and satire, the 1614 *Bartholomew Fair* represents a curious conflation of Shakespearean and Jonsonian comic modes, as several scholars have noticed.[1] *Bartholomew Fair* is, for the purposes of this discussion, most intriguing in its mixed, ambivalent presentation of Ursula, who merges the characteristics of Falstaff, the mythic *and* the satiric androgyne, and even Jonson himself in a confusing welter of valences. *Bartholomew Fair* presents a variety of perspectives on what my last chapter called the "androgynizing" worlds of society and theater: perspectives that include but are not limited to the satirical recoil characteristic of Jonson's earlier comedies.

Significantly, however, Jonson's one pure experiment in Shakespearean androgyny, *The New Inn* (1629), was followed by the most furious and decisive rebuttal he ever wrote of the vain, feminized London world and stage (including his old enemies, the androgynous effeminates): his "Ode to Himself," beginning, "Come, leave the loathed stage" (VI, 492, 1). This poem, which first rehearses Jonson's customary satiric perspective on invalid "androgynous" social theater and then culminates in a worshipful paean to Charles I, represents a peculiar binary mind-set evident throughout Jonson's work: a curious oscillation between satiric disgust with feminized beast-degenerates and Petrarchan-style adulation of idealized, semidivine humanoid figures. Thus near the end of his dramatic career, Jonson reaffirmed the satiric ethos with which he began. "Ode to Himself" recuperates the anti-androgynous principle, in that it resists a vision of flowing, interactive human identity in favor of an idealistic model of reified, self-contained personhood.

My next and final chapter will address the curiously linked perspectives of satiric misogyny and romantic idealization as registered in Jonson's humors drama, particularly with regard to Shakespeare's response to that linkage in the Theater Wars. In that confrontation, Shakespeare clearly rejected these Jonsonian paradigms of personhood, and reaffirmed his mythic androgyne as the appropriate symbol of healthy, interactive human life. But before that, as noted, Shakespeare had demonstrated a keen interest in less positive "Jonsonian" models of androgyny, and it is to Shakespeare's early experimentation with these that I now will turn. I want first to depart from a strict focus on androgyny in order to disclose the characteristics which *The Merry Wives of Windsor* legitimately shares with Jonsonian humors comedy. Thus I hope to demonstrate that in writing this play, Shakespeare was genuinely attempting to embrace the satirical ethic. Ultimately, however, I will discuss the ways in which this Shakespearean "satire" was—wittingly or unwittingly—pulled in the direction of mythic comedy by certain features (perhaps obvious ones) that orient it, despite itself, towards a qualified celebration of the androgynous principle.

I.

The Folger Shakespeare Theater's use of a female actor as Falstaff in its 1990 production of *The Merry Wives of Windsor*, besides its witty reversal of the Elizabethan convention of all-male casting, had this to recommend it: the "distaff" Falstaff, an embodiment of sexlessness, confronted audiences with the curious absence of regenerative possibility that distinguishes *Merry Wives* from standard "Shakespearean" mythic comedy. Unlike (for example) *A Midsummer Night's Dream*, which creates a world capable of transformation and renewal by means of an erotic energy that dominates language and fuels action, *Merry Wives* presents a static community for which transformation is a threat, language lacks creativity, and a dearth of real erotic connective desire parallels the characters' linguistic barrenness. In bourgeois Windsor, the unsavory characters Ford and Falstaff are impelled by jealousy or greed masquerading as eros, while the heroes Mistresses Ford and Page are motivated to protect rather than change their world, by frustrating Ford's and Falstaff's damaging vices and expelling these from the community. The play's language, correspondingly, is not imbued with the poetic power to unite separated beings or to transform them into relational selves; it serves instead repetitively and prosaically to express the villains' unchanging humors, or alternatively is employed medicinally by the heroes to deflate those humors. The consequent absence of transformative and regenerative possibility in both plot and language marks *Merry Wives* as an early experiment in what we now call Jonsonian humors comedy, and demonstrates Shakespeare's early participation in the fashioning of that genre.[2]

The Merry Wives of Windsor seems, in fact, to have been one of the first humors comedies performed in Elizabethan England, and may well have functioned as something of a dramatic model for Jonson's *Every Man in His Humour*, which appeared a year later (and in which Shakespeare the actor played a leading role).[3] *Merry Wives*, apparently written for the 1597 spring Garter Feast at Westminster,[4] was composed about the same time as George Chapman's *Humorous Day's Mirth*, widely considered the first humors play. Whatever the true order of composition, the chronological proximity of Chapman's, Shakespeare's, and Jonson's plays suggests the theater's general interest in the formation of this new type of comedy in the late 1590s; and Shakespeare's appearance in Jonson's *Every Man In* in

1598, coupled with the fact that it was Shakespeare's own Lord Chamberlain's Company that first staged Jonson's play, suggests Shakespeare's particular interest in the form.[5] That Shakespeare's contemporaries, notably Jonson, perceived *Merry Wives* as a humors experiment is suggested by the closing lines of Jonson's 1599 *Every Man Out of His Humour*, when a newly deflated humors character asks for a swell of applause to make him "as fat as Sir John Fal-Staff" (III, 5.11.86-87). Although Anne Barton interprets these lines as Jonson's puzzling gesture toward "an alien popular form: the Shakespearean history,"[6] it seems probable that the "Fal-Staff" invoked is not Prince Hal's companion, but the ludicrous lecher of *Merry Wives*, a character and a play much closer to Jonsonian type.

In participating in the formation of humors comedy, Shakespeare was developing a drama that used language in a way antithetical to its use in mythic comedy. Broadly speaking, the language of mythic comedy opens up realms of imaginative possibility for its characters, while the language of satiric humors comedy serves mainly to express a humors character's imaginative limitations, or, in the mouth of the wit, mockingly to deflate another's humor. Thus Helena's declaration of love for the churlish Demetrius in *A Midsummer Night's Dream*, which asserts that "Things base and vile, holding no quantity, / Love can transpose to form and dignity" (1.1.232–33), contrasts jarringly with the contemptuous sentiment expressed by Truewit toward Jack Daw and Amorous La-Foole at the close of Jonson's *Epicoene*: scoffing at Daw's and La-Foole's "own imagined persons" as valiant lovers, Truewit asserts that the two are in fact merely "they that, when no merit or fortune can make [them] hope to enjoy [women's] bodies, will yet . . . make their fame suffer" (V, 5.4.233–34, 237–39). Whereas Helena's ennobling poetry endows imagination with the power to transform a "base and vile" man to "form and dignity," Truewit's deflationary prose punctures Daw's and La-Foole's imaginary form and dignity and reveals them to be truly base and vile.

In humors comedy, the language of the wit deflates, like a rapier or lance. His sharp words are the verbal deployment of his valorous, contestatory nature. Contrastingly, in the mouth of the foolish, feminized humors character, language is a blunt sword, whose stuntedness expresses mental limitations. We see this in the "tag speech" so common to Jonson's plays, in which a character is marked by the parroting of others' words (Mathew's and Jack Daw's plagiarized poetry in *Every Man In* and *Epicoene*, respectively) or by the mindless repetition of a single phrase (Wasp's "Turd i' your teeth!" in *Bartholomew*

Fair). The closedness and stagnancy of the resulting discourse demonstrate the humor character's imaginative sterility: his or her inability to originate language.

The Merry Wives of Windsor is like Jonson's comedies and unlike most of Shakespeare's in that it develops similar patterns of "boxed-in" discourse. The speech of Nym, Falstaff's disgruntled follower, is dominated by the word "humor" ("The humor rises; it is good. Humor me . . . ! I thank thee for that humor" [1.3.56–57, 64]), a fact which has convinced some scholars that Shakespeare was merely satirizing the new humors genre.[7] But other characters use repetitive speech as well. "Said I well?" the Host of the Garter Inn continually and mechanically asks after he has spoken (1.3.11, 2.1.218, 2.3.89, 95). The Welsh parson Evans and the French physician Caius are also marked by what William Carroll calls an "idiosyncratic verbal quirk,"[8] which is simply their consistent failure to pronounce English correctly. And Mistress Quickly's running-gag malapropisms are a similarly redundant "quirk"; mistaking "allicholy" for "melancholy" (2.4.154), "infection" for "affection" (2.2.115), and "speciously" for "specially" (4.5.111), she earns laughs through the sameness of her errors rather than through linguistic inventiveness.[9] These characters' humor—and their humors —lies in dysfunctional speech rather than in verbal mastery.

The language of the main characters, Mistresses Ford and Page, Ford, and Falstaff, is allowed freer rein, but it, too, is restricted by the humors format of the play. Mistresses Ford and Page, the play's wits, are charmingly inventive in the plots they devise to humiliate Falstaff, but their language, like their plots, is ultimately directed toward destruction rather than creation: the puncturing of Falstaff's silly fantasy of himself as a lover. Their deflationary wit in the play's catastrophe might have inspired the previously cited remarks of Jonson's Truewit to Jack Daw and Amorous La-Foole: "Why, Sir John," the wives ask mockingly,

> do you think, though we would have thrust virtue out of our hearts
> by the head and shoulders, and have given ourselves without scru-
> ple to hell, that ever the devil could have made you our delight?
> (5.5.146–50)

Like Jonson's Truewit, the wives use clever discourse to banish theatrical posing, and to annihilate unwholesome fantasy.

And in humors comedy, fantasy tends to be not only unwholesome but unpoetic as well. Ford's jealous fantasy determines and limits his conversation; he can talk of nothing but Mistress Ford's supposed infidelity, whether in conversation with Falstaff or in anguished soliloquy ("See the hell of having a false woman! My bed shall be abus'd" [2.2.291-92]). And unlike Othello's or Leontes' discourses of jealousy, which reach terrifying imaginative heights,[10] Ford's language shrinks, in comic self-compression, to one obsessively repeated word as his humor escalates: "Cuckold! Wittol!—Cuckold! . . . cuckold, cuckold, cuckold!" [2.2.299, 313-14]). The pattern recurs where, awash in what Evans calls "fery fantastical humors and jealousies" as he fails to locate Falstaff in his wife's buck-basket, Ford screams, "Buck! . . . Buck, buck, buck! ay, buck!" (3.3.170-71, 157-58). In Ford's hysterical repetitions, we hear the ultimate reduction of the human imagination to animal size; he sounds like a chicken. Ben Jonson was later to make standard the correspondence between foolishness and animality; Jonson's Mrs. Otters and Sir Pols, like Shakespeare's Ford, are comically diminished by their association with small, funny beasts. As I have earlier demonstrated, Shakespeare is characteristically apt to dramatize beast metaphors from the mythic erotic tradition, using animals as transcendent signifiers of sublime erotic activity. Jonson, in contrast, habitually employs animals as emblems of the shrunken, degenerate male psyche, "feminized" by its overmastery by sexual (or other) obsession. Shakespeare's Ford is thus surprisingly "Jonsonian": not a potent human beast, empowered by erotic relatedness, but a man psychologically impoverished by the passions in which marriage involves him. Ford is an early type of the mindlessly chattering humors figure, locked into an unimaginative, bestial speech system.

Even Falstaff, whose language is more interesting than anyone else's in *Merry Wives*, is, as most critics acknowledge, a mere verbal shadow of the Falstaff of the Henry plays.[11] Although still capable of outlandish conceits—"My belly's as cold as if I had swallow'd snowballs for pills" (*Merry Wives* 3.5.23)—this Falstaff is unable to construct the imaginative verbal escapes with which he foiled Prince Hal's mockery in the histories. In *1 Henry IV*, when Falstaff is challenged for his cowardly flight from the disguised prince at Gad's Hill— "Come, let's hear, Jack, what trick hast thou now?"—Falstaff improvises an elaborate, fourteen-line response, commencing, "By the Lord, I knew ye as well as he that made ye. Why, hear you, my masters, was it for me to kill the heir apparent?" (2.4.265-69). Later in the same play, after ignominiously collapsing at Shrewsbury, Falstaff similarly gains the prince's indulgence as well as battlefield honors through his preposterous claim to have killed Hotspur (*1HIV* 4.4.138–43). In the Henry plays Falstaff ably plays with others' words, dialogically inverting verbal attacks against him by turning them to excuses for his behavior ("Thou seest I have more flesh than another man, and therefore more frailty" [*1HIV* 3.3.166–67). These imaginative rhetorical defenses contrast markedly with Falstaff's lame responses when confronted with his crimes in *Merry Wives*. In *Merry Wives*'s first scene, for example, when Justice Shallow charges Falstaff with having "beaten [his] men, kill'd [his] deer, and broke open [his] lodge," and demands, "This shall be answer'd," Falstaff briefly and unimaginatively retorts, "I will answer it straight: I have done all this. That is now answer'd" (1.1.111–12, 114–16). And his final gulling at the hands (literally) of the Windsor community—who, disguised as fairies, surround, pinch, and verbally insult him—totally destroys his witty capacity for rebuttal, to the point where he declares his inability to respond: "Well, I am your theme. You have the start of me, I am dejected. I am not able to answer" (5.6.161–62). Pat Carroll, who played Falstaff in the 1990 Folger production, links Falstaff's verbal incapacity in *Merry Wives* with his susceptibility to theatrical neutering; she feels this Falstaff is accessible to a female actor because of the "total de-bristling" of his language. "In the Henry plays," Carroll asserts, "he was always able to get out of it, and it was always with his mouth."[12] That verbally virile Falstaff, continually able to reauthor his relationship to the world with a witty answer, is in *Merry Wives* only the impotent, "dejected theme" of others' mockery. His inability to brandish the satiric verbal weaponry of defensive attack demonstrates his inner emptiness, and foreshadows his later appearance as what my last chapter called the "empty hermaphrodite": the neutered sexual monster who, through vain theatrical posing, becomes feminized and loses all claims to masculinity.

This "total de-bristling" of Falstaff is, of course, the necessary comic result for humors drama, which enacts the healthy purgation of diseased imaginations. Both Falstaff's vain fantasies, called a "dissolute disease" by Mistress Page (3.3.191–92), and what Falstaff calls Ford's "continual 'larum of jealousy" (3.5.71–72) are appropriately mocked and deflated by the events of the play. The deflationary process, effecting as it does the safeguarding of the wives' chastity and reputations, is of the Jonsonian rather than the Shakespearean comic pattern, according to a definition well summarized by F. H. Mares:

> Shakespearian comedy . . . does not assume that the conditions and the requisites of man's welfare have been certainly established, and are therefore a sanctity only to be safeguarded. It speculates imaginatively on modes, not of preserving a good already reached, but of enlarging and extending the possibilities of this and other kinds of good. Hence Shakespearian comedy is not finally satiric; it is poetic.[13]

Another word for the mode Mares calls "poetic" is, of course, "mythic." Ironically, despite Shakespeare's ultimate commitment to poetic or mythic comedy, his *Merry Wives of Windsor* helped originate the antithetical genre of satiric comedy, which is concerned to "safeguard" communal "welfare" and "preserve a good already reached" (we may recall once more the lines from Jonson's *Discoveries* regarding the protection of the originary self). As Anne Barton puts it, in rejecting Falstaff's deluded schemes, Windsor

> simply closes ranks and reaffirms its original values against an outsider. . . . The end of the play does not accord with Shakespeare's usual comic practice. . . . There is no sense that a new or transformed society leaves Herne's oak.[14]

The oak at which the community congregates at the play's end brings to mind the standard Jonsonian images of the integrated self: the "well-timbered gallant," the "piece of cedar" that suggests self-sufficient masculine identity. In *Merry Wives*, the concept of the solid individual self seems analogous to that described in Jonson, but the image involves the integrity, not of male citizens, but of females (a crucial difference to be later discussed). It is the stability and concreteness of Windsor in the specific form of the merry wives' inviolable chastity that Falstaff seems to threaten with destructive change. The satiric construction of hermaphrodism is, we recall, a register of the satirist's fear of "opening" himself to the corrosive presence of a penetrating Other. *Merry Wives* contains an element of this fear, although it problematizes its own satiric ethic by locating the fear of penetration centrally in the ridiculous figure of Ford, himself unmanned by sexual jealousy. The terms with which Ford imagines Falstaff's attack emphasize the likeness of his wife's virtue to an embattled fort: Falstaff's seduction of Mistress Ford could "drive her . . . from the ward of her purity, her reputation, her marriage vow, and a thousand other her defenses, which are now too strongly embattled" (2.2.248-51). The power Falstaff imagines he has (and Ford imagines Falstaff has) to

alter Mistress Ford is a destructive power; it would corrode her
defenses. In Windsor, transformation is to be feared. As William
Carroll observes, "Shapeshifting is bad form."[15]

This fear of change is a logical constituent of drama that presents
selfhood as a fixed good and heroes as consequently bound to defend
their prior integrity against the dangers of imaginative role-play. In
Jonsonian humors drama, make-believe holds little regenerative
power for the community. Falstaff's swaggering "show" of himself as
"young gallant" (2.1.22) and Ford's paranoid dream of himself as
cuckold alienate their subjects from their true selves, and threaten
Mistresses Ford and Page with like losses of self. After reading Falstaff's "mash" note, Mistress Page says,

> [I]t makes me almost ready to wrangle with mine own honesty. I'll
> entertain myself like one that I am not acquainted withal; for sure
> unless he know some strain in me that I know not myself, he would
> never have boarded me in this fury. (2.1.84–89)

The play shrinks from the danger to real identity posed by an imagination that is powerless to generate valid new ways of being and can
only construct false or degraded identities. The comedy's recoil from
imaginative self-creation implies a Jonsonian distrust of the feminizing corrosion of theater, wherein (to invoke *Discoveries* once more)

> every man, forgetful of himself, is in travail with expression of
> another. Nay, we so insist in imitating others, as we cannot (when
> it is necessary) return to our selves: like children, that imitate the
> vices of stammerers so long, till at last they become such, and make
> the habit to another nature. (VIII, 597, 1093–99)

According to this view, theatrical speaking is an anticreative act that
can render only invalid "selves." Such theatrically conceived identities are associated with failed, dysfunctional speech (stammering)
rather than with the synergistic dialogic power unleashed by the disguised transvestite heroines of Shakespeare's later mythic comedies.
In this Jonsonian drama, as in Jonson's own plays, language is limited to a binary capability, exercised in mutually exclusive ways by
what Ann Blake calls "two unchanging groups of fools and clever
men."[16] Used erroneously by the fools, it can miscreate false "selves";
used correctly by clever men (or, in this case, women), it can destroy
the false "selves" so generated.

"Jonsonian" or satiric dramatic language, then, is at best an instrument to protect what is integral and preexistent. It cannot create new worlds or new identities. Characters in humors comedy cannot, as *A Midsummer Night's Dream*'s Helena does with her Demetrius, recast faults as virtues through imaginative poetry; such recasting is a suspect operation that is inevitably foiled by the keen lance of the hero's wit. Reformation is thus only restoration to true form, as when Ford renounces the "here[sy]" of jealousy (*Merry Wives* 4.4.9) and Falstaff is publicly "Falstaffed," simultaneously disclosed and described as "a hodge pudding," a "bag of flax," and a "puff'd man" (5.5.151-52). In Jonsonian fashion, the play strips theatrical pretenses to new identity and restores legitimate, old identity, repeatedly staging a resistance to degenerative metamorphosis.

The theme of expansive, *re*generative metamorphosis through the agency of eros—the hermaphroditic relational power that informs most Shakespearean romantic comedy—is marginalized in *The Merry Wives of Windsor*. The absence of an informing and transforming erotic power parallels (in fact, is) the absence of powerful language. As my second chapter argued, in Shakespeare, the power to unite, transform, and regenerate lovers and communities resides primarily in imaginative, interactive language between human agents who are mutually erotically inclined —who are, in mythic terms, androgynous. The absence of the mythic androgyne in *Merry Wives*, its replacement by the "empty androgyne" of the evolving humors tradition, is analogous to *The Merry Wives of Windsor*'s linguistic rejection of transformation for restabilization.

The primary register of *Merry Wives*'s temporary turn from the androgynous principle is the uncharacteristically sexless solution it provides to its own social ills. Unlike most of Shakespeare's comedies (e.g., *The Comedy of Errors*, *The Taming of the Shrew*, *A Midsummer Night's Dream*, *The Merchant of Venice*, *Much Ado about Nothing*, and *As You Like It*), *The Merry Wives of Windsor* avoids a multiple-marriage or multiple-marital-reunion plot resolution, minimizing the wedding theme by relegating it to the secondary plot involving the "shadowy young lovers," Fenton and Anne Page.[17] The extreme discomfiture of Slender's and Caius's marital hopes through the crossed designs of Page, Mistress Page, and Mistress Quickly, which cause the suitors to "marry" boys dressed as women while Fenton elopes with Anne, dramatizes the resistance to erotic personal and social regeneration that renders this play un-Shakespearean. Indeed, the final scene, in which Shallow's and Caius's "brides" unmask and reveal themselves to be male, looks forward to the denouement of Jonson's

Epicoene, where Morose is similarly un-wived and sexually mocked. Like that of Jonson's play, *Merry Wives*'s comic resolution requires that most characters experience erotic frustration rather than consummation.

But the deeper sterility of both "Jonsonian" dramas lies beneath the obvious turn from erotic connection in the plays' foiled marriages, and has to do with virtually all the characters' lack of significant erotic motive. In this play, as in humors comedy generally, the potent connective force of eros seems hardly to exist.

For example, Slender, Anne Page's most reluctant suitor, is impelled toward courtship by Anne's monetary worth rather than by her personal qualities. When Evans informs him that "seven hundred pounds of moneys, and gold, and silver, is her grandsire upon his death's-bed . . . give," the sluggish Slender shows his first spark of interest: "Did her grandsire leave her seven hundred pound?" (1, 1, 50–54, 64–65). As William Carroll has noticed, this "recurring displacement of natural impulses by commercial self-interest . . . is typical of all the characters in the play except Fenton and Anne."[18]

It is certainly typical of Ford, whose treatment of his wife's chastity as his own threatened personal possession prefigures the obsessive proprietary jealousy of Kitely and Corvino in Jonson's *Every Man In* (folio version) and *Volpone*, respectively. Ford's comment, "I will rather trust a Fleming with my butter, Parson Hugh the Welshman with my cheese, an Irishman with my aqua-vitae bottle, or a thief to walk my ambling gelding, than my wife with herself" (2.2.302–5), reifies his wife's identity by associating it with sexual honor, itself rendered a static commodity by its association with butter, cheese, liquor, and livestock. Ford's fear of identity-fracturing in Mistress Ford—he will not trust his "wife with herself"—echoes Mistress Page's earlier dismayed response to Falstaff's seduction letter: "I'll entertain myself like one that I am not acquainted withal; for sure unless he know some strain in me that I know not myself, he would never have boarded me. . . ." Both Ford and Mistress Page objectify selfhood, expressing the view that displacement from a "true" identity is both possible and unhealthy; one can be "forgetful of himself," to recall Jonson's phrase in *Discoveries*. But Ford surpasses Mistress Page in this objectifying act, reducing his wife's selfhood/sexual honor to his own personal treasure. Like *Every Man In*'s Kitely, who (in Ford-like soliloquy) frames his fears of sexual betrayal in economic terms—"Who will not judge him worthy to be robb'd, / That sets his doors wide open to a thief, / And shows the felon where his treasure lies?" (III, 3.3.15–17)—and like *Volpone*'s Corvino, who locks his Celia in a room like a jewel in a strongbox (V, 2.5), Ford is impelled by miserliness rather than erotic energy. These husbands' sexualization is not erotic, but obsessive-compulsive; the greedy passion marriage inspires in them provides them no legitimate access to their wives' being, it only alienates them from their own, as their reason crumbles. Like Kitely and Corvino, the impassioned Ford represents the principle that, in Anne Parten's words, "it is perfectly possible for a man to be inclined toward jealousy without loving and toward adultery without lusting. A concern for guarding or accumulating wealth supplies an entirely adequate alternate motivation."[19]

Just as Ford lacks authentic erotic motivation, the play as a whole lacks romantic trepidation. The absence of erotic compulsion is emphasized in the characterization of the "softly-sprighted" Slender (1.4.24), who "cannot abide the smell of hot meat" (2.2.285–86) and is reluctant to have anything to do with the young woman he ostensibly courts. Justice Shallow's concern over whether Slender could even perform physically were his suit to Anne successful, implicit in his question, "Cousin Abraham Slender, can you love her? . . . Can you love the maid?" (1.1.232, 243), seems well founded: having successfully obtained an interview with Anne, Slender disclaims all personal interest, saying, "Truly, for mine own part, I would little or nothing with you. Your father and my uncle have made motions" (3.4.62–64).

Finally, the critical attention paid to the Windsor community's repudiation of Falstaff's unwholesome libido —Nancy Cotton calls the public mocking of Falstaff in the play's final scene "symbolic castration," as does Jeanne Addison Roberts[20]—has obscured the fact that that libido has always been mostly bravado, employed in pursuit of cash. Falstaff is "well-nigh worn to pieces with age" (2.1.21–22), "old, cold," and "wither'd" (5.5.153). Falstaff is, in fact, the central symbol of non-erotic or "empty" androgyny in the play. In *Merry Wives*, Falstaff is more Jonsonian than he is Falstaffian. Like Morose's desire in *Epicoene* for a wife, which springs from a miserly wish to disinherit his nephew, Falstaff's sexual stalking of Mistresses Ford and Page is motivated, not by eros, but by a perceived economic necessity; he is "almost out at heels" (or, as Pistol comically observes, "Young ravens must have food") (1.3.31, 35). The true objects of Falstaff's attack are Ford and Page, men "of substance good" (1.3.37) whose wives are only important insofar as they offer access to their husbands' wealth. As in *Epicoene*, an apparent sexual motive masks a genuine financial power play. "I will use her as the key of the cuckoldy rogue's coffer," Falstaff boasts of Mistress Ford (2.2.237–74). Earlier, he has observed that "she has the rule of her husband's purse," and that Mistress Page "bears the purse too; she is a region in Guiana, all gold and bounty. I will be cheaters to them both, and they shall be exchequers to me" (1.3.51–52, 68–71). Falstaff's language here inverts Shakespeare's customary association between water imagery and psychic openness to transformative erotic relationship (Ford's name and his alias, "Brook," also invoke the negative water symbolism of jealous humor as "flood"—recall Cash's lines in *Every Man In* [III, folio 3.3.140–44]). Falstaff's desire to "Sail like my pinnace" (a pun on "penis") to the "golden shores" of Mistresses Page and Ford indicates, instead, the *illusion* of eros, as the "lover" masks his narrow self-interest with the poetry of romantic discovery. For Falstaff, the affair is finally not a contest between him and the wives at all, but between him and their husbands. Thus *Merry Wives* bears a suggestion of what in Jonson's plays is a major plot concern: the competitive homosocial bonding action that defines all-important masculine relationships and dramatizes the distance or "difference" (*Cynthia's Revels* 1.4.52, EMO 3.6.100) between the play's males.

Clearly, Falstaff is not in love. Therefore, so far from indicating an imminent "doubling" of identity in conjugal relationship, Falstaff's cross-dressed body in the play's fourth act merely accentuates his sterile, "neuter" status—his "false staff," as it were. While cross-dressing in mythic comedy opens up new dimensions of relational possibility, Falstaff's cross-dressing, like that of the humorous Jonsonian effeminate, merely confirms sexual foreclosure. Viola/Cesario and Rosalind/Ganymede, we recall, don't lose sexual power as transvestites, but actually initiate erotic action in that garb, demonstrating progress toward relational identities with real male characters. In contrast, Falstaff's disguise as the "fat woman of Brainford" facilitates an escape from erotic connection: he wears it safely to *leave* Mistress Ford, not to approach her, in a way that inverts the function and valence of transvestism in mythic comedy. Falstaff's disguise, like the use to which it is put, reduces his already provisional sexual nature, adding to it another layer of erotic impossibility.

The conspicuous undermining of erotic symbolism here subtly foreshadows the overt inversion of eros in the play's final scene in Windsor Forest, where the evasion of sexual and marital outcomes is accompanied by the visible "draining" of the powerful erotic beast emblem.

In my second chapter, I described the elevation of the symbol of the cuckold to the divine status of the horned erotic beast in *Much Ado about Nothing* and *As You Like It*. In those plays, horned bestiality supports the androgynizing action of the play, suggesting the openness, hazard, risk, divine play, and erotic connectedness available through conjugal relationship. In *Merry Wives*, in contrast, the horned Falstaff—tricked into wearing a deer outfit as the wives' final practical joke—is an antithetical satirical symbol of Jonsonian beastliness, an invalid, degenerative transformation. Falstaff's "horns" augur no induction into relational identity, as they do for Benedick and Touchstone. Instead, like his transvestite disguise, they confirm the play's refusal to grant him the slightest erotic encounter, as the wives show up only to laugh at him.

This scene constitutes the play's most explicit rejection of the fantasy of erotic change, as Windsor repudiates the empty hermaphrodite to affirm its original moral sufficiency. Although critics beginning with Northrop Frye have argued that the Windsor Forest scene ritually transforms Windsor in much the same way that the world of the Athenian wood transfigures Athens in *A Midsummer Night's Dream*,[21] and although, as Peter Evans notes, producers have historically staged this scene so that "Windsor Forest . . . drives in tandem with the wood of Athens,"[22] I believe the scene can best be understood with reference to the differences it invokes between its dramatic world and that of *Dream*, which Jan Kott has called "the most erotic of Shakespeare's plays."[23]

The Windsor Forest episode, in fact, merely parodies the events in the Athenian wood. Whereas *Dream* offers genuine transformation and communal regeneration through the agency of real fairies, who represent authentic human eros, *Merry Wives* resists erotic adventure, exposing it as unhealthy fantasy, and does so through the ministrations of fake fairies who strip Falstaff of his false disguise. William Carroll, who calls *A Midsummer Night's Dream* "the most explicitly metamorphic of Shakespeare's comedies," argues that Bottom's literal transfiguration to an ass parallels Falstaff's metaphorical transformation to a stag in his "Herne the Hunter" outfit. Both transformations, Carroll believes, embody the drama's encounter with the "monstrous," which, we recall, he sees as "the way to marriage, to achieved eros."[24] And it is true that Falstaff's change to a stag is like Bottom's change to an ass in one way: like Bottom, Falstaff *is* an ass, whose theatrical animalization helps to demonstrate that fact; Falstaff himself does finally "begin to perceive that [he is] made an ass" (*Merry Wives* 5.5.119). But Falstaff's monstrousness, unlike Bottom's, has no further value (as William Carroll argues it does); it is a false and, above all, inappropriate monstrousness that lacks the transformative power to move him "to achieved eros." It exposes him as an ass so that he can stop being one, specifically by ceasing to chase the merry wives. Bottom's literal "translation," in contrast, is comically celebrated with an apparently consummated "marriage" to Titania (*Dream* 3.2.197–201). Bottom's sexual encounter with Titania, who, due to Oberon's and Puck's magical ministrations, responds erotically to his monstrousness, thus helps to create *Dream*'s general involvement with marriage and sexual gratification. Ultimately, *Dream* will unite or reunite four couples, three of whom retire "to bed" for "new jollity" at the drama's close (5.1.368, 370). The falsely translated Falstaff's painfully nonsexual encounter with the pinching Windsorites, on the other hand, represents *Merry Wives*' consistent turn from consummation of sexual fantasy, as is fitting for a play wherein such consummation would be transgressive rather than redemptive. Sexual congress between the wives and Falstaff is avoided, as is marital success for two of the three suitors, who end up with male brides. So far from achieving ritualistic sexual renewal through its encounter with the "monstrous," the Windsor community mocks and expels the symbolically half-human beast in deer costume. In this, Windsor's comic world differs from Athens, which assimilates Bottom's sexually charged monstrousness into the overall regenerative pattern of the play. Likewise, it differs from Illyria, where Viola's symbolic double gendering, rendering her in her own terms a "poor monster" (*Twelfth Night* 2.2.34), initiates (through Olivia's arousal) the erotic progress of the play; and even from Padua, where Petruchio, "a very monster in apparel" at his wedding (*Shrew* 3.2.70), behaves like a beast in order to create an opening for Kate's transformation from shrew to wife. Unlike that of Bottom, Viola, or Petruchio, Falstaff's monstrosity lacks sexual potency and creative power; it is a thing to be shunned rather than a valid transformative instrument.

Thus, while the monstrous in "Shakespearean" comedy enhances and symbolizes erotic power, Falstaff's Jonsonian animality, implicit in his stag's antlers, merely demonstrates his weakened and debased humanity. His half-human condition indicates, not semidivinity, but degenerate animality, as it customarily does in Jonson. Falstaff's bestiality is like that of *Volpone*'s Sir Pol, who, fearing arrest for his ridiculous gossip about political conspiracies, hides under a tortoise shell to escape the "authorities" (Peregrine and the disguised merchants). And the fairy pinching scene (a probable influence on *The Alchemist* 3.5), which culminates in the removal of Falstaff's buck-antlers, closely resembles the wits' subsequent discovery of Sir Pol under the shell ("What beast is this?" [V, *Volpone* 5.4.65]).

Falstaff's is indeed a Jonsonian monstrousness, conceived with the skepticism toward the unnatural expressed in Jonson's prologue to *Every Man In*. Jonson there exhorts an audience that has foolishly "graced [stage] monsters" (probably Shakespeare's) to prefer his drama of "men" (III, prologue, line 30). Jonson's "monsters" are consequently, like Falstaff, men and women who act like things they are not—*Bartholomew Fair*'s stinging Wasp, *Volpone*'s Sir Pol (who chatters mindlessly like a parrot), and *Epicoene*'s beastly Lady Centaur and Mrs. Otter, who, in Jonson's terms, act like men. These characters' unnaturalness threatens communal stability; it does not, like Shakespearean monstrousness, facilitate powerful personal and social change.

The Windsor Forest scene thus registers a profound skepticism toward the possibilities of sexual regeneration through the power of the monstrous. Rather than celebrate the half-human, half-divine androgyne, this scene expels the half-human, half-beast humors character, making its monsters representative of corrupt change rather than creative, relational transformation. Repudiating the corrosive threat levied by Master Brook/Ford's and the "lover" Falstaff's theatrical poses, the scene enacts the approved Jonsonian movement back toward the reclamation of solid, legitimate identity.

Generally speaking, erotic energy in humors drama is, like the theatrical postures of Ford and Falstaff, an unrealized phantom; what looks like sex is usually something else, just as what look like wives to *Epicoene*'s Morose and to *Merry Wives*'s Caius and Slender are actually cross-dressed boys, whom the men have inadvertently "married." Humors comedies are finally not about erotic desire at all: they are about passionate greed, which, masquerading as healthy libido, hides a profound relational avoidance that corresponds to these comic worlds' resistance to regenerative change.

Yet the Windsor Forest scene's satirical inversion of the androgynous principle through the mockery of beast-eros and transvestism is compromised by other factors that destabilize this satiric ethos. Primarily, the agency of women in Falstaff's humiliation is what prevents the anti-androgynous principle from fully informing the play. Mistresses Ford and Page may embody a law of solid, self-preservative integrity that is central to their play's satiric resistance to the threat of relational engagement. But, ironically, they also represent the doubling that occurs in marriage. The women's close connection to each other in some ways mirrors the subtly eroticized friendships of Celia and Rosalind; or Hermia and Helena, who grow "like to a double cherry." Like these younger Shakespearean women, the home-grown wives are always already related, in a configuration that (pre-dictably) provokes Ford's irrational sexual envy: Ford tells Mistress Page, "I think if your husbands were dead, you two would marry" (3.2.15). "Be sure of that—two other husbands," Mrs. Page responds (lines 16–17), demonstrating the wives' definitive investment in erot-ic relational identity. Mistresses Ford and Page's self-defensive stance is, in fact, not the satirist's conventional, resolute mooring of his iso-lated self against the pull of the feminized world. Instead, the wives seek finally to protect their marital identity—the androgynous, rela-tional whole from which their selfhood derives.

As feminine wits—*mulieres bonae*—their design succeeds. Rout-ing Falstaff's sexual strategy actually protects and restores their more deeply eroticized conjugal relationships. The Windsor Forest scene performs an *Epicoene*-like evasion of marriage in the action that strips the boy "brides"; yet at the same time it accomplishes, not only the marriage of Anne and Fenton, but the reconciliation of the Fords, as "Master Brook" discovers the groundlessness of his alienating jeal-ousy. The play even ends with a line that explicitly eroticizes the Fords' marital reunion, and that also incorporates a brief reference to the androgynous motif of blurred or "doubled" identity: Ford, referring to his earlier disguise as "Brook," confirms his claim to his wife's body by telling Falstaff that "Master Brook . . . tonight shall lie with Mistress Ford" (5.5.245–46). (We might also mark the para-doxical suggestions of separation/crossing by water implicit in both "brook" and "ford.")

Thus, paradoxically, the play's satirical recoil from sexual engage-ment rebounds on itself. Shakespeare tries to mock eros, but Shake-spearean eros will not be mocked. Significantly, the female wits' victory frustrates the misogynistic motivations of the plays' other characters—such as Falstaff's attempt to bypass the wives' erotic agency, treating them not as human beings but as "key[s]" to their "cuckoldy" husbands' "coffer[s]." In one sense, *Merry Wives* turns satire against itself, punishing Falstaff for his *lack* of real erotic inten-tion and his investment in a competitive homosocial ethic. Similarly, Ford's proprietary jealousy is not cured, as is Corvino's in *Volpone*, by divorce, but by his wife's demonstration of the invalidity of his reductive assessment of her. Ford's satirical use of the "woman-horse" image—"I will rather trust . . . a thief to walk my ambling gelding, than my wife with herself" (2.2.302–5)—is implicitly overturned by the mastery Mistress Ford exerts over Falstaff, Ford, and herself. As in Shakespearean comedy generally, the horse and rider image here proves erotically reversible.

The Merry Wives of Windsor, then, like the anonymous Haec-Vir, records competing perspectives on marital relationship, feminine selfhood, and the androgynous principle. These varying perspectives are inseparable from the divergent contexts that give them distinction and life: the genres of mythic and satiric comedy, which Merry Wives would hybridize. Russ McDonald has observed that in this play Shakespeare was "attempting something different from what [he] did best."[25] Perhaps Shakespeare thought so too: he never tried it again.

II.

The list of satiric inversions of mythic androgyny and mythic inversions of satiric androgyny would be incomplete without the name of Bartholomew Fair's Ursula. Like The Merry Wives of Windsor as a whole, the cross-dressed body of the actor playing Ursula incorporates a set of contradictory mythic and satiric valences. It is, perhaps, not possible finally to derive unitary meaning from this uncharacteristically ambiguous Jonsonian female figure. I would, however, like to offer a reading of Ursula as a Jonsonian dramatic answer to Shakespearean androgynes of various kinds, including his "empty" transvestite, the Falstaff of The Merry Wives of Windsor. Just as the Merry Wives Falstaff turned Shakespeare's customary mythic transvestism inside out, so does Ursula partially invert that Falstaff's satiric valence. Concomitantly, while the androgynous Falstaff challenged the dramatic hegemony of the powerful transvestite within Shakespeare's own comic tradition, Ursula conversely redeems the Jonsonian satiric androgyne from its previously unilateral negative significance. She does so partially by dramatizing an irresistible association: a simultaneously self-mocking and self-approving identification between herself and her creator, Ben Jonson, with the addition of Falstaffian charm.[26]

Over thirty years ago Jonas Barish called attention to the authorial self-mockery evident in Jonson's 1614 Bartholomew Fair. In Barish's

1960 *Ben Jonson and the Language of Prose Comedy*, he notes that Jonson used *Bartholomew Fair* to "heap ridicule on his own lifelong stance as watchdog of public morality."[27] The schoolmaster Wasp, the Puritan minister Zeal-of-the-Land Busy, and the officious judge Adam Overdo, obnoxious authoritarians who ineffectively bluster through the *Bartholomew* landscape, are in Barish's view parodic images of the "satiric commentator" who "remain[s] scornfully aloof, passing judgment": they are "frenzied busybod[ies] whose passionate exposures of folly in others serve only to expose it the more damningly in [them]selves."[28] Thus, according to Barish, *Bartholomew Fair* embodies Jonson's momentary cynicism regarding his own profession of satiric playwright.

But the authorial self-criticism of *Bartholomew Fair* is mitigated, or at least rendered complex and ambiguous, by a central "Jonson figure," Ursula the pig-vendor, whom Barish has unaccountably overlooked. The "bearish" confrontationality implicit in Ursula's name had previously been linked with Jonson's behavior by the rival playwright Thomas Dekker, whose Captain Tucca in *Satiromastix* calls Jonson a "Bear-whelp" (5.2.185) and a "Hunks" (1.2.319) (after Harry Hunks, the most famous victim of the London bear-baitings).[29] But Ursula at least partially redeems Jonsonian bearishness from Dekker's contempt. Like Wasp, Busy, and Overdo, Ursula exposes and repudiates the follies of others; unlike the previous three, however, she chastises only defensively, and does so with a wit, dignity, and power that validate her satirical position. Thus, parodic though she may be, she restores a measure of authority (as opposed to authoritarianism) to the playwright's image. Despite certain misogynistic elements in the presentation of her character, she demonstrates both creative power and nontheatrical integrity, a highly unusual combination for a Jonsonian female. Ursula, in fact, displaces the customary dramatic authority of the Jonsonian male wit, whose power derives from his detachment from the feminized world he mockingly observes. Rather than the marginal locus of a Maciente or Truewit, Ursula occupies the central mediating position of a Portia or Rosalind, serving as the creative center of her play. The cross-dressed actor playing Ursula is, in fact, an atypically powerful Jonsonian queen.

Yet Ursula's comic power differs significantly from the relational force channeled through Shakespeare's female transvestites. She is more cultural critic than romantic facilitator. Like the undisguised female wits of *The Merry Wives of Windsor*, Ursula grows and works from the center of her social environment, yet appropriates the ordinarily

masculine role of clever cynic to do so. Alone among the female characters in Jonson's satiric comedies, and alone among characters of
either sex in *Bartholomew Fair*, Ursula is licensed to perform the
authorial role of satiric commentator, wittily puncturing the theatrical poses of those in her environment. She is *mulier bona*, the female
equivalent of the *vir bonus*, or morally sufficient man who alone can
serve as authentic social malcontent. Like Jonson's other theatrical
spokespersons (Asper/Macilente in *Every Man Out of His Humour*,
Truewit in *Epicoene*, Peregrine in *Volpone*), Ursula is verbally "virile," giving better than she gets in linguistic confrontation with
Bartholomew Fair's witty males, Quarlous and Winwife. As such, she
destabilizes their satiric authority (already undermined by their
shared marital quest), unmooring it with her defensive protection of
her own character and the fair-world she both represents and
metaphorically generates.

For example, when Quarlous and Winwife mock Ursula's "unfeminine" fleshiness, Ursula gives a spirited and imaginative retort that
reduces her attackers to weak and ineffectual "Ha, ha, ha"s (V,
2.5.122). Asserting that she is a "plain plump soft wench o' the sub-
urbs . . . juicy and wholesome," no "thin pinch'd ware, pent up i' the
compass of a dog-collar" (2.5.83–86), Ursula then turns the tables on
the men, attacking the moral insufficiency behind their attractive garments, in a manner usually exercised in Jonson by male wits who
mock effeminate fops: "I ha' seene as fine outsides, as either o'yours,
bring lousy linings to the Brokers, ere now, twice a week," Ursula
sneers (2.5.105–7). With forceful invective, Ursula ultimately drives
the men from her tent: after she calls Quarlous "hedge bird,"
"pannier-man's bastard," "sneer," "dog's head," "Trendle tail," and
"remnant" within a thirty-second, eight-line span (lines 121–28),
Quarlous and Winwife flee in disgrace and fear. "Let's away, her language grows greasier than her pigs . . . . Pray thee, let's go," Winwife
urges (lines 133–34, 138). Ursula is, in fact, the "Bartholomew-wit,"
as her servant Knockem calls her (2.5.102). In interchanges like the
above, she usurps the satirical voice ordinarily given to literate men
in Jonson's plays, and employs this voice (as they do) medicinally to
expose the social pretensions of fellow characters. Ursula might have
served as an inspiration for the defensive words of the Hic-Mulier,
the male-garbed woman in the *Haec-Vir* dialogue, published six years
later: "I stand not with my hands on my belly like a baby at Bartholomew Fair . . . [I] am not dumb when wantons court me." In
confrontation with men, Ursula, like Hic-Mulier, is verbally victori-

ous, able through language to transform her ludicrous bulk to healthy self-sufficiency, and others' "pinch'd"-ness to moral failure.

Ursula's imaginative conversion of fatness to virtue should remind us of the several Jonson poems and epigrams in which the poet defensively celebrates his own inordinate bulk. Jonson consistently employs images of physical weightiness as symbols of goodness, wisdom, and creativity. In "His Excuse for Loving," for example, Jonson refers to the "Language, and the Truth" that "Gives the lover weight" (VIII, 131, 10–12); similarly, in "My Picture Left in Scotland" Jonson argues that his "mountain belly" should be no bar to a woman's appreciation of his merit (VIII, 149–50, 17). Most significantly, we may recall from *Discoveries* the analogy Jonson's definition of the poet forges between hearty eating and the poetic process: the poet "feeds with an appetite, and hath a stomach to concoct, divide, and turn all into nourishment" (VIII, 638, 2473–75).[30] The frequency of flesh and food metaphors in Jonson suggests the degree to which "fatness" was crucial to the playwright's self-image; the pattern also demonstrates Jonson's habitual tendency to make moral, intellectual, and creative capital out of his obesity.

Ursula's skill at this should remind us of someone else, too—as it probably did for her audience. Ursula's ability to make a virtue of obesity was also one of the supreme talents of Falstaff. Not only Ursula's bulk, but her wit and invective are Falstaffian in the older sense: they are reminiscent, not of *Merry Wives*'s empty androgyne, but of the older, verbally virile Falstaff of the Henry plays. In *1 Henry IV*, Prince Hal laughingly observes that Falstaff "sweats to death, / And lards the lean earth as he walks along" (2.2.108–9), and in *2 Henry IV* Falstaff himself speaks of the sweat he discharges, moaning, "My womb, my womb, my womb undoes me" (4.3.12–13, 22). We hear echoes of both Shakespearean passages in Ursula's aggrieved complaint, "I do water the ground in knots as I go" (*BF* 2.2.51–52); her call for "a bottle of ale" to relieve her suffering (line 49) also recalls Falstaff's characteristic plea. Interestingly, an implicit criticism of Falstaff's "over-familiar playing face" in Jonson's 1601 *Poetaster* had additionally noted that Falstaff (or the fat actor playing him) looked "like a mid-wife in man's apparel." The *Poetaster* lines, along with the verbal and physical correspondences between Ursula and Falstaff, indicate the possibility of the pig-vendor as a Jonsonian whim: in a dizzying series of inversions, she seems a cross-dressed male-female Falstaff compounded with a feminized version of Jonson himself. The very complexity of the reversals would seem to move Ursula, and a stage-smart audience's response to her, into the baffling experiential locale of mythic comedy.

We may liken Ursula's pig-tent to the Boar's Head tavern—perhaps even to Jonson's Apollo Room—as the inspirational womb of the comic art of its "ruler." Ursula's tent is the locus of empowerment and intrigue for Bartholomew Fair and thus, by symbolic extension, for the play as a whole. The pig-tent is the hub of the fair's wheel, and in it Ursula sits, turning the dramatic action. Characters gravitate toward her, wishing to "eat of a pig . . . i'the heart o'the fair" (1.5.154–55), and are from thence propelled outward, creatively nourished, to engage in more comic business. Ursula thus emerges as the symbolic mistress and mother of Smithfield. Through her, Jonson temporarily forsakes his habitual association between creative energy and the phallus, ordinarily manifest in the rapier-like language of the male wit. Satirists generally represent their art as a hard instrument, a "whip of steel" (III, *EMO* induction, line 19) that, in deflating humors characters, reveals their "feminine" softness and ultimate vacuity. The steel whip of the satiric male, who is in but not of the feminized world he attacks, is of course analogous to the pen of the isolated satiric poet, the "distant *auctor*" (recalling Liuzza's phrase) who exercises generative power while detached from the social center. Ursula changes all that. Like the wives of Shakespeare's Windsor, she replaces phallic potency with uterine fertility, bringing forth some of the play's controlling schemes (such as Edgworth's thievery) from her own creative center. Her tent is the "very womb and bed of enormity," as Overdo says (2.2.106), and there she squats "with [her] litter of pigs, to grunt out another Bartholomew Fair" (2.3.2–3).

The earthy Ursula as creator of the fair seems, in fact, a calculated alternative to Shakespeare's image of the playwright as magician in *The Tempest*, especially when we take into account Jonson's implicit rejection of *The Tempest*'s supernaturalism in *Bartholomew Fair*'s induction. There, Jonson's spokesman warns the audience not to expect a Calibanesque "servant monster i'the fair," arguing that the playwright "is loth to make Nature afraid in his plays, like those [playwrights] that beget tales, tempests, and such like drolleries" (induction, lines 127–30). Therefore, in place of Prospero, a figure of the dramatist creating through magic, Jonson will "beget" Ursula, who in turn represents the playwright's creativity in terms of human procreation. Ursula, who possesses both a fertile imagination and a potent satirical thrust, embodies suggestions of the playwright's natural power to generate "real" human characters. (Even Ursula's servant

Knockem, whom she calls "Moon-calf" [2.2.45], replaces *The Tempest*'s half-human "moon-calf" Caliban [*Tempest* 2.2.106] with a thoroughly human comic agent.) Jonson seems to have intended Ursula's compounded humanity, represented in her symbolically double gendering, as a partial rebuttal of Shakespeare's general dramatic principles, which occasionally produced magical stage personae.

But in symbolically linking Ursula with female biological generativity, and also giving her the sharp, deflationary wit of the satiric *vir bonus*, Jonson has created a powerful androgyne who in some ways reproduces Shakespeare's androgynous comic creative principle. We may recall, for example, Petruchio's "mother wit" (*TS* 2.1.263), as well as *Love's Labor's Lost*'s description of an intrinsically hermaphroditic human creative power: words are "begot in the ventricle of memory" and "nourished in the womb of [pia mater]" (4.2.68–69). Ursula's androgyny thus makes her the most curious of Jonson's dramatic phenomena: not a Jonsonian rebuttal of Shakespeare, but a Rosalind made over in Jonson's image, who departs from the standard negative Jonsonian caricature of the "mannish" woman (i.e., the woman who vainly aims at "masculine" wit and authority). While female characters such as *Epicoene*'s collegiates abandon passive femininity to exercise "most masculine, or rather hermaphroditical authority" (1.1.75–80), Ursula, though manlike, remains intensely womanly—though in mythic, rather than satiric, terms. She is archetypically identified with Eve, feeling herself "melt[ing] away to the first woman, a rib" in the summer's heat (2.2.50–51). Further, whereas Jonson stresses *Epicoene*'s ladies' abandonment of natural female functions, providing them with "receipts . . . to keep [them]selves from bearing of children" (V, *Epicoene* 4.3.57–58), in *Bartholomew Fair* he uses terms that (however coarsely and comically) associate Ursula with sexual energy, fertility, and creative power. Her tent is, again, the "very womb and bed of enormity"; from it she "grunt[s] out another Bartholomew Fair." But Ursula's figurative maternity is balanced by a "manly" rigor and authority, as she smokes her pipe, monitors her employees, and, exercising the customary confrontationality of the *vir bonus*, beats bothersome male customers.

Yet, just as Shakespeare undermines the satirical ethos of *The Merry Wives of Windsor* with his attractive presentation of the female heroes—in converse manner, rather—Jonson compromises Ursula's comic virtue by emphasizing her unattractiveness to men. As my last chapter argued, Quarlous's and Winwife's radical recoil from her fleshy amorphousness—framed in Quarlous's comment, "he that would venture for't . . . might sink into her, and be drown'd a week, ere any friend he had could find where he were"—rehearses the characteristic satiric male fear of being devoured by the monstrously sexualized woman, as well as the reliance on male ties for the preservation or recovery of the solid masculine self. Further, the arena over which Ursula presides, and which she metaphorically generates, is, after all, the decadent, feminized maze of middle-class London public life (for which Shakespeare's Boar's-Head scenes showed far more sympathy than Jonson does here). Ursula is essentially a part of the "spectacles and shows" of the "turning world" that Jonson rejects in the *Underwood* (VIII, 116, lines 65, 64). Bartholomew Fair is, finally, Vanity Fair; thus, despite Ursula's apparently fertile creative energy, her symbolic vaginal delivery of the fair (2.3.2-3) reiterates the misogynistic equivalence of female "emptiness" with social vanity. Ursula is partially assimilated by this satiric ethic, and by the final symbolic repudiation of false "theater" (such as the Smithfield arena provides) that we see in Leatherhead's manipulation of his puppets in 5.5. In this scene, Puppet Dionysus—who embodies and represents the customary satiric reduction of mythic androgyny figures—comically repudiates the Puritan Zeal-of-the-Land Busy's complaint against actor-transvestites, "who putteth on the apparel of the female" (5.5.99–100), by pulling up his puppet-garment to expose his sexlessness. The gesture recalls the stripping action of *Epicoene*, which reclaims the actual body of the male actor from the feminized theatrical medium, only the puppet's action goes further. Dionysus's self-exposure points to (and argues) the radical vanity and impotence of theatrical illusion itself: a vanity that is writ large in the Smithfield fairgrounds in which Ursula inescapably resides. Thus the puppet's empty "flash" returns the audience to the standard Jonsonian anti-androgynous ethic, which constructs mythic hermaphrodism—and, by implication Ursula—as neutered nothingness, and associates drama's sterility with the vain temptations offered by the fair (and London life) as a whole. Finally, *Bartholomew Fair* is a satire of all human theater, including humors plays like *Bartholomew Fair*.

Self-parody is the ultimate mirror of the satirist's ego, revealing his swollen notion of his own artistic importance. The numerous figures of Jonson in *Bartholomew Fair*, self-mocking or self-congratulatory, reveal the extent to which Jonson identified satire's power with his own. In a sense it is Jonson himself, rather than his play, who "swallows" satire here; the phenomenon of Ursula, like the other Jonson analogues, suggests the assimilation of the world into the self rather than of the self into the world. To the extent that Ursula is mythic, she dramatizes a myth that is predominantly anti-erotic: a myth of the all-consuming self as opposed to a myth of the all-powerful relationship.

Still, there is a trace of eros in Ursula: a momentary, dizzying dissolution of the Jonsonian boundaries between masculine self and feminine Other. Massively fat and proud of her bulk, a devourer of food and drink, a satiric commentator on the characters who float through her tent, and the metaphorical creator of events, "grunt[ing] out another Bartholomew Fair," Ursula—like Jonson's poem to William Burlase describing his own swelling "womb"—demonstrates Jonson's occasional capacity to imagine him*self* female. Thus, despite the instinctive misogyny with which her character is drawn, Ursula paradoxically expresses an unusual Jonsonian dream: a vision of an artistic power that is simply human, rather than psychologically male.

The anomalous Ursula was a rare instance of Jonson's willingness to experiment with three-dimensional stage females: that is, with female figures whose characterization involved either moral complexity or behavioral choice. Such beings are practically absent from the Jonsonian catalog of Lady Wouldbes and Dol Commons and their opposite numbers, the Celias and Dame Pliants. Customarily, Jonson locks female characters into fixed positions, presenting them as either aggressive interlopers in male territory or passive repositories of "soft virtues." By this means he exercises the satirical anti-androgynous principle, which not only precludes a relational zone in which genders can merge, but which misogynistically genders the qualities of ingenuity, choice, and self-mastery as male.

One very late play, however, the 1629 *New Inn*, curiously departs from the satirical ethical norm that, with the partial exception of *Bartholomew Fair*, had informed Jonson's comic work for over three decades. *The New Inn* is generally considered artistically secondary to most of Jonson's other comic work, and it was resoundingly unsuccessful in the theater.[31] The play is, however, worthy of attention with regard to its (for Jonson) uncharacteristic investment in the related ideas of positive feminine power and the androgynous principle. Specifically, *The New Inn* is un-Jonsonian in that, registering its female characters' agency and wit in their demonstrated ability to pose and function as males, it overtly exploits the Shakespearean model of mythic hermaphrodism, derived partly from Plato's androgyny myth.

Indeed, so pronounced and self-conscious are its mythic androgyny motifs that *The New Inn* seems one of several possible things: a determined "proof" that Jonson could do romantic comedy, too; an uncharacteristically subtle parody of Shakespearean method; or (strangest of all) a recantation of a lifelong misogyny registered in thirty years of fiercely articulated and upheld dramatic principles. The plot of *The New Inn* conforms to the standard mythic-romantic model, involving several pairs of lovers who are united, at the Light Heart Inn, partially through the enabling power of transvestite disguise. In standard Shakespearean fashion, the chief wits are women, most notably the disguised nurse (the lost wife of Good-stock, the inn's host), Frances (Good-stock's disguised daughter), Lady Frampul (another lost daughter), and Lady Frampul's servant, Pru. Much of the action involves Pru's presiding over a kangaroo court wherein the play's chief male suitor, Lovel, is required to prove his belief in the sovereign powers of romantic love. Ultimately, both the young lovers Lady Frampul and Lovel, the severed couple Good-stock and his wife, and Pru and Frances and their respective suitors are joined and rejoined through the "alchemy" of eros (VI, 3.2.55).

Lovel's long speech on love in Pru's mock court rehearses the standard tropes and myths of Platonic androgyny and the Orphic Hymns, sacred to mythic comic convention, and also asserts the mythic valences of Renaissance metaphors associated with the hermaphroditic joining of unlike beings. Lovel explicitly describes the "fable of Plato's" (3.2.86) that

> man and woman
> Were, in the first creation, both one piece,
> And being cleft asunder, ever since,
> Love was an appetite to be rejoin'd.

(lines 79–82)

Lovel expands on this myth, describing Platonic androgyny with adjectives reminiscent of the Orphic Hymns' praise of the cosmic generative force. Love is

> circular, eternal;
> Not feign'd, or made, but born: And then,
> so precious,
> As nought can value it, but itself. So free,
> As nothing can command it, but itself,
> And in itself, so round, and liberal,
> As where it favors, it bestows itself.

(lines 107–12)

Lady Frampul's response to this speech explicitly invokes the alchemical metaphor, which was, we recall, imaginatively linked during the Renaissance to erotic hermaphrodism:

> How am I changed! by what alchemy
> Of love, or language, am I thus translated!
> His tongue is tip'd with the Philosopher stone,
> And that hath touch'd me thorough every vein!
> I feel that transmutation o'my blood,
> As I were quite become another creature. . . .
>
> (lines 171–76)

The dialogue's self-conscious embrace of the tropes of mythic androgyny, along with its inversion of the symbolism of alchemy—one of Jonson's standard metaphors for bogus social transformation—suggests Jonson's willful departure from the satirist's deflationary, separatist skepticism regarding the possibilities of relational connection. Thus the speech tempts us to read as Jonson's the later plea of Lord Latimer, one of the inn's guests:

> What penance shall I do, to be receiv'd,
> And reconciled to the Church of Love?
> . . . .
> For I have trespass'd, and blasphemed Love.
> I have, indeed, despis'd his Deity,
> . . . .
> Now I adore Love. . . .
>
> (3.2.216–27)

But, as usual with Jonson, things are not that simple. For this "romantic" comedy incorporates within itself certain standard satirical motifs. For one thing, Jonson's inclusion of the character Nick Stuff re-presents the negative image of Sir Voluptuous Beast, which stages marriage not as an expansive relational opportunity but as an arena for depraved sexual theater. Stuffe uses his occupation as tailor to enact licentious role-play, dressing his wife in the finery of the upper-class women whose clothes he makes and then pretending that she is one of those women when he makes love to her.[32] Here Jonsonian satire pulls away from the explicit romanticism of the play's main plot, replacing erotic energy with an image of what to Jonson was degrading sexual contact. Another incongruous satiric element is Pru's strangely deviant desire to dress up the pretty serving boy, Frances, as a girl in 2.1. Although Frances (unbeknownst to Pru) is a girl anyway, the audience does not know this at this point in the play; thus the scene replicates some of the Swiftian comic horror of *Epicoene*'s first scene, where Clerimont's "engle" (the later Epicoene) complains that the ladies dress him in their outfits and play with him. The *New Inn* scene partially registers *Epicoene*'s misogynistic construction of "humors" women as gender-transgressive sexual beasts, seeking to appropriate a properly male sexual dominance. Here, even before the transvestite disguise is dropped, its relational work accomplished, that disguise's mythic symbolism is curiously inverted. Jonson's refusal to allow full audience complicity in Frances's transvestite disguise—his withholding of the fact that she *is* in disguise for much of the play—crucially prevents this transvestite from assuming the symbolic powers of Shakespeare's mythic androgynes.[33] Audiences see Julia, Portia, Rosalind, Viola, and Imogen as women *before* they assume male garb; thus these characters' transvestite attire, once assumed, takes on for watchers the "doubling" relational valence appropriate to the imminent conjugal unity these characters represent. In contrast, for most of Jonson's *New Inn*, the audience simply sees a boy actor. Thus the androgynous principle, though eloquently described in Lovel's "court" (and courting) speech, is never integrated into the play's formal design.

Whether intended as a proof of dramatic versatility, a parody of Shakespearean motifs, or a recantation of harsh satirical skepticism, the problematically hybrid *New Inn* publicly failed on all three counts. At the play's first performance at Blackfriars, it was "hissed off the stage before the actors got as far as the epilogue," to quote Rosalind Miles.[34] The public rejection of Jonson's version of mythic androgyny ironically provoked his bitter return to satirical virulence and the anti-androgynous principle, as exemplified in the poem that he wrote and appended to the folio version of the play (reviving a version of ancient Aristophanic tradition). The very title, "Ode to Himself," indicates its renewed embrace of the closed, self-protective, masculinist satirical position (although the poem's publication ironically confirms that that position was defined, not in isolation, but by aggressive public attack of a degraded world). In "Ode," Jonson reiterates his age-old scorn for the womanlike "plush and velvet men" of the theater (VI, 492–93, 32): gaudily dressed actors, playwrights, and audience members who merge without distinction into an amorphous welter of brainless foolery. Against these, Jonson urges his own satiric self-sufficiency. Beckoning himself back from an imaginary selfhood to a presumably originary identity, he confirms his own integrity and self-control. The poem's first line, implicitly delivered from the social margin that is Jonson's own legitimate center, directs this redemptive retreat from theater's corrosive seductions: "Come, leave the loathed stage" (line 1).

This poem's final verse is instructive in the connection that it indicates between this satirical scorn for a corrosive, feminized social environment and the veneration of an idealized Other. Jonson ends his philippic by veering suddenly into worshipful praise for Charles I, whom he metaphorically places above and outside the illicit theatrical arena of London society. In his last lines, Jonson presents a reified image of an inhumanly perfect overlord, and urges himself to forswear play-writing to "sing"—perhaps in court masques—"The glories" of this king: "His zeal to God, and his just awe o'er men" (VI, 94, lines 51–53). The poem's ultimate reference to the constellation known as "Charles['s] . . . Wain" (line 60) merges the image of the monarch with that of the changeless stars. The trope confirms the idealized Charles as inspirational source, but precludes all possibility of close interactive contact with him: he becomes inhuman, a static emblem of virtue. Thus "Ode to Himself" swings between the binary alternatives of satiric misanthropy/misogyny and Petrarchan-style worship of an apotheosized thing.

The oscillation between these extremes is evident in much of Jonson's work—*Epicoene*, for example, reverses the swing of the "Ode" from depravity to perfection, moving from Clerimont's fantasy of the naturally ideal woman (V, 1.1.91ff.) to Truewit's articulated nightmare about her aging body (4.1.35ff.). But two additional examples will be sufficient to underscore the connection between Jonson's Petrarchan propensities and his satirical misogyny, which last—as I hope I have demonstrated—is fundamentally associated with his habitual resistance to the androgynous principle. *Cynthia's Revels*, a play produced nearly thirty years before the disastrous public reception of *The New Inn*, dramatizes a vain, degraded court world inhabited by lecherous women and feminized, clothing-obsessed men (Amorphus and Asotus, we may recall, live there). This world is mediated for the audience through the satirical commentary of Crites, a Jonson analogue: a wise philosopher whom the degenerate characters pointedly ignore. But ultimately, the virgin moon-goddess Cynthia—an obvious figure of Elizabeth I—arrives to banish the humors figures and their patron deity, Cupid ("vanish, hence, away" [IV, 5.11.89]), to reconsecrate the court to learning and to restore the dignity of Crites. Cynthia's final lines provide Crites/Jonson with the compensatory approval that, in "Ode to Himself," Jonson derives from the reified image of Charles I:

> Nor are we ignorant, how noble minds
> Suffer too much through those indignities,
> Which times, and vicious persons cast on them
> . . . .
> Cynthia shall brighten, what the world made dim.
>
> (5.6.102–11)

Thus within this humors play, predominantly populated by Jonson's usual feminized males and lecherous, "hermaphroditic" women, Jonson ultimately incorporates the countervailing figure of virginal feminine perfection, allowing it to cancel through inversion the theatrical unreality of the sexualized characters.

A more curious oscillation between satiric sexual disgust and Petrarchan veneration of virgins is found in a comparison of two of Jonson's poems. Jonson's vindictive epigram attacking Cecilia Bulstrode, we recall, articulated the standard themes of satiric misogyny, representing the poet Bulstrode as an aggressively sexualized, "masculine" monster engaged in a figurative literary rape: a "Court Pucelle" who could "force a Muse, / And in an epicoene fury [could] write news." Yet in 1609, when Bulstrode died, Jonson radically reversed this literary image in a poetic encomium. His later poem, so far from accusing its subject of degraded femininity, presents her as the sum of womanly perfections. The poem renders Bulstrode

> a Virgin; and then, one
> That durst be that in court: a virtue alone
> To fill an epitaph. But she had more.
> . . . .
> She might have claimed to have made the Muses four,
> Taught Pallas language, Cynthia modesty,
> As fit to have increased the harmony
> Of spheres, as light of stars; she was earth's eye;
> The sole religious house and votary,
> With rites not bound, but conscience. Wouldst thou all?
> She was Cil Bulstrode. In which name, I call
> Up so much truth as, could I it pursue,
> Might make the fable of good women true.
>
> (VIII, 371, 3–14)

Alive, she was a whore; dead, she is a virgin goddess. Like *Cynthia's Revels*, the paired poems "On the Court Pucelle" and the Bulstrode "Epitaph" oscillate between the binary feminine images of "pucelle" and asexual deity. The literal personality of Bulstrode, the represented subject, remains almost thoroughly unaccessed, as Jonson reproduces the two models of womanhood available in satire's repertory. In these models are registered both satirical recoil from a fantastic demon-woman and longing for a perfect female figure who is equally unreal.

These models are antithetical, but alike in that they are both reified images of human identity. The idealized emblem of virginal female purity is analogous to Jonson's basic satiric vision of the male self as a rooted, free-standing entity, defined in antithesis to the feminized pull of a degenerate social environment. This self's oppositional Other is, of course, some form of androgynous "pucelle": a liquid, theatrical, and sexually interested humors figure, such as the man who has lost his solid center through "amorous" fascination with women, or the woman who, aping male physical and sexual aggression, tries vainly to enact centered selfhood. Since the identity of the ideal virgin female, like that of the *vir bonus*, is defined in opposition to the sexualized denizens of a corrupt world, her image confirms the satirist's vision of a world in which constructive erotic identity is impossible. What for Shakespeare is the mutual, interactive inclination of humans toward relational identity is for Jonson the parasitical inability to stand on one's own feet, registered in a reprehensible submission to the temptations of the world. In Jonsonian satire, Eros becomes Cupid—a degenerate carnal force that must be banished by the virtuous scorn of the sexual puritan.

"Ode to Himself," in adapting the Petrarchism of *Cynthia's Revels* to the veneration of a male monarch, duplicates these binary oppositions of Jonson's earlier satiric work, and confirms his irresistible satiric compulsion. A renewed analysis of Jonson's earliest humors plays, with specific regard to the connection they reveal between romantic idealism and satiric scorn, will be the project of the next chapter, for it was in this early period that Jonson achieved mastery in the mode that Shakespeare, ironically, helped to create with *The Merry Wives of Windsor*. Meanwhile, after *Merry Wives*, the work of Shakespeare himself demonstrated increasing distrust of the reified models of human selfhood on which Jonson's satire depended. Shakespeare—who was singularly uninterested in permanent virginity[35]—uses the 1598 *Much Ado about Nothing* to demonstrate that fixed, parodic models of human identity ("Lady Disdain" [1.1.118] and "Monsieur Love" [2.3.36]) inhibit authentically interactive, erotic human relationship. *Much Ado* also posits a generic opposition between satire and eros, providing its heroes with access to conjugality only through their abandonment of previous satiric postures. Benedick's insight regarding the creative inefficacy of satire concludes the play: "Dost thou think I care for a satire or an epigram? No. . . . since I do purpose to marry, I will think nothing to any purpose that the world can say against it" (5.4.102–6). The 1601 *Troilus and Cressida* even more strongly suggests the dangerous cultural implications of satire, and of satirical drama in particular, representing the enervating effect of Patroclus's theatrical "paradoxes" (parodies) of Greek commanders on the soldiers besieging Troy (1.3.184). *Hamlet*, produced in 1600 or 1601, also posits a connection between satiric animus, spiritual enervation, and social impotence. Early in *Hamlet*, Rosencrantz delivers some famous lines by means of which Shakespeare's contemporary London briefly intrudes into Hamlet's late-medieval Denmark: upon arrival at Elsinore, Rosencrantz blames the decline of "the tragedians of the city" (2.2.371) on a "late [theatrical] innovation" (line 374), the "eyrie of children" (line 377), or boys' acting companies like Jonson's, who—as Shakespeare's audience knew—performed only comic plays. Rosencrantz's oblique comment, in other words, presents Jonsonian satire not just as bad comedy, but as degraded tragedy. The apparently offhand remark merges with *Hamlet*'s sustained exploration of satiric melancholy's tragic potential, as Shakespeare links the puritanical mind-set of the play's "bitter jester,"[36] Hamlet himself, to radical psychological withdrawal, to moral dysfunction, and even to madness.

Such was the origin of Shakespeare's entry into the Theater Wars. Just as they publicly aired their experiments with each other's evolving comic forms, Shakespeare and Jonson literally staged their methodological differences between 1599 and 1601, as both dramatists incorporated the tensions between mythic comedy and satire into the very structure of their plays. The competing principles of androgynous comedy and misogynist satire were, as I have indicated, crucial elements in the *poetomachia* that erupted in London playhouses during this period; *Hamlet*'s commentary on satire constituted just one part of Shakespeare's response to Jonson and his merry band of rival parodists. In my final chapter, besides exploring another Shakespearean response, I hope to demonstrate how Jonson's and Shakespeare's antithetical theories of comic androgyny, integral to their roles in the

Theater Wars, actually assisted in the clarification of these play-wrights' competing comic philosophies. Like the satirist who defines himself against an oppositional world, Jonson and Shakespeare became their artistically polarized selves largely by means of this fight.[37] On the other hand, *The Merry Wives of Windsor, Bartholo-mew Fair*, and *The New Inn* indicate their authors' recurrent open-ness to dialectical play.

5

"That Reason Wonder May Diminish": The Androgyne and the Theater Wars

> He was (indeed) honest, and of an open, and free nature: had an excellent fantasy; brave notions, and gentle expressions: wherein he flow'd with that facility, that sometime it was necessary he should be stop'd. . . .
>
> —Ben Jonson on Shakespeare

> And will you have poor woman such a fixed Star, that she shall not so much as move or twinkle in her own sphere?
>
> —*Haec-Vir*

An oblique line in the anonymous play *The Return from Parnassus, Part II*, produced early in 1602 at St. John's College, Cambridge, implicates Shakespeare in the "War of the Poets" that had recently enlivened the London stage. This famous quarrel had most obviously and explicitly raged between Ben Jonson, John Marston, and Thomas Dekker, who—reviving a tradition as old as Aristophanes' *Frogs*— satirically attacked one another in successive London stage productions between 1599 and 1601. But in a now-famous passage from *Parnassus II*, an actor impersonating Will Kempe awards Shakespeare laurels in the dubious dramatic contest. Beginning, "Few of the university [men] pen plays well; they smell too much of that writer Ovid, and that writer Metamorphoses, and talk too much of Proserpina and Jupiter," Kempe then gloats, "Why, here's our fellow Shakespeare puts them all down, aye, and Ben Jonson too." "Kempe" further boasts that Shakespeare has given Jonson a much deserved "purge" (II, 4.3.1766-73).

The comment has prompted a wealth of interpretations within the numerous twentieth-century "readings" of the Renaissance *poetomachia*. In her biography of Jonson, Rosalind Miles suggests that the lines probably refer to *Troilus and Cressida*, but may signify the

1601 staging by Shakespeare's Lord Chamberlain's Men of Dekker's *Satiromastix*, which viciously lampooned Jonson and ended the Theater Wars.[1] Favoring Miles's latter suggestion, David Farley-Hills even speculates that the *Parnassus* lines refer to Shakespeare's skill not at writing, but at acting: Shakespeare may have played the part of Jonson (as Horace) in *Satiromastix*.[2] On another track, Henk Gras has recently argued that *Twelfth Night* was Shakespeare's foray into the conflict, and was designed specifically to respond to Jonson's insults regarding Shakespeare's Ovidianism. Gras asserts that in *Twelfth Night* "Shakespeare, using the means rejected by Jonson, shows that [Ovidian] romantic comedy as distinct from humour comedy can indeed reform men and manners, and can do so without becoming didactic."[3] Like Miles, however, Alfred Harbage, J. B. Leishman, George Rowe, and James P. Bednarz think it likely that "*Troilus and Cressida* is the 'purge'"[4] that "Kempe" mentions, since in that play the combative instinct is so discredited as to call all wars—real or literary—into serious question. Rowe sees in *Troilus and Cressida*'s satiric treatment of competition the suggestion "that the goals sought by rival poets at the end of Elizabeth's reign might not be worth attaining."[5] Most thoughtful and compelling of all these readings is Bednarz's recent essay entitled "The Literary Context of *Troilus and Cressida*." Bednarz first documents Jonson's numerous literary assertions of his own "poetic authority," born of "an inner voice of conscience" that is "the sole arbiter of identity."[6] Bednarz then carefully examines *Troilus and Cressida*'s critique of Jonson's view, evident in the hollow grandiosity of Ajax's similar claims to self-sufficiency, as well as in Ulysses' countervailing demonstration of "the dependence of the individual on the 'applause' of spectators who determine his significance."[7]

My purpose here is not to refute these critical positions (with the qualified exception of Gras's argument), since all are arguable and are not, in any case, mutually exclusive. Indeed, given the lively inter-theatrical conversation regarding dramatic method that informed the early Jacobean theatrical environment, it is likely that audiences would have expected a play to comment on rival dramatic approaches almost as a matter of course. Rosencrantz's earlier-mentioned mockery of the performing "children, little eyases," popular boys' companies like Jonson's, is a case in point. In fact, though our historical tendency has been to isolate and examine particular Shakespeare comedies in competitive attempts to solve the *Parnassus* mystery, it now seems clear that Shakespeare's "purge" consisted of a barrage of joking theatrical responses to Jonson delivered in several plays produced around 1600, and even that more than one play was indicated in the remark of "Kempe." Thus, rather than countering other critical speculations, I want merely to propose the addition of another play, *As You Like It*, to the list of probable Shakespearean interventions in the Theater Wars, and to propose its consideration as a referent of the *Parnassus* remark. Produced, like *Twelfth Night*, at the height of the *poetomachia*, in late 1599 or early 1600,[8] *As You Like It* (also like *Twelfth Night*) uses mythic romantic comedy to mock the methods and aims of Jonsonian satire. Further, analogies between *As You Like It* and Jonson's 1599 *Every Man Out of His Humour*—Jonson's first salvo in the war—indicate that Shakespeare fashioned *As You Like It* specifically to reject the satiric method demonstrated and championed by that play.[9]

As You Like It's pervasive antagonism not just to satire but to the Petrarchan strain of much Elizabethan poetry links it with other Shakespearean plays of this three-year period, all of which attack men's unnatural idealization of women. And when we take into account Shakespeare's near-obsessive focus in 1599–1601 on the twin evils of Petrarchan idolatry and humoral satire—personified by Troilus and Thersites, Orsino and Malvolio, and Orlando and Jaques, among others—sense is made of the first lines of the *Parnassus* comment: "Few of the university pen plays well, they smell too much of that writer Ovid, and that writer Metamorphoses, and talk too much of Proserpina and Jupiter." These lines tend to be overlooked by scholars; indeed, as noted above, Henk Gras reads the "Kempe" comment as a defense of, not an attack on, Ovidianism. And it is indeed difficult to conceive how a criticism of Ovid could be logically linked by the *Parnassus* playwright to praise of Shakespeare, a writer so obviously influenced by Ovid's *Metamorphoses*.[10] However, despite *As You Like It*'s clear investment in "erotic beast" myths, the play manifests an equally obvious skepticism regarding another Ovidian motif. The following lines from Ovid's *Amores* provide an example of the particular poetic mode and mind-set that Shakespeare, in the late 1590s, was learning increasingly to distrust:

> What shall I say this means, that my couch seems so hard, and the coverlets will not stay in place, and I pass the long, long night untouched by sleep, and the weary bones of my tossing body are filled with ache?—for I should know, I think, were I in any wise assailed by love. . . . (I, 2, lines 1–8)

No love is worth so much—away, Cupid with the quiver! —that
so often my most earnest prayer should be for death. (II, 6, 1–2)

she was dazzling fair, and her fairness was mingled with rosy red—
the rosy red still glows in her snowy cheeks. Her foot was small—
her foot is still of daintiest form. . . . She had sparkling eyes—like
stars still beam the eyes by which she has often falsely lied to me.
Surely, even the immortal gods indulge the fair in swearing false,
and beauty has its privilege divine. (III, 3, 1–13)

We may note that as early as the 1593 *Two Gentlemen of Verona*,
Shakespeare had demonstrated cynicism toward the Petrarchan melancholy that derived from Ovidian verses like these (1.1.30ff., 3.269–
70). Even more significantly, we may recall that as far back as the
early comedy *Love's Labor's Lost* Shakespeare had begun to associate this mode with the scholarly, satirical bent of the social critic
(remember Berowne's hybridized satiric/romantic discourse in *Love's
Labor's Lost* 3.1). That Shakespeare still associated satiric rancor
with romantic pain late in his career is evident from the passage in
the 1609–10 *Cymbeline* when Posthumus, maddened by Imogen's
alleged infidelity, vows to "write against" and "curse" women (2.5.32–
33). The linkage was an astute one: although Shakespeare might not
have been familiar with Archilochus, that primal satirist's work confirms the origin of critical invective in frustrated eros. We remember
that, in verse predating Ovid's by eight centuries, Archilochus complains of "the passion of love that has twisted its way beneath [his]
heartstrings . . . stealing the soft heart from inside [his] body" (no.
26); his next verse fragment beseeches Apollo to "single out the guilty
ones; / destroy them" (no. 27). Thus, paradoxically, the earliest satire
provided both the prototype for the Ovidian/Petrarchan love-sufferer
and the model for the speaker's reclamation of hard, confrontational
masculinity from Cupid's theft of his "soft heart." *As You Like It,*
more overtly than any other Shakespearean play, stages this age-old
connection between love-longing and satiric spleen, dramatizing the
paradoxical link between the romantic poet's self-obsessed, antirela-
tional discourse and the social reformer's angry rhetoric. In doing so,
the comedy expresses Shakespeare's complex but coherent ambivalence toward the variant romantic attitudes found in the work of
"that most capricious poet, honest Ovid" (*AYLI* 3.3.7). Shakespeare's
play also discloses his clear antipathy toward both Petrarchan and
satiric dramatic formulae. Dismissing both the anticomic impulses of

romantic idealization and satiric misogyny, Shakespeare dismisses, or "purges," Jonson.

The poets' war was, in fact, inspired by such broad theoretical differences regarding comedy as this thesis suggests; therefore the playwrights' staged caricatures are properly regarded as satiric embodiments, not merely of each other, but of each other's competing comic strategies. Thus the attacks were also defenses: by lampooning mythic romance in *Every Man Out*, Jonson argues the artistic superiority of his new humors drama; conversely, by mocking satire in *As You Like It*, Shakespeare champions mythic comedy. Both playwrights' assertions of methodological superiority rest on their ideas regarding their plays' moral effects on theater audiences; it will therefore be helpful to clarify the distinctions between Jonson's and Shakespeare's views in this regard.

I.

Jonson's satiric approach, which criticized social foolishness from a learned, isolated, embattled, and intrinsically misogynistic perspective, invoked tension and distance between playwright and audience, as well as between audience members themselves. Jonson's emphasis on scholarship as the avenue to moral health secured him in a scholarly context discussed in earlier chapters: the tradition of antifeminist writing originating with the classics and running through medieval patristic writers to Renaissance scholars. According to this tradition (mocked by Shakespeare in *Love's Labour's Lost*) disdain for feminine charm is a feature of male psychological strength. We may recall the recoil from the corrosive effects of feminine allurement evident in Jonson's "Song: That Women Are But Men's Shadows," where he writes that "men at weakest, [women] are strongest, / But grant us perfect, they're not known." The satirist's writings in particular, we recall, were to be "strong and manly" (VIII, 585, 797), and the distinguishing characteristic of the mind that would produce "manly" satire was—logically—continual defensiveness. Jonson required both himself and his audience to be perennially armed, not only against women's charms, but against the seductive power of ignorant views. The prologue to the 1600 *Cynthia's Revels*, a play that constituted a second Jonsonian blast in the poets' war, makes the satirist's classic exclusionary plea for the reasoned approval of the wise few: Jonson's Muse "shuns the print of every beaten path,"

Nor hunts she after popular applause,
Or foamy praise, that drops from common jaws:
The garland that she wears, their hands must twine,
Who can both censure, understand, define
What merit is. . . .

                                        (IV, lines 10–20)

Thus Jonson's satiric outlook, a corollary of his scholastic isolationism, urges individual masculine judgment and censure of the vain,
irrational, "feminized" world that his theater audience inhabits and
that his plays dramatize. Accordingly, Jonson's plays are frequently
introduced by authorial spokesmen who urge *male* audience members to judge his plays from a detached, reasoning perspective, and
to avoid the seductive, "feminizing" corruption of opinion sharing.
For example, the 1614 *Bartholomew Fair*'s Scrivener, an authorial
spokesman, proposes to his hearers that

> every man here, exercise his own judgment, and not censure by con-
> tagion, or upon trust, from another's voice, or face, that sits by him
> . . . also, that he be fixed and settled in his censure, that what he
> approves, or not approves today, he will do the same tomorrow
> . . . and not . . . be brought about by any that sits on the bench
> with him, though they indict, and arraign plays daily. (VI, lines
> 97–104)

The seventeenth-century judiciary was, of course, composed exclusively of men; Jonson's courtroom metaphor thus (inaccurately) presents the Hope Theatre audience as an all-male judgmental body.[11]
Yet in it, according to Jonson's peculiar model for justice, all juries
are hung: allowing one's judgment to be influenced by others is an
effeminate weakness that radically threatens one's integrity. To try
on another's viewpoint is to affect a humor. Like wearing a false costume, the action is "feminine . . . , / And far beneath the dignity of
a man" (Jonson, IV, *Poetaster* [1601], "To the Reader," lines 178–79).
Thus *Every Man Out of His Humour*'s inductive spokesman Asper,
like *Bartholomew Fair*'s Scrivener, criticizes the "infectious" (line
174) playgoer who

> us[es] his wryed looks
>   . . . to wrest, and turn
> The good aspect of those that shall sit near him,
> From what they do behold. . . .

                                        (III, lines 181–84)

Such a playgoer is "monstrous" (line 177) in that his presence fosters an illegitimate, hybridized opinion of the play; those sitting near him are moved to praise or blame not by their own judgment, but by his. This parasitical opinion sharing is distinct from the model of legitimate learning that we may recall from Jonson's *Discoveries*: a slow process that involves the gradual, rational assimilation of ideas into the psyche. In contrast, the contagious audience response is emotional and immediate, received communally in the living moment of the dramatic action, not earned individually over time. As we know, Jonson's publication of his plays along with additional printed material implicitly—and sometimes explicitly—directed them to private readers, rather than to superficially related audience members whose unitary responses dissolved the contestatory difference vital to the Jonsonian concept of manhood. (Recall the lack of "difference between" the fashionable courtiers in both *Cynthia's Revels* and *Every Man Out*, explored in my third chapter.) It was effeminate communal audience response that (to Jonson's mind) ruined *The New Inn*'s critical reception thirty years later; Jonson's folio version of that play included poems ridiculing his audience members and the "weak, sick, queasy age" that produced them (which suggests that Jonson's famous encomium to Shakespeare, beginning "Soul of the Age!" [VIII, 390ff., 17], was not as big a compliment as it seemed). Recoil from the mingled, relational audience response that occurred in the moment of theatrical production—fear that emotional community, rather than rational individualism, would rule his viewers' thought and behavior—underlay Jonson's repeated warnings to audience members to ignore each other's responses (in effect, to pretend they were not a theater audience).

When we turn from the stern directives of "Asper" in *Every Man Out*'s induction, which demand the playgoers' mutual disregard, to the friendly audience address of Rosalind in *As You Like It*'s epilogue, we encounter the radical antithesis of Jonson's view. For through the boy playing Rosalind—himself a kind of hybrid sexual "monster" (to recall *Bartholomew Fair*'s Scrivener's word)—Shakespeare urges the commingled audience response that Jonson abhors. "I charge you, O women, for the love you bear to men, to like as much of this play as please you; and I charge you, O men, for the love you bear to women . . . that between you and the women the play may please," Rosalind "conjure[s]" the Globe playgoers (lines 12–17, 11). Rejecting the satirist's isolated, scholastic, rational, masculine model of moral education as inappropriate for the theater,

Shakespeare proposes that the fundamentally *ir*rational erotic sensibility that connects audience members should serve as a communal basis of judgment. Rosalind's promise that *As You Like It*'s experiential lesson will transcend sexual barriers is framed in procreative terms: pleasure in the play, inspired by sexual love, will be engendered "between you [men] and the women." In other words, rather than establishing distinct Jonsonian intellectual identities, the Shakespearean method will unite audience members as well as actors in non-intellectual erotic consensus (even Rosalind himself/herself offers to kiss the men to facilitate this! [lines 18–20]).

I suggest that *As You Like It*'s Rosalind, both in her double-gendered "Ganymede" role and in her invitation to others, here and within the play proper, to embrace erotic relationship as the antidote for human suffering, represents and validates the Shakespearean mythic comic method, and specifically rejects the detached, misogynistic, and isolating satiric approach of *Every Man Out of His Humour*. Rosalind's victory is achieved on two fronts. First, she vanquishes the satirical Jaques, who, in his vain attempts to reform men and manners, constitutes Shakespeare's mocking response to Asper/Macilente, *Every Man Out*'s cynical hero and authorial spokesman. And second, she repudiates the Ovidian/Petrarchan impulse that has frozen *As You Like It*'s lovers in postures of frustrated longing, and replaces Petrarchism with genuine dialogic engagement. In *Every Man Out*, Asper—who becomes "Macilente" in the play proper—shatters the romantic idealism that motivates lovers, but puts nothing in its place. Thus his satire rejects not only idealistic love-longing, but the possibility of love itself. But Rosalind/Ganymede goes one step further than Asper/Macilente, associating isolated Ovidian/Petrarchan yearning with the equally sterile self-love of the satirical reformer and banishing both in favor of interactive romantic relationship. *As You Like It* thus incorporates and then dismisses a complex of values intrinsic to *Every Man Out*'s satiric mode: frustrated romantic idealism and its corollary, cynical misogyny.

We may trace the linked modes of romantic idealization and misogyny that Shakespeare discerned in *Every Man Out* in the path the later, more familiar play *Epicoene* describes from praise of the naturally perfect woman in 1.1 to disgust with the real female body in 4.1. In *As You Like It*, Shakespeare discredits both modes and replaces both faulty Ovidianism and satire with his preferred theatrical antidote: the doubled metamorphic beast of both Ovidian and classical myth, the erotic androgyne.

II.

Anne Barton's observation that in *As You Like It* "a structure of cunningly juxtaposed characters and attitudes . . . becomes a substitute for plot"[12] applies equally to *Every Man Out*'s great stage-parade of fools; the plays' structural similarity invites, for us as well as for Shakespeare's audience, comparison between the denigration of romantic *attitudes* in Jonson's play and the triumph of romantic *interaction* in Shakespeare's. In *Every Man Out*'s court and country, characters wander alone, in pairs, or in groups, combining, recombining, and spying on one another; their encounters stimulate, expose, and ultimately deflate their swollen humors. Romantic fantasy is a central butt of ridicule, as worshipful longing impels the lovelorn Puntarvolo, Deliro, and Fastidious Brisk to extremes of absurd posturing before scornful mistresses.

Every Man Out repudiates these characters' romantic delusions through the schemes of a witty intriguer, introduced in the induction as "Asper." Described in the character list as "eager and constant in reproof, without fear controlling the world's abuses," Asper is the embodiment of Jonson's Juvenalian impatience with the world's "hateful luxuries" (III, induction, line 24) and "lusts" (line 36), vowing to "strip the ragged follies of the time, / Naked" (lines 17–18). To this end he calls, in proper Jonsonian fashion, for an audience of detached, discriminating men who will respond rationally and not emotionally to his dramatic lesson: "attentive auditors" who have "come to feed their understanding parts" (lines 201, 203). Asper also presents himself as a doctor, calling on the individual audience member to be a "patient" who does not "reject all physic, / 'Cause the physician tells him, you are sick" (lines 189–90).

To achieve his cures Asper enters the play as Macilente, a deserving, "well travail'd" (2.6.74), but unappreciated scholar bent on exposing the vanities of the uneducated. Macilente is, in the courtier Carlo Buffone's words, a "lean mongrel" who "carries oil and fire in his pen, [which] will scald where it drops" (1.1.212–15); he is a "lank raw-bon'd anatomy" who "walks up and down like a charg'd musket[;] no man dares encounter him" (4.4.25–26). Buffone's mockery of Macilente's thin frame recapitulates what were apparently common insults to Jonson (in *Satiromastix*, Dekker calls Jonson a "hungry-faced" and "hollow-cheeked scrag").[13] By associating these insults with Buffone's cowardly recoil from Macilente's "scald[ing]" pen, Jonson turns the tables on his rivals, suggesting that they are buffoons and invalid audiences for his satire ("patient[s]" who "reject . . . physic") and also effeminate cowards, who shrink from manly physical combat. (Significantly, the play's final line, wherein Macilente, as Asper, claims that audience applause may "make leane Macilente as fat as Sir John Fal-Staff" [5.11.86–87], highlights Shakespeare's inclusion among the rivals addressed.)

Curiously, however, Buffone and the other humors characters co-operate with Macilente's satiric project, which is the medicinal indict-ment of romantic illusion through the moral devaluation of women. The men ally themselves almost in the manner of *Epicoene*'s "wit club" of Clerimont, Dauphine, and Truewit. Though themselves in-fected with vanity and love-longing, Buffone and Fastidious Brisk jeer at the knight Puntarvolo's courtly idolatry of his "splendidious" wife (2.2.79): Buffone calls it "a tedious chapter of courtship, after Sir Lancelot and Queen Guenever" and wonders "in what dull cold nook he found this lady out?" "'Slud," he says, "I think he feeds her with porridge, I: she could ne'er have such a thick brain else" (2.3.67–73). Conversely, Puntarvolo helps Macilente expose the ignorance of Saviolina, the "self-conceited" gentlewoman Fastidious Brisk blindly worships (4.8.56). Puntarvolo's scheme, which reveals Saviolina's inability to recognize a disguised farmer posing as a nobleman, links seductive feminine posturing with other forms of invalid social role-play and indicts both.[14]

The curious doubling of the roles of Brisk, Buffone, and Puntar-volo—victims of romantic delusion who yet function dramatically to dispel such illusion—is mirrored in Macilente's own ambivalence toward romance. Macilente's chief design is to expose Fallace, Deliro's adored but unfaithful wife, as shallow and unworthy, thereby puncturing Deliro's infatuation with her. To Deliro's claim that Fallace is so "rare," "true," and "pure" (2.4.38) that "no man can be worthy of her kindness" (2.4.31), Macilente objects, "Is't possi-ble, she should deserve so well, / As you pretend?" (2.4.49–50); later he interrupts Deliro's rapturous praise of "such a wife" with

Such a wife? Now hate me, sir, if ever I discern'd any wonder in your wife. . . . I have seen some that ha' been thought fairer then she, in my time; and I have seen those, ha' not been altogether so tall, esteem'd properer women; and I have seen less noses grow upon sweeter faces . . . the gentlewoman is a good pretty proud hard-favour'd thing, marry not so peerlessly to be doted upon. . . .
(4.4.45–54)

But Macilente's plot to expose Fallace is, in fact, motivated by his own frustrated passion for her ("How long shall I live, ere I be so happy / To have a wife of this exceeding form?" he complains in an aside [2.4.135–36]). Macilente's ultimate reduction of Fallace is thus a self-curative process. Through her public devaluation he dispels not only her husband's romantic obsession, but his own. Having provided Deliro with ocular proof of his wife's infidelity and witnessed her banishment from the stage ("Out, lascivious strumpet" [5.11.17]), Macilente pronounces himself cured of the envious desire that prompted his satiric surgery. "Why, here's a change," he observes.

> Now is my soul at peace.
> I am as empty of all envy now,
> As they of merit to be envied at.
> My humour (like a flame) no longer lasts
> Than it hath stuff to feed it. . . .
>
> (5.2.54–58)

For Macilente, as for his fellow intriguers, distrust of women is strangely connected to the fantasy of feminine perfection. When *Every Man Out of His Humour* was played before Elizabeth I, Macilente's epilogue, quoted above, was followed by a speech in which he praised the queen's "perfections" (line 13) and credited her with a sovereign power over his soul:

> Never till now did object greet mine eyes
> With any light content: but in her graces,
> All my malicious powers have lost their stings,
> Envy is fled my soul, at sight of her,
> And she hath chas'd all black thoughts from my bosom,
> Like as the sun doth darkness from the world.
>
> (lines 1–6)

The idealized vision of Elizabeth is not incidentally inspired, but deeply predicted, by the play's sardonic recoil from human women. The movement these paired speeches indicate from satiric disgust to stunned admiration prefigures the pattern of Jonson's earlier discussed poems about Cecilia Bulstrode, the first of which denigrates her as a whore, while the second, written safely after her death, elevates her to virgin sainthood. Like the Bulstrode poems, the two *Every Man Out* epilogues demonstrate a paradoxical Jonsonian dualism, joining the contrary impulses of scornful repudiation and awestruck adoration. Alice Birney has commented on "the old golden ideal every satirist has within him or the utopian vision which he at some time conceives."[15] For Jonson, this vision became the static image of what was in his terms the perfect female, a disillusioned response to the flesh-and-blood ones he knew. This "golden ideal" is indeed "conceived within" the satirist, to use Birney's words: a male-generated phantom, it, like satire, is born of the frustrating conflict between the wished-for and the real.

Romantic longing is thus the contradictory subtext of Macilente's satiric misogyny, and is in fact what produces his misogyny. The woman's inevitable failure to live up to the Ovidian/Petrarchan standard implicit in male desire results in the profound masculine disillusionment at the heart of humors satire. Thus Jonson's final solution to the problem of romantic idealism is the public debunking of romantic relationship (Deliro's "cure" necessarily involves his repudiation of his wife). Like the wise audience member whose solitary judgment is untainted by the "contagion" of another's presence, the masculine satirist's victory is achieved when he finally stands alone, untainted by the desire for connection—most particularly, for connection with women. So far is Asper/Macilente from human relationship at the play's end that he longs for the other characters' annihilation: "It grieves me / To think they have a being. . . . / let them vanish, vapors" (5.11.62–65). Thus Jonson proposes isolation as the satirist's essential psychological condition.

Macilente's self-liberating release of Fallace and company has its curious counterpart in Troilus's psychological dismissal of Cressida in *Troilus and Cressida*, proposed by Bednarz as a specific Shakespearean rejoinder to *Every Man Out*'s moral arguments. After witnessing Cressida's incriminating tryst with Diomedes, Troilus tears her love-letter and throws its empty words into the air, declaring, "Go, wind, to wind" (5.3.110). Initially the very type of the Petrarchan idolater, suffering in the "open ulcer" of his heart for a "pearl"-like and "stubborn-chaste" Cressid (1.1.53, 100, 97), Troilus is now a world- and woman-hating soldier: an Archilochan battle-seeker who misperceives wise Cassandra as a "foolish, dreaming, superstitious girl" (5.3.79). Bednarz's analysis of *Troilus* does not discuss Troilus's transformation, focusing instead on the Ulysses plot's rebuttal of *Every Man Out*'s claims regarding self-determined authorial identity. But the Troilus plot is an essential part of this play's anti-Jonsonianism, for Troilus's swing from idolatry to misogyny mimics the anti-erotic path taken by Macilente/Asper, restaging

Macilente's journey not as progress but as a fruitless shuffle between the walls of a blind alley. Thus Troilus's characterization equally challenges the Ovidian/Petrarchan ethos of woman-worship and *Every Man Out*'s suggestion that rational virtue is achievable through a profound distrust of feminine charm. Further, while Ulysses' mockery of boastful Ajax and Achilles in *Troilus* demonstrates "the social determination of [male] value" in defiance of Jonson's "aggressive self-assertiveness,"[16] Cressida's virtual disappearance into the category of "whore" (*TC* 5.2.114) once Troilus rejects her argues for a balance between the ethic of self-definition and social valuation. For while Ulysses' revelations mock the satirist's belief in a world where value is entirely self-generated, Cressida's story dramatizes the pathetic erasure of feminine selfhood in a world where human worth is entirely defined by men. Both Ovidian-Petrarchism and satiric misogyny would construct such a world, as *Troilus and Cressida* makes clear.

While *Troilus and Cressida* stages the destructive effects on both sexes of *Every Man Out*'s Petrarchism and misogyny, *As You Like It* presents a more hopeful response to Macilente's romantic-satiric ethic: one which resurrects feminine agency within a shared human search for authentic identity. *Troilus and Cressida*'s final act presents a Cressida who, accepting male-authored judgments of her worth, becomes radically inaccessible even to herself, speaking fewer and fewer lines until she disappears from the script entirely nine scenes before the play's close.[17] But the female hero of *As You Like It* resists such erasure by conspicuously foiling exclusively masculine attempts to define her or her gender. In the process, she undermines both Ovidian/Petrarchan and satiric claims to an isolated male self—that is, to masculine claims of total self-definition—shattering the oppositional paradigm of self and Other on which both Petrarchism and satire depend. Macilente/Asper, we recall, defends the self-made man in *Every Man Out*'s conclusion, when he reclaims his own psychic stability by imaginatively dismissing both feminine and "feminized" influences on his emotional state. In *As You Like It*, Shakespeare chooses a mythic warrior to destabilize the limited and lonely vision of self thus constructed: the powerfully connective androgyne, Rosalind/ Ganymede.

III.

Like the characters of *Every Man Out*, the people of *As You Like It*'s Arden wander aimlessly through their fictional world, highlighting each other's foolishness; however, the results of their interactions differ radically from the Jonsonian outcomes described above. Romantic humors such as Orlando's "quotidian of love" for Rosalind (3.2.365), Silvius's inordinate passion for Phebe, and Phebe's obsession with Rosalind/ Ganymede are dispelled not, as in Jonson, to restore lovers to singleness and sanity, but to allow authentic sexual connection in marriage to occur between appropriate partners. The primary agent by whom *As You Like It* repudiates Jonson's repudiation of romance is, of course, Rosalind/Ganymede, the androgynous hero who combines all humors and antitheses within her own person, and employs them medicinally to "cure" the socially alienated characters in her environment. As Anne Barton observes, Rosalind is able to resolve others' conflicts because within herself, "warring opposites are reconciled and live at peace."[18] Rosalind is a doting lover who yet possesses a detached, amused perspective on love; she is also a female fugitive whose male costume enables her to exercise a masculine boldness and authority. Though like Macilente a kind of social physician, Rosalind fixes herself and other characters in a manner radically different than his: one which asserts the curative value of romantic interaction over that of satirical deflation. Unlike the voyeuristic, margin-dwelling Macilente, who begins and ends *Every Man Out* in the satirist's customary position of social detachment, Rosalind works from the center. She is, as I argued earlier, always already deeply involved in human relationships—first with her cousin Celia, with whom she is "coupled and inseparable" (1.3.76), and increasingly with Orlando, whom she finally marries. Further, she is herself impelled and empowered by erotic feeling for Orlando, and initiates Phebe's and Silvius's "cures" by (inadvertently) arousing Phebe's sexual interest. Macilente, in contrast, positions himself in psychological isolation from a vain social world, ultimately disentangling himself from it emotionally as well by ceasing to envy it; additionally, so far from embodying love-longing, he is (as we've seen) the instrument by which Jonson ridicules romantic yearning. Rosalind too deflates romantic "delirium," calling Phebe's Ovidian/Petrarchan love-verse "railing" (4.3.46) and Orlando's analogous poeticizing a "tedious homily of love" (*AYLI* 3.2.155–56). However, Rosalind differs fundamentally from Macilente in that she enables *actual* love, involving friendship and erotic fulfillment, to replace poetic illusion.

Thus, while Macilente's satiric treatment of Deliro's obsession with Fallace ("Such a wife? Now hate me, sir, if ever I discern'd any wonder in your wife") has its analogue in Rosalind's mockery of

Silvius's passion for Phebe, Macilente's and Rosalind's goals differ. Macilente's satiric manner objectifies the adulterous woman, treating her as an aspect of her husband's humor: Deliro is the patient, Fallace the disease. Macilente's lancing, medicinal lines are accordingly directed to Deliro, their aim being (in the manner of the later *Epicoene*) to divest him of both unwholesome fantasy and unwholesome wife. In contrast, Rosalind's blunt claim that she "see[s] no more in [Phebe] than in the ordinary / Of nature's sale-work" (3.5.42–43) is directed at "proud and pitiless" Phebe herself (line 40), and is intended, by puncturing the shepherdess's own inordinate self-regard, to prepare her for a relationship with the doting Silvius.

> But, mistress, know yourself, down on your knees,
> And thank heaven, fasting, for a good man's love,
> For I must tell you friendly in your ear,
> Sell when you can, you are not for all markets.
> Cry the man mercy, love him, take his offer;
> Foul is most foul, being foul to be a scoffer.
>
> (3.5.57–61)

In this way *As You Like It* rejects the antiromantic, antimythic, antiandrogynous action of *Every Man Out*, which aims to destroy false connections between sham lovers rather than to replace inauthentic with legitimate human bonds.

Like Jonson's Asper, who becomes Macilente, Shakespeare's Rosalind assumes an alternative persona to achieve a social cure. But Shakespeare's cure is Jonson's disease. *Every Man Out's* dialogue presents eros as an unhealthy contaminant, to the point where its Sogliardo, a "new-created gallant" (like the newly gentrified Shakespeare in 1601) is derided for his "villainous Ganymede," or attractive male companion (4.3.81, 83). *As You Like It* turns the tables both on Jonson's language and his diagnosis of social ills by making "Ganymede" the disguise that cures all the lovers in the play, including Rosalind herself. In *As You Like It*, "Ganymede" is the curative androgynous principle: the paradoxical double-genderedness that male costume permits symbolizes the heterogenous erotic community that its wearer creates, and to which he/she appeals in the play's epilogue. Rosalind's disguise enables her to orient herself as well as Phebe toward nonillusory sexual relationship, for it allows her to befriend and talk with Orlando, and thus to explode the static image of the remote and beautiful female authorized by both Ovidian and

Petrarchan convention (*AYLI* 3.2, 4.1).[19] The analogue to Orlando's logorrheic versifying, as he "carve[s] on every tree / The fair, the chaste, and unexpressive she" (3.2.9–10), is Rosalind's own lovesick silence ("Cupid have mercy, not a word?," Celia teases her when she first falls in love [lines 1–2]). As I suggested in chapter 2, the conversation Rosalind's "maleness" allows between herself and Orlando frees them *both* from verbal conditions that are fundamentally "unexpressive" and detached. By her androgynous persona, both within the play and in its epilogue, Rosalind indicates the symbiotic joining of male and female opposites, or marriage— a symbiosis achieved through *dialogue* between lovers—as the mechanism that can end self-obsessed longing and resolve psychic conflict. *As You Like It* is less concerned with the reformation of men and manners than with the transformation of both male and female psyches, so that all are drawn from isolated solipsism into interaction and relationship.

This action necessarily involves the comic deflation of the two essentially misogynistic modes of being that characterized male thought in *Every Man Out*: Ovidianism/Petrarchism and satiric posturing. *As You Like It* links and then repudiates both modes, first by exposing and thus undermining the dehumanizing stereotypes of conventional romantic discourse, and next by replacing that discourse with the action and symbols of authentic erotic engagement—the Rosalind/Ganymede-Orlando dialogue and, ultimately, the four onstage marriages—in defiance of the satirical standoffishness of the play's own "melancholy Jaques" (*AYLI* 2.1.41). It is, in fact, through the presentation of Jaques and Rosalind's repudiation of what might be called his "Petrarchan satiric mode" that Shakespeare completes his response to *Every Man Out*'s misogynistic isolationism.

Both James Bednarz and O. J. Campbell have noted Jaques's similarity to "the English satirists whose works streamed from the press during the years from 1592 to 1599."[20] (Bednarz even notes the repetition of Jaques's name in that of Ajax—"a jakes"—the Jonson analogue in *Troilus and Cressida*.)[21] As were the Elizabethan satirists Hall, Marston, Chapman, Guilpin, and Jonson, Jaques is "melancholy's own," voicing "profound dissatisfaction with life in bitter diatribes."[22] Like Macilente, who enters *Every Man Out* railing against social injustices—the unworthy man "thought wise and learn'd," the man who is "rich, / And therefore honour'd" (1.21, 22)—Jaques first appears on stage deriding the evils of the "infected world" (*AYLI* 2.7.60). And like Asper, Macilente's initial persona,

Jaques appeals to an audience of wise men capable of recognizing and reforming their own faults. Asper vows to show "Good men, and virtuous spirits, that loathe their vices" the "time's deformity / Anatomiz'd in every nerve, and sinew" (*EMO* induction, lines 134, 120–21); Jaques similarly claims that "The wise man's folly is anatomiz'd / Even by the squandering glances of the fool" (*AYLI* 1.7.56–57). Jaques justifies his attacks by a standard Jonsonian expedient, claiming their nonspecificity (and also reiterating Jonson's customary obsession with sartorial vanity):

> Why, who cries out on pride
> That can therein tax any private party?
> ·
> What woman in the city do I name,
> When that I say the city-woman bears
> The cost of princes on unworthy shoulders?
>
> (2.7.70–76)

Jonson, staging himself as "The Author," speaks similar lines in his epilogue to the 1601 *Poetaster*, where he claims to have "used no name," and that he "spare[s] the persons, and . . . speak[s] the vices" (lines 84–85); Jaques's lines also echo in the induction to *Bartholomew Fair*, when Jonson's Scrivener derides the "politic picklock of the scene, so solemnly ridiculous, as to search out, who was meant by the Gingerbread-woman, who by the Hobby-horse-man," etc. (VI, 138–40). These defenses are authoritative within Jonson's own dramatic contexts; however, in chaotic Arden Jaques's Jonsonian confrontationality occurs as absurdly free-floating, unconnected to other characters' experience or discourse. Jaques preaches not to a wise, attentive audience but to a band of festive lords more concerned with merriment than moral improvement; his anomalous presence in their midst is accentuated by the discrepancies between their conversation and his. Jaques's question, "Why, who cries out on pride . . . ?" is, in fact, an illogical response to Duke Senior's accusation, immediately preceding:

> For thou thyself hast been a libertine,
> ·
> And all th' embossed sores, and headed evils
> That thou with license of free foot hast caught,
> Wouldst thou disgorge into the general world.
>
> (2.7.65–69)

For Jaques, in general, is talking only to Jaques. He functions as both questioner and respondent in his solitary satiric diatribe:

> they that are most galled with my folly,
> They most must laugh. And why, sir, must they so?
> The way is plain as way to parish church. . . .
>
> (lines 50–52)

> Or what is he of basest function,
> That says his bravery is not on my cost,
> Thinking that I mean him, but therein suits
> His folly to the mettle of my speech?
> There then! how then! what then? Let me see wherein
> My tongue hath wrong'd him. . . .
>
> (lines 79–84)

Jaques's verbal floundering in this passage's penultimate line suggests a pedantic speaker vainly searching for another interested discussant. He evades the real dialogue in which other Arden characters engage: of the Duke he says, "I have been all this day to avoid him. He is too disputable for my company" (2.5.34–35), and when Rosalind tries to talk to him, he leaves (4.1). His own best (and his only) student, he represents the self-involved rhetorical mode of the Elizabethan satirical reformer. Jaques is here reminiscent of *Love's Labour's Lost's* pompous Don Armado, and also of John Marston's self-questioning, self-answering authorial voice in *The Scourge of Villainy*:

> Thinke you a satire's dreadful sounding drum
> Will brace itself? and deign to terrify,
> Such abject peasants' basest roguery?
> No, no, pass on, ye vain fantastic troop. . . .
>
> (p. 4)

Jaques's real audience is, as noted, not the "wise man" whose folly he seeks to "anatomize" (line 56), but a group of merrymakers who view Jaques himself as a figure of fun. Duke Senior "loves to cope him in these sullen fits" (2.2.68), and the duke's lords, regaling the duke with a tale of having "[stolen] behind" Jaques as he gazed at a dying deer, appropriate and frame Jaques's satirical comment on the scene to make Jaques, rather than the deer, the object of mockery:

> DUKE S.:   But what said Jaques?
> Did he not moralize this spectacle?

1. LORD: O yes, into a thousand similes.
            First, for his weeping into the needless stream:
            "Poor deer," quoth he, "thou mak'st a testament
            As worldlings do, giving thy sum of more
            To that which had too much."

(2.2.44–49)

Jaques's reported lines overturn one of Shakespearean comedy's most common metaphors of erotic surrender and resurrection (one that Jonson almost invariably used negatively): the dissolution of the self within a stream or sea (e.g., *Comedy of Errors* 1.2.35–40, *Tempest* 1.2.397–405). Jaques's words, in fact, convert this mythic trope to something more like Asper's extended simile defining "Humour" in *Every Man Out*'s induction: "a quality of air or water" existing "in every human body" that "flow[s] continually / In some one part" because it "want[s] power to contain itself" (lines 89–101). Yet the lord telling the story adds that Jaques himself, hypocritically reproducing the "moralized" action of the deer's weeping, "Stood on the' extremest verge of the swift brook, / Augmenting it with tears" (lines 42–43). These lines further conflate the image of mocker and mocked. In this reported scene (Jaques's own introduction into the play), the lords are hidden; Jaques is thus first presented as a solitary figure, preaching by the banks of a stream to an indifferent nature and a hidden, amused audience.

Ensuing scenes reinforce that image. Jaques continues his one-man dialogue throughout the play, to no didactic effect. His melancholy set pieces fall like stones, ignored by those around him: his famous twenty-seven-line exposition of the seven ages of man concludes, not with applause or agreement, but with an interruption, as Orlando and old Adam enter and are welcomed by Duke Senior (2.7.139ff.). Jaques's appearance on stage with other characters merely highlights his isolation and ineffectuality in their world, as when he eavesdrops and jeers as Touchstone successfully woos Audrey (3.3). While Macilente's cynical voyeurism in *Every Man Out* is instrumental to revelations that resolve his and the play's plot, Jaques's spying, like his satirical pronouncements, has no effect on the marital action of *As You Like It*. Touchstone will wed Audrey with or without Jaques's "counsel" (3.3.95), and Orlando will not be talked out of his "mad humor of love" (3.2.418), despite Jaques's mockery of his obsession (3.2.253–92).

Jaques's mockery is, in fact, at times simply baffling to both the characters and the Globe audience. For example, Jaques's chant

> Ducdame, ducdame, ducdame!
> Here shall he see
> Gross fools as he
> And if he will come to me

provokes Amiens's puzzled question, "What's that 'ducdame'?" (2.6.54–58). Jaques's response, "'Tis a Greek invocation, to call fools into a circle" (lines 59–60), seems metatheatrically to suggest Asper's self-imposed satirical duty in *Every Man Out*, a play that was performed by the Lord Chamberlain's Men at the Globe to a "circle" of playgoer-fools (it was not until after the production of *Every Man in His Humour* that Jonson defected to the indoor theater across the Thames, Blackfriars).[23] Arthur Gray has suggested that the mysterious "Ducdame" was Shakespeare's way of parodying Jonson's continual "Damme," and even (somewhat cruelly) Jonson's alleged stutter.[24] Whatever the word's true meaning (if it has one), its irreducible mystery within the scene reinforces the play's suggestion of Jaques's inability to win others to his satirical perspective, as he vainly tries to persuade the altar-bound lovers that they are fools.

As You Like It's third act constructs a crucial link between this Macilente-like, satirical perspective on love and the obsessive, idealistic Ovidian longing that impels Orlando, Silvius, and Phebe. Rosalind's rejection of Phebe's Petrarchan verses puzzles the love-struck Silvius:

ROS. (*Read.*)   "Art thou god to shepherd turn'd,
                      That a maiden's heart hath burn'd?"
                      Can a woman rail thus?

SIL.   Call you this railing?

ROS. (*Read.*)   "Why, thy godhead laid apart,
                      Warr'st thou with a woman's heart?"
                      Did you ever hear such railing?
              . . . .

SIL.   Call you this chiding?

                                         (4.3.40–64)

But the association of Phebe's worshipful poetry with "railing" (a standard Elizabethan description of satiric language) is comprehensible. Both are discursive modes that objectify their subjects and that prevent their authors from encounter and engagement with the real. From their respective margins, both *As You Like It*'s Jaques and *Every Man Out*'s Macilente regard a world of fops and fools that they have no wish to join (Macilente is in fact "cured" when he sees other characters as "vapors," or unreal things, and "begin[s] to pity 'em" [*EMO* 5.11.65, 62]). Rosalind's jeers at Phebe's verses point to the fact that ridiculous idealization of the beloved similarly marginalizes the lover: Ovidian/Petrarchan discourse, by presenting a static image of the beloved as a cruel and remote deity, traps the speaker in a condition of separateness and discontent, an isolated melancholic stance that mirrors that of the satirical reformer.[25]

As You Like It's linkage between love-longing and satirical melancholy is most evident in the thematic association it forges between Orlando and Jaques. For one thing, Orlando's love verse to Rosalind (more accurately, *about* Rosalind) sounds strikingly like Jaques's rehearsal of the "seven ages" of man that end in "mere oblivion" (2.7.143, 165):

> Tongues I'll hang on every tree,
> That shall civil sayings show:
> Some, how brief the life of man
> Runs his erring pilgrimage,
> That the stretching of a span
> Buckles in his sum of age;
> Some, of violated vows
> 'Twixt the soul of friend and friend;
> But upon the fairest boughs
> Or at every sentence end,
> Will I "Rosalinda" write. . . .
>
> (3.2.127–37)

Orlando's scornful litany followed by his sudden reversion to the idealized name of "Rosalinda" rehearses *Every Man Out*'s final swing from satiric disgust to reverential worship of an idealized image, who exists above and apart from the unappreciative world. Thus Orlando's love poetry itself prepares us to view him and Jaques as analogues when they meet later in this scene. Despite their mutual dislike, "Signior Love" and "Monsieur Melancholy" emerge in this scene as opposite sides of the same coin (3.2.292, 294). Each seeking solitude and shunning the other's company, the pair's mutual indictment does little more than reinforce their likeness, as does their reduction of each other to two-dimensional humors characters.

JAQ.   Will you sit down with me?
And we two will rail against our mistress the
world, and all our misery.

ORL.   I will chide no breather in the world but myself,
against whom I know most faults.

JAQ.   The worst fault you have is to be in love.

ORL.   'Tis a fault I will not change for your best virtue.
I am weary of you.

JAQ.   By my troth, I was seeking for a fool when I found
you.

ORL.   He is drown'd in the brook; look but in, and you
shall see him.

JAQ.   There I shall see mine own figure.

ORL.   Which I take to be either a fool or a cipher.

JAQ.   I'll tarry no longer with you. Farewell, good
Signior Love.

ORL.   I am glad of your departure. Adieu, good Monsieur
Melancholy.

                                      (3.2.277–94)

Orlando's weariness with Jaques's sermonizing recapitulates Rosalind's impatience with Orlando's own "tedious homily of love" that "wearie[s its] parishioners," expressed earlier in this scene (lines 155–56). Further, Jaques's word "rail" and Orlando's "chide" prefigure Rosalind's and Silvius's conversation in the following act, which describes Phebe's love poetry in these terms. Like Rosalind's and Silvius's dialogue, Jaques's and Orlando's exchange links the melancholic modes of love-longing and satiric enmity, accentuating the self-indulgent, isolating tendencies of each. Jaques describes the despised world as a "mistress," invoking the likeness between his melancholy and the misery of the distressed Petrarchan lover. The characters' position by the reflective brook further suggests their mirroring, and Orlando's insulting advice to Jaques recalls the Narcissus myth, the archetypal paradigm of self-obsessed longing (Jaques, we recall, was first introduced as a man alone with his reflection, standing "On th' extremest verge of the swift brook, / augmenting it with tears" [2.1.4243]).

Through Orlando and Jaques, Shakespeare re-presents *Every Man Out*'s Deliro and Macilente, personifications of the socially detached modes of love-longing and satiric melancholy. But Shakespeare places his characters in a context that mocks Macilente's—and, by extension, Jonson's—satire, repudiating its medicinal benefits. In *Every Man Out*, the humors formula works: Macilente cures Deliro's and his own obsession by disclosing Fallace's deceptiveness. But in *As You Like It*, "Macilente" and "Deliro" collide ineffectually, and separate, unaltered, in a condition of mutual antipathy.

What Jaques the satirist cannot do, however, Rosalind the androgyne can. On the heels of Jaques's exit from this scene, Rosalind advances to accost Orlando. Their ensuing dialogue initiates her "remedy" for the "quotidian of love" that shakes them both (lines 368, 365). Rosalind's cure is not, in fact, the fickle response of the cruel Petrarchan mistress that she threatens to enact in order to "wash [Orlando's] liver . . . clean" of any "spot of love" (lines 422, 424). Rather than "now like him, now loathe him; then entertain him, then forswear him," Rosalind instead persistently and consistently engages Orlando in a witty conversation that, by cynically reiterating the standard tropes of Ovidian/Petrarchan convention, highlights these tropes' fictionality. Rosalind/Ganymede's words here and her subsequent impersonation of Orlando's "'fair . . . Rosalind'" (3.2.95) consistently present the "cruel mistress" in histrionic terms, as something "imagine[d]" and "apish" (performed) (3.2.408, 412); thus the mistress's image is displaced by an active (and acting) human agent capable of involving Orlando himself in the dramatic process. Unlike *Every Man Out*'s Macilente, who presents a sermon to deflate Deliro's romantic obsession (*EMO* 2.4), Rosalind performs the androgynous principle she represents, using baffling dialogic give-and-take to dissolve the barrier between lover and beloved enforced by the Ovidian/Petrarchan model and to begin the lovers' mutual transition from self-enclosed separateness to interactive relationship. Macilente's satiric scheme is completed by Deliro's repudiation of his marriage ("Out, vile strumpet"); Rosalind's "cure," in contrast, ends with her and Orlando's wedding, which dramatically registers the unity they have achieved.

A passage in Rosalind's and Orlando's initial dialogue also confirms *As You Like It*'s association between the invalid discourses and postures of satirical and amorous melancholy. Rosalind/Ganymede tells Orlando how she (posing as a woman) once drove a former "suitor" from "his mad humor of love to a living humor of madness, which was, to forswear the full stream of the world, and to live in a nook merely monastic" (3.2.418–21). The lines recall Jaques's repudiation of the merging of self and stream in 2.1, and also predict Jaques's ultimate removal to a "nook merely monastic" at the play's end. There, he vows, he will join the "convertite" Duke Frederick, who—according to Rosalind's weirdly inverted chronology—is the "old religious uncle" who

> was in his youth an inland man, one that knew courtship too well, for there he fell in love. I have heard him read many lectures against it, and I thank God I am not a woman, to be touch'd with so many giddy offenses as he hath generally tax'd their whole sex withal. (3.2.344–50)

Courtly lovers and melancholic woman-haters are both "inland men," mired in recalcitrant misogyny and clinging to personal genderedness, unable or unwilling genuinely to interact with the female "objects" their discourses frame. Their final condition is figured in Jaques's stubborn positionality at *As You Like It*'s end as, abandoning the wedding celebration, he sits alone in an abandoned (but dry) cave (5.4.196).

These scenes' verbal and stage tropes enact an interpretive battle between Jaques and Rosalind over the valences of land and water images. For Jaques, as for Jonson, groundedness is safety, and watery dissolution is perilous surrender to a corrupt and feminized world. For Rosalind, as for Shakespeare, to be safe is to be "land-locked" and alone, while to risk watery self-abandon is to gain a larger and more powerful relational identity. Rosalind's willingness to assume, and her ability to promote, such risk is figured in her own cross-dressed body. Again, we may recall Gayle Whittier's words regarding the symbolic configuration of water and mythic androgyny:

> [T]he androgyne's body seems still in motion, challenging the perceived world of settled objects, replacing stability with progressive

activity. . . . That is why many representations of sublime androgyny place the androgyne near a pool or stream of water, fluid, ele-
mentally essential, and shapeless. . . .

Thus Rosalind's enigmatic story about her "land-locked" uncle, her
transvestism, and her physical proximity to the stream combine in a
subrational invitation to Orlando (who has also claimed to be "inland
bred" [2.7.96]) to leave his solitary life. Fortunately, Orlando heeds
the warning, choosing to acquiesce in the compulsion of authentic
eros and to abandon fatuous *amor*—or perhaps the compulsion of
eros overrides his own choice. For Orlando is saved, not through his
reasoned absorption of a "tedious homily," but through his willingness to *be* absorbed by a mythic paradox: to forsake the illusionary
"Rosalinda" in order to play with the real girl. Thus Rosalind wins
her interpretive battle with Jaques—and with Jonson—through erotic
subliminal suggestion. Jaques and Macilente end high and dry, but
Rosalind returns Orlando (and herself) to "the full stream of the
world."

Thus *As You Like It* confronts the repentant, de-monsterized
Macilente, cured both of his satiric frenzy and his emotional bondage
to society in *Every Man Out*'s final scene, with the unrepentant,
healthy "monstrousness" of the androgynous Rosalind, whose cross-
dressed body symbolizes both heterosexual marriage and her own
embedment in a matrix of gendered social relationships. Comparing
the two plays' epilogues is instructive with regard to the competing
symbolism of the pivotal characters who speak them. At *Every Man
Out*'s close Macilente acknowledges that he "was Asper at the first"
(5.11.76); Rosalind similarly invokes the audience's sense of her doubleness by beginning her final speech as "the lady the epilogue" (epilogue, line 1) and ending it as a boy actor ("If I were a woman . . ."
[line 18]).[26] But Macilente's doubleness—his twin romantic and
satiric passions—have both disappeared by means of his satiric cure;
thus his final lines cement him in his present single identity, disclosing that he will not resume the role of Asper, furious poet. In visual
as well as thematic contrast to the solitary, black-garbed, obviously
male Macilente, the white-wedding-gowned boy-girl Rosalind who
delivers *As You Like It*'s epilogue asserts both the power and the possibility of reconciliation between genders and other warring opposites, through the agency not of scorn but of love. We recall her lines'
erotic suggestion (and their contrast with Jonson's appeal to individual, masculine audience judgments): "I charge you, O women, for

the love you bear to men, to like as much of this play as please you; and I charge you, O men, for the love you bear to women . . . that between you and the women the play may please" (epilogue, lines 12–17). Thus the epilogue urges upon the audience the "remedy" with which Rosalind cured Orlando's loneliness within the play proper: mutual, interactive engagement, to be produced by the dialogic marriage of male and female minds.

In short, Rosalind's epilogue prescribes the emotional audience consensus that Jonson's dramatic spokespersons explicitly abhorred. Her lines present, not a rational "masculine" argument, but an irrational "feminine" conjuration ("My way is to conjure you, and I'll begin with the women" [AYLI epilogue, lines 11–12]). Neither Asper nor Macilente, concerned to get "every man out of his humor," begins or ends with the women. For Jonson, audiences who count are male, and among them opinion-borrowing, like mind-changing, is capitulation to emotionality, which is moral illness. To submit to such seductive conjuration is (to recall *Poetaster*'s epilogue) "feminine . . . , / And far beneath the dignity of a man."

A curious analogy between Rosalind's epilogic appearance and a passage in *Every Man Out* introduces us to the specific issue that Jonson would have taken with Shakespeare's epilogue, and also indicates that by structuring his epilogue as he did, Shakespeare might have been tempting Jonson's further spite. In *Every Man Out*'s second act, the courtier Fastidious Brisk defends his ornate, effeminate attire with this comment: "[Y]our good face is the witch, and your apparel the spells, that bring all the pleasures of the world into their circle" (III, 2.6.37–39). Brisk, of course, is the butt of Jonson's mockery here; Jonson fashioned this remark, just as Jaques fashions "Ducdame!," to strike at the vanity of a circle of fools: specifically, the Globe's feminized, clothing-obsessed audience members, some of whom, seated on stage, might have resembled Brisk.[27] But Rosalind's final conjuration, reminiscent of both Brisk's lines and Jaques's earlier "Greek spell to call fools into a circle," inverts the negative suggestion of both. Recuperating the age-old symbolism of the mythic hermaphrodite, Ganymede/Rosalind's charm displaces Jonson/Jaques's curse, investing both her boy actor's feminine apparel and the Globe's circle of heterogenous playgoers—and actors—with creative relational power, or eros.

That Jonson was not (or perhaps that he was) amused was indicated by the 1601 *Poetaster*, Jonson's next and most violent salvo in the *poetomachia*, delivered from the hostile ground of Blackfriars.

Poetaster was introduced by an "armed prologue" (later mocked by Shakespeare in his prologue to *Troilus and Cressida*)[28] who faced down the "dangerous age . . . / Forty-fold proof against the conjuring means / Of base detractors, and illiterate apes" (lines 6, 8–9). The reference to "conjuring means" recalls Rosalind's final address to the Globe patrons, tempting us to read the subsequent line as an insult to Shakespeare: the social-climber Sogliardo, the "base detractor" and "illiterate ape" who had recently mocked Jonson by an illegitimate theatrical method, appealing to an effeminate "transsexual" audience consensus rather than to reasoned, manly discretion. In any case, the distance between *As You Like It*'s androgynous Rosalind and *Poetaster*'s prologue militant, like that between Rosalind and *Every Man Out*'s Macilente, is the distance between a mythic location of identity in double-gendered erotic relationship and a satiric construction of identity as concrete, isolated, embattled, discriminating, and resolutely male.

Through the androgynous Rosalind, Shakespeare thus confronts Jonson the *vir iratus*, and inverts a militant and masculine satiric tradition. Shakespeare's action in the Theater Wars linked Jonson's satiric stance with the very Ovidian/Petrarchan dazzlement Jonson's *Every Man Out* mocked, suggesting that satiric spleen, like the stylized mournfulness of conventional love discourse, was sterile, self-reflexive, and socially useless.

In dramatizing the cultural bankruptcy of both Ovidian/Petrarchan idolatry and satire at the turn of the seventeenth century, Shakespeare involved himself in social currents that extended beyond the theater world. It is likely that at this late moment in the reign of a visibly aging queen, the once potent image of a celestial and all-powerful virgin beauty had lost much of its political and theatrical power to awe. *As You Like It*, in fact, discloses the intrinsic instability of the symbol that had legitimized Elizabeth I's rule for four decades. And in combining its general attack on this symbol with a specific jab at Jonson's satiric method, *As You Like It* may have enacted a still larger historical inevitability. D. A. Beecher has recently surmised that

> erotic melancholy was destined to lose its credibility as a motivational force in theatrical love plots at the same general moment in medical history that the system of humoral medicine upon which it was based itself came under professional attack. But it is more probable that the entire sequence of pathological causation lost its viability through literary over-exposure and metamorphosis,

through the creation of increasingly urbane, witty and sceptical heroines, and through the discovery of a possible reinterpretation of the entire paradigm.[29]

Ironically, however, Shakespeare, in staging Rosalind and his other mythic androgynes, was not discovering a new paradigm, but recovering and reinterpreting an old one. And by 1599, because of the popularity of the new humors genre, this stage revival of mythic androgyny necessarily involved the rebuttal of humors comedy's almost equally ancient, oppositional tradition of learned misogyny, with its unhealthy Ovidian-Petrarchism. Rejecting Jaques, *As You Like It* also rejects as "tedious homily" (*AYLI* 3.2.155) both the sterile litanies of love and the "physic of the mind" that *Every Man Out*'s Asper promises (induction, line 132). In their place, *As You Like It* offers a closing "wedlock-hymn" in order "That reason wonder may diminish" (5.4.137, 139). This last line's amphibology is consistent with the play's central paradox. On one level, it refers to the characters' impending comic anagnorisis, as disguises are dropped and questions answered. On another, it contains a meaning consistent with Rosalind's reference to "conjur[ing]" in the play's epilogue: it suggests the diminishment of reason, tool of the satiric reformer, by the application of wonder, aroused by the contemplation of eros in action. *As You Like It*'s final lines may not have pleased Jonson; they did, however, conform to the poetic standards of Jonson's other adversary Thomas Dekker, who urged the "perfect poet" to inspire his audience "T'Applaud, what their charm'd soul scarce understands."[30]

Epilogue

In the exchange of theatrical hostilities known as the Theater Wars, the satirist himself became a central figure of ridicule. Marston's Chrisoganus in *Histriomastix*[1] and Lampatho in *What You Will*, Dekker's Horace in *Satiromastix*, and "Furor Poeticus" in the anonymous *Parnassus* plays are all specific parodies of Jonson's satirical zeal. The proliferation of such satirist-parodies indicates the increasingly self-reformative inclination of dramatic satire itself during this period. A passage from Marston's 1600 *Jack Drum's Entertainment* (also aimed at Jonson) creates a sense of satirical energy collapsing in on itself:

> Why should thou take felicity to gall
> Good honest souls? And in thy arrogance
> And glorious ostentation of thy wit
> Think God infused all perfection
> Into thy soul alone, and made the rest
> For thee to laugh at? Now, you censurer,
> Be the ridiculous object of our mirth ....
>
> (5.16–21)[2]

Lines like these enact the customary satiric thrust outward against a foreign antagonist, but simultaneously indicate the satiric genre's gradual turn inward, as it begins to interrogate its own ethos. Jonson himself, whose later *Bartholomew Fair* proved his talent for self-mockery, more frequently exploited the poetomachic forum to attack his methodological allies—satirical playwrights like Dekker and Marston—than to mock Shakespeare's methods; two celebrated examples are his parodies of Marston as Crispinus in *Poetaster* and Carlo Buffone in *Every Man Out of His Humour*.[3]

But curiously interwoven into this "satirists' war" was a thread of awareness of the alternative principle of mythic comedy, and its— to the satirist—threatening power to absorb and transform the satirical paradigm. Paradoxically, an early-seventeenth-century epigram

198

by Endymion Porter, "Upon Ben Jonson and his zany Tom Randolph" (a poet friend of Jonson's), frames an argument that both records and repudiates the satiric values of learnedness, self-centeredness, and male sexual dominance, in an affirmation of the subsuming power of a mythic communal ethic of artistic appreciation:

> E'en Avon's Swan could not escape
> These letter-tyrant elves;
> They on his fame contrived a rape
> To raise their pedant selves.
> But after-times with full consent
> This truth will all acknowledge—
> Shakespeare and Ford from Heaven were sent,
> But Ben and Tom from college.[4]

Porter's poem brings us back to Shakespeare. Any close analysis of Shakespeare's plays will reveal the few years spanning the turn of the seventeenth century as the period of his most intense interest in the satirical form. "Interest," of course, does not signify adulation or emulation (although it occasionally may, and for Shakespeare occasionally did). The interest in satire that marks many of Shakespeare's plays of this period—*Much Ado about Nothing*, *As You Like It*, *Twelfth Night*, *Hamlet*, and *Troilus and Cressida*—was registered in a complex dramatization of the fear beginning to emerge in metasatirical diatribes such as Marston's in *Jack Drum* (quoted above): an increasing skepticism regarding the possibilities of the satiric mode to foster cultural health. In all of the above plays, Shakespeare implicitly argued the inability of the satirist (Benedick, Jaques, Malvolio, Hamlet, Thersites) to connect with his human environment in any genuinely contributory way, at least while positioned in the self-alienated, misogynistic framework of satirical perspective. The satirist's key characteristic in *As You Like It* and *Twelfth Night* is his ineffectuality. Ignored by his fellow characters, he is resoundingly defeated by the androgynous principle that informs both plays. To adapt James Bednarz's statement regarding Marston's caricature of Jonson in *Histriomastix*, the Shakespearean satirist's "didactic program is . . . called into question by its failure to command moral authority and to cement meaningful social relationships capable of justifying his vocation."[5]

Nor do the satirical Jaques or the puritanical Malvolio successfully mediate the play's action for the theater audience—the "fools" in the "circle"—as they wish to do. Instead, they themselves are mediated by the play's powerful androgynes (Maria, *Twelfth Night*'s "Penthesilea," or Amazon [2.3.177], is one), who construe them as sterile anomalies in a fertile mythic-comic environment. The Shakespearean satirist is at best a null factor, and at worst a debilitating force, as the last comedy in this antisatirical "series," *Troilus and Cressida*, suggests. In *Troilus and Cressida*, Thersites—a voyeur like Jaques, but, partly due to his assumption of the powerful scene-closing positions previously held by Shakespeare's androgynes, a more successful audience mediator than either Jaques or Malvolio—reduces all human striving to humorous symptoms of diseased psyche and spirit. Most harmfully, Thersites' cynical perspective on the Greeks and Trojans transforms eros from a genuine relational force to lecherous self-indulgence ("nothing but lechery! all incontinent varlots!" [*TC* 5.1.97– 98]).

More poignantly than they dramatized satire's cultural sterility, Shakespeare's comedies of this period revealed—as did certain features of Jonson's life—the frightening power of the satirical perspective, once embraced, to imprison its holder in solitude. Jaques and Malvolio particularly represent the satirist in a solipsistic condition, his recursive energies endlessly circulating in a sad parody of the circular androgynous ideal. Shakespeare dramatizes the satirist's difficulty in breaking out of his interpretive framework in the denouements of both *Twelfth Night* and *As You Like It*, as these plays' satiric figures are invited into communal celebration, but choose instinctively—almost uncontrollably—instead to remain in marginalized, voyeuristic postures (in Malvolio's case, to plot active revenge [*Twelfth Night* 5.1.378]). *As You Like It*'s conclusion is particularly revelatory of Shakespeare's grim prognosis for the would-be social reformer. Here, Jaques resists the Duke's plea, "Stay, Jaques, stay," with the comment, "To see no pastime I. What you would have I'll stay to know at your abandon'd cave" (5.4.194–96). Jaques's preference for knowing rather than having—for rational, solitary interpretation, away from and after the event, rather than for shared and immediate experiential being—is a final proof of the anti-androgynous principle that has motivated him throughout the play. As such, the line and its context confirm not only Shakespeare's skepticism regarding satire's social power, but his doubts about anti-androgyny's spiritual healthfulness for the individual who clings to it.

Still, and importantly, these Shakespearean doubts are for the most part comically rendered, demonstrating (as did *The Merry Wives of*

Windsor) Shakespeare's willingness to play with, or dialogically engage, the antithetical philosophical position. The same can be said of much of Jonson's treatment of Shakespearean characters and themes, despite Jonson's explicitly and frequently articulated distrust of such psychic interplay.

The circumstance suggests a possibility implicit in the androgynous principle itself, and raised not only by a poem like Porter's, which somewhat fatuously celebrates mythic comedy's subsuming power, but by satirical lines like those in Marston's *Jack Drum*, which criticize the satirist for positing his difference from the rest: for thinking and acting like "God infused all perfection / Into thy soul alone, and made the rest / For thee to laugh at." The satirical ethos, as we have seen, was fully based on this notion of the satirist's positional and psychological difference from others. The threat mythic comedy held for satire was not its repudiation of this notion of personal difference, but its assimilation of that notion into the myth's larger paradox: the androgynous principle's proposal that despite our real differences, we are all related, and the same. ("Difference," as Catherine Belsey says, "*co-exists* with multiplicity and love"[6] [my emphasis].) "The myth is the central informing power that gives archetypal significance" to all "phases" of experience, including the satiric, as Northrop Frye has written.[7] Thus Jaques and Malvolio are not repudiated, but recontextualized, by their mythic-comic antagonists, as, despite their attempts at radical withdrawal, they are absorbed into the comic pattern of their plays. The mythic-satiric antagonism is, finally, a one-sided argument.[8] The satirist may choose to ignore the myth, but the myth confirms his place within it.

Doubtless unwittingly, Jonson himself, by means of the Theater Wars, his mythic-comic experiments, and even his anti-androgynous satires, confirmed his place within the androgyny myth. He was, in a sense, the "thin-bearded hermaphrodite" that a rival poet once insultingly called him,[9] as well as the double-gendered hero of *Bartholomew Fair*: a living example of recurrent dialogic engagement in the relational context of his heterogenous social environment. The ultimate generosity Jonson demonstrated in his ode to Shakespeare, entitled, "To the memory of my beloved," suggests that Jonson's recollection of this all-defining social context survived his dominant impulse toward satiric withdrawal.

This complicated relationship of Jonson's to the "feminized" society he criticized is deeply implicated in his own misogynistic, antitheatrical attitudes. Laura Levine notes the paradoxical belief in real androgynous transformation that underlay Jonson's and other Renaissance writers' antitheatrical stances, stating that the fear "that a man can be turned into a woman is a version of the more basic 'magical' idea that a given person can be turned into another person."[10] In other words, the fear that motivates satire's repeated assertions of personal autonomy is, finally, an unintentional homage to the mythic view that none of us is wholly self-contained. Thus satiric recoil from the stage transvestite or other androgynous figure ultimately destroys its own hypothesis of men's free-standing integrity, implicitly confirming that, despite men's and women's—and men's and men's, and women's and women's—physical divergence, we lack discrete underlying selves. This ontological riddle recurrently asserts itself through the uncontrollable workings of the erotic process, whose goal is simply life. To adapt a newly popular phrase, human heterosexuality, now as in classical and Renaissance times, is "compulsory" for the same reason it has always been compulsory for most: not because we choose it, but because it chooses us, and creates the world through us. Yet in mythic terms, as Plato reminds us, "compulsory" heteroeroticism is not the essential conferrer of human identity. Eros, by definition, transcends the sexual categories it generates. Erotic myth simply points to the pursuit of relatedness—to the search for our birthright that proves we've misplaced it—as the defining human action. The androgyne figures this paradoxical and necessary assertion of our shared selfhood. According to its myth—according even to the satirical representations that unwillingly confirm its significance—physical separateness, not androgynous capability, is our fundamental illusion.

Notes

Notes to the Introduction

1. See, for example, Ann Jones and Peter Stallybrass's "Fetishizing Gender: Constructing the Hermaphrodite in Renaissance Europe," in *Body Guards,* ed. Julia Epstein and Kristina Straub (New York: Routledge, 1991), pp. 80–111, as well as Robert Kimbrough's discussion of the two words in "Androgyny Seen through Shakespeare's Disguise," *Shakespeare Quarterly* 33 (1982): 21 n. 8. My discussion of the symbolic literary use of androgyny inclines toward Kimbrough's (with the exception of his above-referenced footnote, which summarizes the Renaissance medical implications of the words "androgyny" and "hermaphrodism"). But my discussion differs fundamentally in approach from that of Jones and Stallybrass, who focus on the effects of classical and Renaissance biological (and literary) texts on definitions of physical "maleness" and "femaleness." My concern, unlike theirs, is not with androgyny/hermaphrodism as a biological category, but as an artificial symbol of a heterosexual relationship or of a psychological condition.

2. Phyllis Rackin, "Androgyny, Mimesis, and the Marriage of the Boy Heroine on the Renaissance Stage," in *Speaking of Gender,* ed. Elaine Showalter (New York: Routledge, 1989), p. 113.

3. See Ken Ringle, "Into the Heart—and Soul—of Africa: Laurens van der Post's Spiritual Quest as Writer, Hunter, Soldier & Humanist," *The Washington Post,* 26 June 1993. In a section entitled "The Fall of Eros" in his recent *Love and Friendship* (New York: Simon and Schuster, 1993), the late Allan Bloom also defines the Greeks' expansive notion of eros.

4. Cynthia Secor, quoted in Kimbrough, "Androgyny Seen," p. 19.

5. Edmund Spenser, *The Faerie Queene,* ed. A. C. Hamilton (New York: Longman, 1977). Other references to *The Faerie Queene* are also to this edition.

6. *The Orphic Hymns: Text, Translation, and Notes,* trans. and ed. Apostolos N. Athanassakis (Atlanta: Scholars Press, 1977). All references to the hymns are to this edition.

7. Marjorie Garber, *Vested Interests: Cross-Dressing and Cultural Anxiety* (New York: Routledge, 1992).

8. Alfred Harbage, for example, speaks of "two distinct theatrical traditions in England. . . . romantic, idealistic, positive, and often patriotic and religious drama," and "satirical comedy." Quoted in R. A. Foakes, "The Profession of Playwright," in *Modern Shakespearean Criticism,* ed. Alvin B. Kernan (New York: Harcourt Brace Jovanovich, 1970), p. 145 n. 1.

9. The seminal work clarifying this likeness is Jonas Barish's *Anti-theatrical Prejudice* (Berkeley: University of California Press, 1981), especially chapters 4 and 5.

10. The satirist's explicit self-identification with his work also facilitates—and, I would argue, justifies—interpretations of his own life and psychology as they relate to his productions, a critical practice notoriously difficult to perform with Shakespeare.

11. Rackin, "Androgyny, Mimesis, and the Boy Heroine," p. 120.

12. Brian Vickers, *Appropriating Shakespeare: Contemporary Critical Quarrels* (New Haven: Yale University Press, 1993), p. xii.

13. The popular critical assumption of a controlling Renaissance misogyny has led to readings of the culture as a whole that occasionally defy common sense. For example, current scholarship has made much of a single account, found in the writings of the French physician Ambroise Paré, of a sixteenth-century girl's alleged transformation into a boy as a result of strenuous athletic activity: a story that several critics insist demonstrates a prevailing Renaissance fear that women could turn into men, and vice versa. (See, for example, Jones and Stallybrass, "Fetishizing Gender," pp. 84–85; Thomas Laqueur, *Making Sex: Body and Gender from the Greeks to Freud* [Cambridge: Harvard University Press, 1990]; and Phyllis Rackin, "Historical Difference/Sexual Difference," in *Privileging Gender in Early Modern England* [Kirksville, Mo.: Sixteenth-Century Journal Publishers, 1993], p. 51.) This popular critical assumption seems to be gaining strength despite the great number of mythic texts ranging from Homer to Plato to Genesis (all surely more widely read during the Renaissance than Paré) that treat man and woman as divinely separated, biologically distinct entities. One would think, at any rate, that since transformations like the one Paré describes never actually happened in anyone's experience, the average sixteenth-century man or woman probably proceeded through a life that involved marriage and procreation untroubled by the poststructurally assigned fear of turning into a member of the opposite sex. The theory of homologous male and female sexual organs, never widely held even by Renaissance scientists, had in fact been almost completely abandoned by 1600, as is made clear in Ian Maclean's well-researched *The Renaissance Notion of Woman* (New York: Cambridge University Press, 1980), p. 33. See also Linda Woodbridge's *Women and the English Renaissance: Literature and the Nature of Womankind, 1540–1620* (Urbana: University of Illinois Press, 1984) for a balanced discussion of Renaissance notions of sexual difference.

14. Anne Hollander, "Dragtime: The Professor, the Transvestite, and the Meaning of Clothes," *The New Republic*, 31 Aug. 1992, 34.

15. See, for example, Catherine Belsey's "Disrupting Sexual Difference: Meaning and Gender in the Comedies," in *Alternative Shakespeares,* ed. John Drakakis (London: Methuen, 1985), p. 167.

16. Paulos, *The Greek Anthology,* ed. Peter Jay, trans. Andrew Miller (New York: Oxford University Press, 1973), p. 348.

Notes to Chapter 1

1. Kimbrough, "Androgyny Seen," p. 20.

2. See Wendy Doniger O'Flaherty, *Asceticism and Eroticism in the Mythology of Siva* (London: Oxford University Press, 1973), p. 170.

3. See Matthew Hodgart, *Satire* (New York: World University Library, 1969), p. 20.

4. Joan Westcott, "The Sculpture and Myths of Eshu-Elegba, the Yoruba Trickster," *Africa* 22 (1962): 336–54, quoted in ibid.

5. Edgar Wind, *Pagan Mysteries in the Renaissance* (London: Faber and Faber, 1958), p. 173.

6. Origen, *Homilies on Genesis and Exodus*, trans. Ronald E. Heine (Washington, D.C.: Catholic University Press, 1981).

7. Kimbrough, "Androgyny Seen," p. 19 n. 5.

8. Midrash, commentary on Genesis, Rabbah 8:1, quoted in ibid.

9. Joseph Campbell, from *The Hero with a Thousand Faces*, Bollingen series (Princeton: Princeton University Press, 1949, 1972), pp. 152–53; quoted in Kimbrough, "Androgyny Seen."

10. Plato, *Symposium*, trans. and ed. Alexander Nehamas and Paul Woodruff (Indianapolis: Hackett, 1989). All references to the *Symposium* are to this edition.

11. For an impressive analysis of various aspects of divine necessity according to Greek thought, see Bernard Williams, *Shame and Necessity* (Berkeley: University of California Press, 1993), especially chapters 5 and 6.

12. Homer, *The Odyssey*, trans. Robert Fitzgerald (New York: Vintage Books, 1990). My references to Homer are all to this edition.

13. Sophocles, *Oedipus the King*, in *The Three Theban Plays*, translated by Robert Fagles, introduction and notes by Bernard Knox (New York: Viking Press, 1982). All references to Sophocles are to this edition.

14. Euripides, *The Bacchae*, trans. William Arrowsmith, in *Euripides V*, ed. David Grene and Richmond Lattimore (Chicago: University of Chicago Press, 1968). All references to *The Bacchae* are to this edition.

Thomas G. Rosenmeyer writes, "Dionysus, who is Euripides' embodiment of universal vitality. . . . appears to be neither woman nor man; or, better, he presents himself as woman-in-man, or man in-woman, the unlimited personality." Quoted in Carolyn G. Heilbrun's *Toward a Recognition of Androgyny* (New York: Harper Colophon, 1974), p. xi.

15. See William Harlan Hale, *Ancient Greece* (New York: American Heritage Press, 1970), p. 27.

16. Euripides, *Hippolytus*, trans. David Grene, in *Euripides I*, ed. David Grene and Richmond Lattimore (Chicago: University of Chicago Press, 1955). References to *Hippolytus* are all to this text.

17. Plato, *Phaedrus*, trans. Lane Cooper, in *Phaedrus, Ion, Gorgias, and Symposium, with passages from the Republic and Laws* (Ithaca: Cornell University Press, 1985), p. 38.

18. Ovid, *Heroides and Amores,* trans. Grant Showerman, ed. T. E. Page, E. Capps, and W. H. D. Rouse (New York: G. P. Putnam's Sons, 1931). All references to *Amores* are to this text.

19. Ovid, *Metamorphoses*, trans. Rolfe Humphries (Bloomington: Indiana University Press, 1957). Unless otherwise noted, all references within my text to the *Metamorphoses* are to this edition.

20. Ovid, *Heroides and Amores.*

21. Stevie Davies writes that Apuleius's work "cast[s] white light over the world of *A Midsummer Night's Dream*" (Davies, *The Feminine Reclaimed* [Lexington: University Press of Kentucky, 1986], p. 22).

22. Apuleius, *Metamorphoses*, vols. 1 and 2, trans. and ed. J. Arthur Hanson (Cambridge: Harvard University Press, 1989). All quotations of Apuleius are from this text.

23. The Hindu myth of Siva interestingly conflates the symbolism of androgyny,

the horse, and water to convey a sense of an ever-changing life force. In one episode Siva takes the form of a female underwater horse, or what Wendy O'Flaherty calls a "submarine mare," to perform sexual exploits. See O'Flaherty, *Asceticism and Eroticism,* p. 170.

24. Davies, *The Feminine Reclaimed,* p. 23.

25. Quoted by Richmond Lattimore in his notes to *The Frogs,* by Aristophanes, trans. Richmond Lattimore, in *Four Plays by Aristophanes,* ed. William Arrowsmith, Richmond Lattimore, and Douglass Parker (New York: New American Library, 1962), p. 587 n. 497.

26. In Arthur Golding's 1567 translation, Hermaphroditus's plea is "That whoso comes within this well may be so weakened there, / That of a man but half a man he may from thence retire" (book 4, lines 477–78; spelling modernized). (See Golding's *Metamorphoses,* ed. John Frederick Nims [New York: Collier-Macmillan, 1967].) In reading the Hermaphroditus tale as an example of the mythic paradigm that glorifies androgyny, I take issue with Ann Jones and Peter Stallybrass's observation that Hermaphroditus ends as "an effeminized boy, who remains alone" ("Fetishizing Gender," p. 97). It seems to me that the story's point is that Hermaphroditus is not alone, and never will be again. This is, indeed, to borrow Jones and Stallybrass's phrase, "a problem of male identity" (p. 97), but it is a necessary problem, unless a man opts for Hippolytus's militant celibacy—which (as Euripides suggests) causes other problems.

27. Gayle Whittier, "The Sublime Androgyne Motif in Three Shakespearean Works," *Journal of Medieval and Renaissance Studies* 19, no. 2 (Fall 1989): 186.

28. Nehamas and Woodruff's introduction to the *Symposium* provides an excellent analysis of Alcibiades' reversal of the anticipated erotic role-playing between himself and Socrates (see previously cited edition).

29. See Don Cameron Allen, *Mysteriously Meant: The Rediscovery of Pagan Symbolism and Allegorical Interpretation in the Renaissance* (Baltimore: Johns Hopkins University Press, 1970), p. 180.

30. Aeschylus, *The Libation Bearers,* trans. Richmond Lattimore, in *Aeschylus I: Oresteia,* ed. David Grene and Richmond Lattimore (Chicago: University of Chicago Press, 1953).

31. See Edith Hamilton's *Mythology: Timeless Tales of Gods and Heroes* (New York: New American Library, 1969), pp. 52–54.

32. Claude Lévi-Strauss, "The Structural Study of Myth," in Thomas A. Sebeok, ed., *Myth: A Symposium* (Bloomington: Indiana University Press, 1958), p. 64. I should point out that Lévi-Strauss's linguistic model, while useful in some respects to illuminate the power of dialectic, is ultimately problematic when applied to myth, due to his insistence that the meaning of the mythic synthesis can be reduced to the sum of its dialectical parts, and ultimately to nonmeaning. In fact, myth combines oppositional terms in order to achieve a meaning both greater than and wholly unlike that suggested by each term alone (e.g., "unity" as opposed to "separateness"). As Brian Vickers points out, when verbal "elements are combined a meaning is produced, which is not 'reducible' in any simple sense to its component parts" (Vickers, *Appropriating Shakespeare,* p. 16). See also Victor Turner, *The Ritual Process: Structure and Anti-Structure* (Chicago: Aldine, 1969), for a discussion of this paradox.

33. Jonathan Swift, *Gulliver's Travels and Other Writings,* ed. Louis A. Landa (Boston: Houghton Mifflin, 1960), p. 110.

Horace's dialogues are an exception that proves this rule about satiric animus. As Raman Selden has observed, the dialectical method that Horatian satire employs softens his satirical edge, introducing a hint of moral relativism that mitigates the narrator's condemnation. Dialogue allows Horace to avoid "direct moral reprehension" (Selden, *English Verse Satire: 1590–1765* [London: George Allen and Unwin, 1978], p. 22) and enables him to engage in "witty self-depreciation" (ibid., p. 28), but in so doing it blurs both his moral and his narrative persona in a way that prevents the ideal satiric erection of a virtuous speaker, separate and free from the social situation he describes.

34. For a discussion of the distinctions between choral lyrics, lyric monodies, and the simpler iambic style, see Richmond Lattimore's preface to *Greek Lyrics,* trans. Richmond Lattimore (Chicago: University of Chicago Press, 1960). My quotations of Archilochus and Semonides all derive from this edition.

35. Aristophanes, *The Frogs,* trans. Richmond Lattimore, in *Four Plays by Aristophanes,* p. 582. (All citations of *The Frogs, The Clouds,* and *Lysistrata* are from this edition.) Aristophanes' skepticism regarding the power of dialogic give-and-take to promote genuine moral insight can be seen in many of his plays, perhaps most famously (and hilariously) in the ludicrous conclusions reached through the sophistical conversations of moral reprobates in *The Clouds.*

36. *The Clouds,* trans. William Arrowsmith, in ibid., p. 62.

37. The phrases are Hugh Walker's, from his *English Satire and Satirists* (New York: Octagon Books, 1972), p. vi.

38. Jonas Barish, *The Anti-theatrical Prejudice,* p. 85.

39. See the play's description of effeminate Kallias, "the son of Ponyplay," who "has gone to sea and the ships with a lionskin over his hips" (p. 512). The physical cowardice of Dionysus (who also wears a lion skin) is comically dramatized in the play's middle section (pp. 514–30); Dionysus later agrees when Euripides calls him an idiot (p. 545). Euripides himself is seen praying, not to fertile Dionysus, but to "Socket of the tongue" and "sensitory nostrils" (p. 543).

40. Lucian, *Satirical Sketches,* translated and introduced by Paul Turner (Baltimore: Penguin Books, 1961), pp. 51–52. All references to Lucian are to this edition.

41. Hodgart, *Satire,* p. 123.

42. Aristophanes, *Lysistrata,* trans. Douglass Parker, in *Four Plays by Aristophanes,* pp. 401–2.

43. Aristophanes, *Thesmophoriazusae,* in *Aristophanes: The Eleven Comedies,* trans. anon. (New York: Liveright, 1943), p. 285.

44. See Hamilton, *Mythology,* p. 177.

45. Whereas Aristophanes satirically inverts Atalanta's story to demonstrate male recoil from erotic contact, Plato invests Atalanta with divine hermaphrodism and uses her as a symbol of hopeful regeneration. The myth of Er that concludes Plato's *Republic* recounts how in the afterworld, given the choice to return to life in a new body, Atalanta "saw great honors being given to a male athlete" and "chose his life, unable to pass them by" (a mythic innovation that would doubtless seem poignant to many female athletes). See *The Republic,* trans. G. M. A. Grube (Indianapolis: Hackett, 1992), 10:620b.

46. Horace, *Horace's Satires and Epistles,* trans. Jacob Fuchs (New York: W. W. Norton, 1977).

47. Juvenal, *The Satires of Juvenal,* trans. Rolfe Humphries (Bloomington: University of Indiana Press, 1958). All references to Juvenal's work are to this text.

48. Persius, *Satires*, in *Juvenal and Persius*, trans. G. G. Ramsay (Cambridge: Harvard University Press, 1930). All references to Persius are to this text.

49. Martial, *Epigrams*, vol. 1, trans. Walter Ker (London: G. P. Putnam's Sons, 1925), p. 211. All references to Martial are to this text.

50. Robert C. Elliott, *The Power of Satire: Magic Ritual. Art* (Princeton: Princeton University Press, 1960), p. 292.

51. Thomas MacCary, *Friends and Lovers: The Phenomenology of Desire in Shakespearean Comedy* (New York: Columbia University Press, 1985), p. 62.

52. Davies, *The Feminine Reclaimed*, p. 4.

53. Ibid., p. 14.

54. See ibid., 5; see also Elizabeth Ann Ambrose's descriptions of the importance of the Hermetica to sixteenth-century authors in *The Hermetica: An Annotated Bibliography*, an edition of *Sixteenth-Century Bibliography* 30 (1992): 7–8.

55. Edgar Wind, *Pagan Mysteries in the Renaissance* (New Haven: Yale University Press, 1958), p. 174.

56. Davies, *The Feminine Reclaimed*, pp. 4, 6–7, 17.

57. Marsilio Ficino, *Commentary on Plato's Symposium*, translated and introduced by Sears Jayne (Columbia: University of Missouri Press, 1944), p. 160.

58. "Now, some people are pregnant in body, and for this reason turn more to women and pursue love in that way, providing themselves through childbirth with immortality" (Diotima's speech in Plato, *Symposium* 209A). A more blunt statement of man's primary generative role is found in Apollo's words in Aeschylus's *Eumenides*, "The mother is no parent of that which is called / her child, but only nurse of the new-planted seed / that grows. The parent is he who mounts" (lines 658–60). See *Aeschylus I: Oresteia*, trans. Richmond Lattimore, previously cited.

59. Davies, *The Feminine Reclaimed*, p. 1.

60. Ficino, *Commentary*, p. 60.

61. From book 2, chapter 6, of Pico della Mirandola's *Heptaplus*, trans. Douglas Carmichael, in *On the Dignity of Man and Other Works* (New York: Bobbs-Merrill, 1940), p. 104.

62. See Antonio Beccadelli, *L'Ermafrodito*, introduced by Angelo Ottolini (Milan: Studio Editoriale Corbaccio, 1922).

63. The anecdote concerning Elizabeth in armor is discussed by Susan Frye in "The Myth of Elizabeth at Tilbury," *Sixteenth-Century Journal* 23 (Spring 1992): 95–114. I thank Dr. Susan Krantz for calling my attention to the story via her work on Mary Frith.

64. Wind, *Pagan Mysteries*, p. 75 n. 1.

65. See Jeanne Addison Roberts, *The Shakespearean Wild: Geography, Genus Gender* (Lincoln: University of Nebraska Press, 1991), esp. pp. 67–70, and Gayle Whittier, "The Sublime Androgyne Motif in Three Shakespeare Works," cited earlier in this chapter.

66. See Barthelemy Aneau, *Picta Poesis* (London, 1522) and Johannes Sambucus, *Emblemata* (London, 1564).

67. Davies, *The Feminine Reclaimed*, p. 7.

68. Thomas Elyot, *The Boke Named the Governor*, ed. Donald W. Rude (New York: Garland Press, 1992), book 2, lines 20–23, p. 162. R. S. White also comments on the parallel between Elyot's, Lyly's, and Shakespeare's attitudes towards erotic metamorphosis in "Metamorphosis by Love in Elizabethan Romance, Romantic

Comedy, and Shakespeare's Early Comedies," *Review of English Studies* 35 (1984): 14–44.

69. Philip Sidney, *Selections from Arcadia and Other Poetry and Prose*, ed. T. W. Craik (New York: Capricorn Books, 1966).

70. See Juliet Dusinberre, *Shakespeare and the Nature of Women* (London: Macmillan, 1975), esp. chapter 4, "Femininity and Masculinity"; Marianne Novy, "Shakespeare's Female Characters as Actors and Audience," in *The Woman's Part: Feminist Criticism of Shakespeare*, ed. Carolyn Ruth Swift Lenz, Gayle Greene, and Carol Thomas Neely (Urbana: University of Illinois Press, 1980), pp. 256–70; Phyllis Rackin, "Androgyny, Mimesis, and the Marriage of the Boy Heroine" (cited earlier); Jean Howard, "Cross-Dressing, the Theater, and Gender Struggle in Early Modern England," *Shakespeare Studies* 39 (Winter 1988): 418–40; Kathleen McLuskie, "The Act, the Role, and the Actor: Boy Actresses on the Elizabethan Stage," *New Theatre Quarterly* 3 (1987): 120–30; Ann Jennalie Cook, "'Bargaines of Incontinencie': Bawdy Behavior in the Playhouses," *Shakespeare Studies* 10 (1977): 271–90; Catherine Belsey, "Disrupting Sexual Difference" (cited earlier); Robert Kimbrough, "Androgyny Seen" (cited earlier); Steve Brown's "The Boyhood of Shakespeare's Heroines: Notes on Gender Ambiguity in the Sixteenth Century," *SEL* 30 (1990): 243–63; Laura Levine, "Men in Women's Clothing: Antitheatricality and Effeminization from 1579 to 1642," *Criticism* 28 (1986): 121–43; Susan C. Shapiro's "Amazons, Hermaphrodites, and Plain Monsters: The 'Masculine' Woman in English Satire and Social Criticism from 1580-1640," *Atlantis* 13 (1987): 65–76 . . . and the list continues. Many of these scholars make, as I do, the point well articulated by Jeanne Addison Roberts in her recent *The Shakespearean Wild*: that the gender-baffling androgyne was a natural character for the evolving theatrical medium because "ambivalences are at home in drama. Its dialectical nature makes it a particularly useful forum for the exploration of . . . [c]ultural assumptions, uncertainties, and dilemmas" (p. 8).

71. Kent Cartwright, "The Humanism of Acting: John Heywood's *The Foure PP*," *Studies in the Literary Imagination*, Spring 1993, 21.

72. Ibid.

73. John Lyly, *Gallathea*, in Russell Fraser and Norman Rabkin, eds., *Drama of the English Renaissance*, vol. 1 (New York: Collier-Macmillan, 1976), pp. 126–44. All references to *Gallathea* are to this edition.

74. See n. 10, p. 127 of *Gallathea* in ibid.

75. In "John Lyly's *Gallathea*: A New Rhetoric of Love for the Virgin Queen," Ellen Caldwell interprets the play as (among other things) a suggestion that even Elizabeth should marry. In Kirby Farrell et al., *Women in the Renaissance* (Amherst: University of Massachusetts Press, 1988), pp. 69–87.

76. See Peter Saccio, *The Court Comedies of John Lyly* (Princeton: Princeton University Press, 1969), p. 99.

77. Peter Saccio also notes the "allegorical significances" of *Gallathea*'s gods (p. 104), although he objects to interpretations of them as "personifications of states of mind" (p. 105). I interpret Lyly's Poseidon, Agar, and Eros as separate personifications, not of characters' subjective mental states, but of a divine erotic force that exists in nature and that it is unhealthy to resist. Although Saccio says that Lyly's "gods are not Homer's" (p. 104), I believe my description fits the original Eros and Aphrodite also. Lyly's gods *are* Homer's, and Euripides', and also Ovid's.

Gallathea restages the Ovidian lesson of Lyly's *Love's Metamorphosis*, wherein Fidelia's transformation into a tree is a result of her unnatural resistance to the erotic force embodied by an amorous satyr.

78. William Shakespeare, *The Riverside Shakespeare*, ed. G. Blakemore Evans (Boston: Houghton Mifflin, 1974). All references to Shakespeare's works are to this edition.

79. Rackin, "Androgyny, Mimesis, and the Boy Heroine," p. 121.

80. G. K. Hunter, *John Lyly: The Humanist as Courtier* (New York: Routledge, 1962), p. 306.

81. See Leah Scragg, *The Metamorphosis of Gallathea: A Study in Creative Adaptation* (Washington, D.C.: University Press of America, 1982), esp. pp. 11–12; Shakespeare's interest in *Gallathea* was also noted in Kent Cartwright's "*Gallathea's* 'Drama of Ideas' and *Twelfth Night*," a paper presented at the 1992 meeting of the Shakespeare Association of America. For a broader (and alternative) discussion of Lyly's influence on Shakespeare's staging of gender differences, see David Bevington's "'Jack Hath Not Jill': Failed Courtship in Lyly and Shakespeare," *Shakespeare Survey* 42 (1990): 1–13.

82. Rackin, "Androgyny, Mimesis, and the Boy Heroine," p. 113.

83. John Marston, *The Scourge of Villainy*, ed. G. B. Harrison (Edinburgh: University of Edinburgh Press, 1966), p. 3. Marston's spellings have been modernized, along with the spellings of his contemporaries. All references to Marston's nondramatic satires derive from this work.

84. Jones and Stallybrass, "Festishizing Gender," p. 97. Phyllis Rackin makes a similar claim in "Historical Difference/Sexual Difference."

85. Jeanne Addison Roberts, "Animals as Agents of Revelation: The Horizontalizing of the Chain of Being in Shakespeare's Comedies," *New York Critical Forum* (1980): 79–96.

86. Thomas Dekker, *Satiromastix. or the Untrussing of the Humorous Poet*, in *Jonson's Poetaster and Dekker's Satiromastix*, ed. Isiah H. Penniman (Boston: D. C. Heath, 1913), pp. 265–446.

87. Joseph Hall, *Mundus ater et idem* (London, 1609).

88. See Jonas Barish's seminal *The Anti-theatrical Prejudice*, especially chapter 4, "Puritans and Proteans." See also the previously cited studies by Jean Howard, Laura Levine, Steve Brown, and Phyllis Rackin. The argument is by now a familiar one, but another summary of it can be found in Peter Stallybrass's "Patriarchal Territories: The Body Enclosed," in *Rewriting the Renaissance: The Discourses of Sexual Difference in Early Modern Europe* , ed. Margaret Ferguson et al. (Chicago: University of Chicago Press, 1986), pp. 123–42.

89. See Barish, *The Anti-theatrical Prejudice*, pp. 45–59, for a summation of these complaints. Ironically, a comparison of Pico's and Ficino's dependence on Origen and Philo with William Prynne's and Anthony Munday's reliance on Augustine and Tertullian demonstrates that both mythic and satiric androgyny could be validated with reference to early Christian theology.

90. Barish, *The Anti-theatrical Prejudice*, p. 44.

91. Anthony Munday, *A Second and Third Blast of Retreat from Plays and Theaters* (New York and London: Johnson Reprint Co., 1972).

92. Stephen Greenblatt, *Shakespearean Negotiations* (Berkeley: University of California Press, 1988), pp. 126, 129.

93. Philip Stubbes, *The Anatomy of Abuses* (London: Richard Jones, 1583).

94. William Prynne, *Histriomastix: The Player's Scourge, or Actor's Tragedy* (New York and London: Johnson Reprint Co., 1972), p. 201.

95. Ibid.

96. Munday writes witheringly of the "harlots, utterly past all shame" who try to "be as an object to all men's eyes" (*Second and Third Blast*, p. 89).

97. Quoted in Barish, *The Anti-theatrical Prejudice*, p. 85.

98. Prynne, *Histriomastix*, p. 200.

99. Levine, "Men in Women's Clothing," p. 123.

100. Munday, *Second and Third Blast*, p. 89.

101. Barish, *The Anti-theatrical Prejudice*, p. 85.

102. Joseph Hall, quoted in Selden, *English Verse Satire*, pp. 88–89.

103. Ian Maclean's *Renaissance Notion of Woman* discusses the link between misogyny and scholasticism in the Renaissance, as does Peter Holbrook's "Lyly, Shakespeare, and the Poetics of Gender," a paper presented at the Shakespeare Association's 1992 meeting in Kansas City, Missouri.

104. George Chapman, *Sir Gyles Goosecappe*, 1.4.134–36. From *The Plays of George Chapman: The Tragedies, with Sir Gyles Goosecappe*, ed. Allan Holaday (Cambridge: D. S. Brewer, 1987).

105. Barish, *The Anti-theatrical Prejudice*, p. 22. Although Barish finds this resistance in Plato, linking Renaissance antitheatricalism to Platonic doctrine, I would hold that Renaissance antitheatricalism is essentially resistant to the dialectical movement intrinsic to Plato's works—a movement that ironically destabilizes Socrates' valuation of the timeless and immutable.

106. Selden, *English Verse Satire*, pp. 18, 22, 52.

107. Everard Guilpin, *Skialetheia*, Shakespeare Association Facsimiles no. 2 (London: Oxford University Press, 1931).

108. All references to Jonson's work are to the text in *Ben Jonson*, ed. C. H. Herford, Percy Simpson, and Evelyn Simpson, 11 vols. (Oxford: Clarendon Press, 1925–52). I will cite poems and prose by volume, page, and line numbers, and plays by volume, act, scene, and line numbers.

109. James B. Bednarz credits Jonson with the invention of the character sketch. See Bednarz, "Shakespeare's Purge of Jonson: The Literary Context of *Troilus and Cressida*," *Shakespeare Studies* 21 (1993): 193.

110. Roy Michael Liuzza, "*Sir Orfeo*: Sources, Traditions, and the Poetics of Performance," *Journal of Medieval and Renaissance Studies* 21, no. 2 (Fall 1991): 269.

111. Ibid.

112. *Hic-Mulier, or The Man Woman: Being a Medicine to Cure the Coltish Disease of the Staggers in the Masculine-Feminine of our Times. Also Haec-Vir; or The Womanish-Man: Being an Answer to a Late Book Entitled Hic-Mulier* (London, 1620, facsimile ed., Yorkshire: Scholar Press, 1973). All references to *Hic-Mulier* and *Haec-Vir* are to this text.

Notes to Chapter 2

1. Stevie Davies eloquently describes the essentially comic nature of Shakespeare's androgynous (or, to use her word, "geministic") principle, writing that the theme of self-sacrificial relationship as humanity's ultimate expression "is played out in all genres, bloodily and terribly in history and tragedy, but more hopefully

in comedy, which seeks in the darkness of human identity to read the braille of clues and intuitions imprinted on the deepest self, as to how to redress the lost balance of gender" (*The Feminine Reclaimed,* p. 111).

2. Some of the more noteworthy recent discussions of Shakespeare's transvestite heroines as challenges to or affirmations of conventional gender stereotypes include Catherine Belsey's "Disrupting Sexual Difference" (cited in my chapter 1); Barbara Bono's "Mixed Gender, Mixed Genre in Shakespeare's *As You Like It,*" in Barbara K. Lewalski, ed., *Renaissance Genres* (Cambridge: Harvard University Press, 1986), pp. 189–212; Nancy K. Hayles's "Sexual Disguise in 'As You Like It' and 'Twelfth Night,'" *Shakespeare Survey* 32 (1979): 63–72; Leah Marcus's "Shakespeare's Comic Heroines, Elizabeth I, and the Political Uses of Androgyny," in Mary Beth Rose, ed., *Women in the Middle Ages and the Renaissance: Literary and Historical Perspectives* (Syracuse, N.Y.: Syracuse University Press, 1986), pp. 135–53; Kenneth Muir's "Males as Females on Shakespeare's Stage," in T. R. Sharma, ed., *Essays on Shakespeare in Honour of A. A. Ansari* (Meerut, India: Shalabh Book House, 1986), pp. 1–7; and Peter Erickson's *Patriarchal Structures in Shakespeare's Drama* (Berkeley and Los Angeles: University of California Press, 1985). W. Thomas MacCary's *Friends and Lovers*; David Bevington's "'Jack Hath Not Jill'"; Phyllis Rackin's "Androgyny, Mimesis, and the Marriage of the Boy Heroine"; Robert Kimbrough's "Androgyny Seen"; Jean Howard's "Crossdressing, the Theatre, and Gender Struggle in Early Modern England"; and Steve Brown's "The Boyhood of Shakespeare's Heroines" have been cited previously. This, however, is merely a short sampling of titles; contemporary critical interest in this subject is apparently boundless.

3. Richard D. Altick, "Symphonic Imagery in *Richard II,*" in *Richard II,* ed. Kenneth Muir (New York: Signet, 1988), p. 200.

4. Thelma Greenfield, "The Dreaming Audience in Shakespeare's and Lyly's Plays," paper presented at 1992 meeting of Shakespeare Association of America.

5. Jeanne Addison Roberts also notes the implied connection between the Minotaur and Petruchio's reference to the maze in "Horses and Hermaphrodites: Metamorphoses in *The Taming of the Shrew,*" *Shakespeare Quarterly* 34 (Summer 1983): 165. This essay has been reprinted with some changes in Roberts's *Shakespearean Wild.*

6. "Habitual association" is Altick's phrase, which he uses to describe the clustering of images in *Richard II* (p. 210).

7. I owe the term "liminal" to Victor Turner's *Ritual Process: Structure and Anti-Structure.*

8. The Falstaff of the Henry plays (distinct from his incarnation in *The Merry Wives of Windsor*) is associated with androgynous creative power from his first appearance on stage. In *1 Henry IV* 1.2 Prince Hal links Falstaff with the androgynous sun, "himself a fair hot wench in flame-color'd taffata" (lines 9 10), and Falstaff defines himself by means of a cluster of androgyny symbols, identifying himself and his gang as "Diana's foresters . . . minions of the moon . . . govern'd, as the sea is, by our noble and chaste mistress the moon" (lines 25–29). In *2 Henry IV* Falstaff complains "My womb, my womb, my womb undoes me" (4.3.22). In *1 Henry IV*'s long tavern scene, Falstaff tells Hal to "spit in my face, call me horse" (2.4.194), but Hal instead calls him "horse-back-breaker" (lines 242–43); the interchange adds the reversible horse-rider image to Falstaff's symbolic attributes. I am grateful to a student of mine, B. C. Boyd, for pointing out another androgynous archetype for the

Falstaff-Hal relationship, which is Hercules' education by a centaur. For an alternative discussion of Falstaff's androgyny, see Valerie Traub's "Prince Hal's Falstaff: Positioning Psychoanalysis and the Female Reproductive Body," *Shakespeare Quarterly* 40 (1989): 456–74.

9. The tennis pun is accidental, but it fits the play (see 1.2.258ff.).

10. See William Carroll, *The Metamorphoses of Shakespearean Comedy* (Princeton: Princeton University Press, 1985), pp. 142, 147.

11. Jan Kott, *Shakespeare Our Contemporary*, trans. Beleslaw Taborski (Garden City, N.Y.: Doubleday, 1964), p. 212. Much of the paragraph in which I cite this reference follows the wording of Grace Tiffany, "Falstaff's False Staff: 'Jonsonian' Asexuality in *The Merry Wives of Windsor*," *Comparative Drama* (Fall 1992): 254–70.

12. Kent Cartwright notes "the incompleteness and longing that haunt *Twelfth Night*" (tying this mood to Lyly's *Gallathea*), in "*Gallathea*'s 'Drama of Ideas' and *Twelfth Night*," 2. Also, Jeanne Addison Roberts has remarked on *Shrew*'s "theme of deferred sexual consummation," which begins with the Sly episode (*The Shakespearean Wild*, p. 60).

13. Meres called Shakespeare his age's Seneca and Plautus, masterful in both tragic and comic form (*Palladis Tamia: Wit's Treasury*, London, 1598).

14. Stevie Davies describes the characteristic failure of the Shakespearean tragic male to risk the "self-defending . . . ego" for the embrace of relationship (*The Feminine Reclaimed*, p. 11). The possibility of androgynous "embrace" for Othello is suggested in Desdemona's wish "that heaven had made her such a man" as Othello (*Othello* 1.3.163); her amorous statement, recalled by Othello before the Venetian council, expresses the Shakespearean lover's characteristic desire not only to have but to *be* the beloved. Ultimately, Othello's "self-defending ego" violates the androgynous union to which he and Desdemona initially aspire.

15. I assert this against the currently popular and, in my view, radically misguided notion expressed in Phyllis Rackin's recent "Historical Difference/Sexual Difference" that "man's desire for a woman, now coded as a mark of masculinity, is repeatedly associated in Shakespeare's plays with effeminacy" (p. 39). To support this idea Rackin simply dismisses the genre of comedy as nonrepresentative of what she calls "the dominant discourse, which was also the discourse of patriarchal dominance" (pp. 52–53), and instead focuses on the tragedies and histories, pointing to Romeo pining for Rosaline as a type of effeminacy (p. 39) and Hotspur fleeing Kate on his horse as an example of heroism (p. 60 n. 52). Against such arguments, I would point to the arbitrariness of privileging historiographical over comic discourse, and would also claim that careful, nonselective readings of all the plays disclose that Shakespeare never invalidates erotic love, but simply distinguishes real eros from the kind of silly Petrarchan love-longing Romeo expresses for Rosaline, as numerous critics have shown (see, for example, Barbara Bono's previously cited essay). Hotspur, of course, is not the ideal man of the Henry plays; Rackin's discussion of the histories unaccountably focuses on Hotspur and Falstaff rather than on the eroticized Hal/Henry, the plays' central figure.

16. In this I agree with Linda Bamber, who, defending Shakespeare's vision of the woman as exotic other, states that "Men must write as men." See Bamber's *Comic Women, Tragic Men: A Study of Gender and Genre in Shakespeare* (Stanford, Calif.: Stanford University Press, 1982), p. 5.

17. See Roberts, *The Shakespearean Wild*, p. 67.

18. Ibid., p. 68.

19. William Carroll, *The Metamorphoses of Shakespearean Comedy*, p. 147.

20. Roberts, "Horses and Hermaphrodites: Metamorphosis in *The Taming of the Shrew*," *Shakespeare Quarterly* 34 (1983): 160. This essay is reproduced, with some changes, in Roberts's *Shakespearean Wild*.

21. For a discussion of the significance of twinship to "fusion" with the significant other in *Twelfth Night*, see Barbara Freedman's "Separation and Fusion in *Twelfth Night*," in Maurice Charney and Joseph Reppen, eds., *Psychoanalytical Approaches to Literature and Film* (Madison, N.J.: Fairleigh Dickinson Univeristy Press; London and Toronto: Associated University Presses, 1987), pp. 96–119.

22. Heilbrun, p. 29.

23. Barbara Bono's "Mixed Gender, Mixed Genre" provides an excellent discussion of Rosalind's overturning of the Arden lovers' limiting, stylized love discourse. See also Kimbrough, "Androgyny Seen," p. 29.

24. See Robert N. Bellah et al., *Habits of the Heart: Individualism and Commitment in American Life* (Berkeley: University of California Press, 1985), p. 122.

25. MacCary, *Friends and Lovers*, p. 58.

26. Paraphrased from G. K. Hunter's "Lyly's Survival in the Boys' Theatre 1600–1610," a paper delivered at the 1992 meeting of the Shakespeare Association of America.

Notes to Chapter 3

1. For the seminal discussion of the analogies between Jonson's satirical response to the institution of theater and the attitudes of classical and Renaissance antitheatricalists, see Jonas Barish's "Jonson and the Loathed Stage," chapter 5 in Barish's *The Anti-theatrical Prejudice*. Although Jonson's puritanical moralism and his investment in the Juvenalian satiric tradition have long been noted, relatively few scholars have explored Aristophanes' important influence on Jonson, and none have done so with specific regard to the two playwrights' representations of androgyny or sexual behavior. Coburn Gum's *Aristophanic Comedies of Ben Jonson* (Paris: Mouton, 1969) is one of the few studies comparing the formal dramatic techniques of these two satiric masters.

2. Mary Beth Rose, *The Expense of Spirit: Love and Sexuality in English Renaissance Drama* (Ithaca: Cornell University Press, 1988), p. 59.

3. See Thomas F. Greene, "Ben Jonson and the Centered Self," *Studies in English Literature. 1500–1900* 10 (1970): 325–48.

4. Ronald Huebert, "'A Shrew but Honest': Manliness in Jonson," *Renaissance Drama* 15 (1984): 38, 32.

5. See Barish, *The Anti-theatrical Prejudice*, p. 150, and Alexander Leggatt, *Ben Jonson: His Vision and His Art* (New York: Methuen, 1981), p. 13, for discussions of the antitheatricalism of this epigram and scene.

6. Steve Brown, relying heavily on the theories of Michel Foucault, argues that Renaissance society in general was sympathetic to the male practice of keeping a "ganymede" or erotic boy, and suggests that *Epicoene* reflects this indulgence toward "a variety of [what later came to be known as] gender disorders," treating them with "playfulness" as mild "frailties of the flesh" (see Brown's earlier-cited "The Boyhood of Shakespeare's Heroines," pp. 254 and 258). Although Brown would doubtless find my analysis "compromised by . . . radical essentialism and sal-

vationist zeal," which is how he describes Phyllis Rackin's work on *Epicoene* ("Boyhood," pp. 259–60), I would still like to point out the cruelty intrinsic to his celebration of *Epicoene's* patriarchal sexual ethic. Brown's study implicitly approves *Epicoene's* treatment of both women *and* boys as sexual objects, and seems to suggest that in condoning these sexual practices (which he by no means proves that they did), Renaissance people were higher-minded than we. The moral dangers of such critical "indulgence" towards violent sexual behaviors is evident from Brown's blithe citation of an instance during the Renaissance when a man was hanged for having had sex "with Barnaby Wryght, aged five years," which Brown sees as a lamentable example of the encroaching medical distinction of "perversion" (p. 249). To Brown, the man's execution may have constituted oppressive policing of "the frailties of the flesh"; most contemporary (and presumably most Renaissance) people, "essentialist" or otherwise, would recognize the action as punishment for child abuse. Brown's studied and stunning obtuseness regarding the Wryght case justifies George Orwell's famous comment, "There are some ideas so preposterous that only an intellectual could believe them."

7. C. G. Thayer also refers to the fundamental similarity between Aristophanes' and Jonson's social rules for women, calling *Epicoene* "Aristophanic" in its presentation of "the monstrous regiment of women" (see Thayer's *Ben Jonson: Studies in the Plays* [Norman: University of Oklahoma Press, 1963], p. 84). Although Aristophanes clearly *likes* women more than did Jonson, his plays, like Jonson's work, ultimately present feminine dominance as a chaotic reversal of the natural social order. *Ecclesiasuzae* and *Thesmophoriasuzae* especially ridicule feminine social aggression.

8. Barbara Millard demonstrates how the play's masculinist ethic first limits women's available roles, so that they must devote their energies to seduction, and then punishes them for their efforts. See Millard's "'An Acceptable Violence': Sexual Contest in Jonson's *Epicoene*," *Medieval and Renaissance Drama in England* 1 (1984): 143–58. See also Fran Dolan's recent discussion of cultural attitudes towards cosmetics during the Renaissance, "Taking the Pencil out of God's Hand: Art, Nature, and the Face-Painting Debate in Early Modern England," *PMLA* (March 1993): 224–39. Dolan argues, like Millard, that the Renaissance patriarchal ethic "constructs the display or spectacle [of beauty] as feminine and the spectator as masculine, associating pleasure and desire with the feminine and rendering them suspect" (p. 227). See also the similar argument of Shirley Nelson Garner in "'Let Her Paint an Inch Thick': Painted Ladies in Renaissance Drama and Society," *Renaissance Drama* 20 (1989): 123–39.

9. Rosalind Miles, *Ben Jonson: His Life and Work* (New York: Routledge and Kegan Paul, 1986), p. 91.

10. Quarlous's horrified recoil from Ursula is in fact reminiscent of Syracusan Dromio's fear of Luce, the overweight kitchen-maid who claims him as mate in Shakespeare's *Comedy of Errors*: Dromio "know[s] not what use to put her to but to make a lamp of her and run from her by her own light" (3.2.96–98). However, the satiric image of marriage *Errors* presents through Luce and Dromio, low-comic characters who inhabit that play's subplot, is overturned by the more serious marital action of the play's main plot, which dramatizes Adriana's reconciliation with her husband and Syracusan Antipholus's surrender to Luciana's mermaid charms. *Bartholomew Fair* also leads some characters to marriage, but Quarlous's engagement to Dame Purecraft (a pragmatic rather than a romantic alliance), and even

Winwife's pursuit of Grace Wellborn, is not central enough to the play's action to shift its genre from satire to romance, or even romantic farce. It is also true, as David Bevington pointed out in a response to this book in manuscript, that Shakespeare's sympathy for mythic marital androgyny deepened over time, and is more powerfully expressed in his 1590s comedies than in early works such as *The Comedy of Errors*. The radical gap between Shakespeare's and Jonson's general attitudes towards the androgyne may become evident when we consider that Luce's analogue Ursula, born midway through Jonson's dramatic career, was (as my fourth chapter will argue) one of the most sympathetic "manlike" females ever to grace Jonson's comic stage.

11. Also noted in Leggatt, *Ben Jonson*, p. 15.

12. John Rainolds, *The Overthrow of Stage Plays* (New York: Johnson Reprint Co., 1972).

13. Leggatt, *Ben Jonson*, p. 123.

14. For many of these references to water as image of threatening flood, I am indebted to Leggatt's second chapter, entitled "That Dead Sea of Life" (especially pages 59–60).

15. Miles's book returns recurrently to this theme (see, for example, her pages 64 and 112–13).

16. Sidney, *Selections from Arcadia*, p. 83.

17. *The Three Parnassus Plays*, ed. and intro. J. B. Leishman (London: Ivor Nicholson and Watson, 1949). All references to the *Parnassus* plays are to this edition.

18. John Marston, *Histrio-Mastix*, facsimile ed. (London: Thomas Thorp, 1610).

19. In a talk at the Folger Shakespeare Library in Washington, D.C., in June 1993, William B. Ashworth argued that at the turn of the seventeenth century—a central period of Jonson's literary production—animal symbolism was becoming increasingly undermined by the development of modern zoology, which looked at animals as objects in nature rather than as symbols of human qualities. Although animal emblemature is integral to Jonson's comic art, his reductive treatment of mythic beast-divinity may owe something to this scientific trend.

20. In regard to the satirical combative ethic, Jonson's life imitated his art, as several scholars have noted. William Drummond records Jonson's proud claim that "He had many quarrels with Marston, beat him, and took his pistol from him, wrote his Poetaster on him; the beginning of them were that Marston represented him in the stage." See William Drummond, *Ben Jonson's Conversations with William Drummond of Hawthornden*, ed. R. F. Patterson (London: Blackie and Son, 1923), pp. 26–27. Ronald Huebert argues convincingly that the value Jonson assigned to combativeness derived from his own violent choler ("'A Shrew,'" p. 33); I would suggest, as do Raman Selden, Robert Elliott, Matthew Hodgart, and Hugh Walker, that Jonson's choler was a necessary part of his satiric temperament. Finally, Jonson's preference for male over female society is well documented (Rosalind Miles speaks of Jonson's "violent revulsion from the female sex" [*Ben Jonson*, p. 175], and also observes that "As a married man, Jonson . . . made a very good bachelor" [p. 25]). The famous "Tribe of Ben," the informal all-male literary and drinking society over which Jonson ruled, demonstrated the comfort he took in exclusively male society. For a detailed discussion of the "Tribe of Ben," see chapter 12 of Miles's book.

21. Eve Sedgwick, *Between Men: English Literature and Male Homosocial Desire* (New York: Columbia University Press, 1985), p. 1.

22. See footnote 447 to *Cymbeline* in *The Riverside Shakespeare*, ed. G. Blakemore Evans (previously cited), p. 1560.

23. In Brian Vickers's words, "*Imitatio*, once fully absorbed or metabolized, could lead to . . . invention, but undigested, it could only be superficial, resulting at best in pastiche" (208). For a more extended discussion of literary *imitatio*, see George Pigman's "Versions of Imitation in the Renaissance," *Renaissance Quarterly* 33, no. 1 (Spring 1980): 1–32. Kathleen E. Marley has discussed *imitatio* with specific regard to Jonson in "'A big fatt man, that spake in Ryme': Ben Jonson and the Grotesque Dinner of Patronage," a paper presented at the Sixteenth-Century Association's annual meeting in Atlanta, October 1992.

24. Barish, *The Anti-theatrical Prejudice*, pp. 151–52.

25. Huebert, "'A Shrew,'" p. 36.

26. Jean Howard's reference to "the man playing Epicoene" (Howard, "Cross-Dressing," p. 430) is misleading in this regard.

27. My argument bears some resemblance to that of Jean Howard, who contends that in *Epicoene*, "male crossdressing becomes a way to appropriate and then erase the troubling figure of a wife" (ibid., p. 430).

28. Rose, *The Expense of Spirit*, p. 49.

Notes to Chapter 4

1. See, for example, Thomas Cartelli, "*Bartholomew Fair* as Urban Arcadia: Jonson Responds to Shakespeare," *Renaissance Drama* 14 (1983): 151–72; James Robinson, "*Bartholomew Fair*: Comedy of Vapors," *Studies in English Literature* 2 (Spring 1961): 65–80; and George Rowe, *Distinguishing Jonson: Imitation, Rivalry, and the Direction of a Dramatic Career* (Lincoln: University of Nebraska Press, 1988), pp. 141–42.

2. Scholars have traditionally assumed that Shakespeare's experimentation with "humors" in *Merry Wives* was parodic rather than straightforward and have dated the play correspondingly. Sydney Musgrove, for example, dates the composition of *Merry Wives* after that of Jonson's *Every Man in His Humour* because of Nym's excessive use of the word "humor," which he sees as Jonsonian leg-pulling (*Shakespeare and Jonson* [Auckland: Auckland University College, 1957], p. 6). This view is also expressed in O. J. Campbell, *Shakespeare's Satire* (Hamden, Conn.: Archon Books, 1963). More recently Russ McDonald, supporting the now-favored early 1597 date for *Merry Wives* (which would place it just before Jonson's play), has nevertheless argued that Shakespeare may have been straightforwardly imitating Jonson, with whose developing work he was probably familiar, and that the result was a hybrid drama blending the romantic with the humors form (*Shakespeare and Jonson/Jonson and Shakespeare* [Lincoln: University of Nebraska Press, 1988], chapter 2). Herford and Simpson briefly comment on *Merry Wives* as a humors play, and Jeanne Addison Roberts plausibly suggests that "the composition of Chapman's *A Humorous Day's Mirth* [and of *Merry Wives*] would have been almost simultaneous and would probably show a common trend rather than influence in either direction" (*Shakespeare's English Comedy: The Merry Wives of Windsor in Context* [Lincoln: University of Nebraska Press, 1979], p. 47).

3. See McDonald, *Shakespeare and Jonson*, p. 31; also Ben Jonson, *Ben Jonson*, ed. Herford and Simpson, I:18.

4. See Anne Barton's introduction to *Merry Wives* in *The Riverside Shakespeare*, especially pp. 266–87.

5. See McDonald, *Shakespeare and Jonson*, p. 5. McDonald also notes (p. 192n) a claim made by Nicholas Rowe in his 1709 biography of Shakespeare that Shakespeare had personally "recommended" the production of Jonson's play.

6. Anne Barton, *Ben Jonson, Dramatist* (Cambridge: Cambridge University Press, 1984), p. 73.

7. See my above lengthy note regarding scholars' responses to this play. Although Nym is obsessed with the word "humor," virtually all the other characters use the term as well, suggesting the play's general concern with humors theory. Unfortunately, the traditional critical insistence on polarizing Shakespeare's and Jonson's art, while justifiable in many respects, has blinded us to this concern and to the real role Shakespeare seems to have played in developing the drama that became "Jonsonian." Russ McDonald is one of the few critics who has suggested Shakespeare's straightforward interest in the humors genre (see *Shakespeare and Jonson*, especially p. 34). I, of course, am one of the culprits who are concerned primarily to stress the divergence of Shakespearean and Jonsonian forms and ideas. Still, I would argue that Shakespeare arrived at a clear ethos of mythic androgyny partly by testing himself in the alternative humors tradition.

8. William Carroll, "'A Received Belief': Imagination in *The Merry Wives of Windsor*," *Studies in Philology* 74 (1977): 200.

9. McDonald, *Shakespeare and Jonson*, p. 39, reiterates Carroll's claim that Ford's and Mistress Quickly's language reveals their "creative energy" (Carroll, "A Received Belief," p. 201). Obviously, I disagree.

10. Compare, for example, Othello's expansive metaphorical treatment of Desdemona's supposed guilt in *Othello* 4.2 and Leontes' similarly poetic accusation of Hermione in *The Winter's Tale* 1.2 with Ford's repetitive "Cuckold! Cuckold!" and "Buck, buck, buck!" Characteristically, Shakespeare explores sexual jealousy's tragic rather than its comic potential. Othello's and Leontes' imaginations, though no less diseased than Ford's, empower and unleash verbal skills in a romantic style more characteristically "Shakespearean."

11. Barton, for example, sees the "Windsor version of Sir John" as "tame and unresourceful compared with his far greater self of Eastcheap, Shrewsbury, Gaultree, and even Gloucestershire" (introduction to the Riverside *Merry Wives*, p. 287). See also H. B. Charlton's *Shakespearian Comedy* (New York: Macmillan, 1938), which describes the Falstaff of *Merry Wives* as a "cynical revenge which Shakespeare took on the hitherto unsuspecting gaiety of his own creative exuberance" (p. 193).

12. Telephone interview with Pat Carroll (1 November 1990).

13. Quoted in Charlton, *Shakespearian Comedy*, pp. 277–78.

14. Barton, introduction to the Riverside *Merry Wives*, p. 288; see also Peter Erickson, "The Order of the Garter, the Cult of Elizabeth, and Class-Gender Tension in *The Merry Wives of Windsor*," in *Shakespeare Reproduced: The Text in History and Ideology*, ed. Jean E. Howard and Marion F. O'Connor (London: Methuen, 1987), pp. 116–40.

15. Carroll, "'A Received Belief,'" p. 196.

16. Ann Blake, "'Sportful Malice': Duping in the Comedies of Jonson and Shakespeare," in *Jonson and Shakespeare*, ed. Ian Donaldson (Canberra: Humanities Research Centre, 1983), p. 133.

17. Anne Barton, "Falstaff and the Comic Community," in *Shakespeare's "Rough Magic*," ed. Peter Erickson and Coppélia Kahn (Newark: University of Delaware Press, 1985), p. 142.

18. William Carroll, "'A Received Belief,'" p. 188. Carroll further notes that "Page's ultimate taunt is not that Falstaff is impotent, but that he is 'as poor as Job' (V, v, 156). That is the sterility best understood in the relentlessly middle-class Windsor" (ibid.). However, having contended that Falstaff's motive is economic rather than sexual, Carroll confuses the issue by characterizing Falstaff as a "too-visible reminder of folly and sexual license," a "presumably tumescent buck" who "represents an aspect of man that Ford . . . would prefer to suppress" and "embodies the possibilities, often dangerous ones, of change and transformation" (p. 196). In his later *Metamorphoses of Shakespearean Comedy*, previously cited, Carroll likens Falstaff to other creative agents in Shakespearean mythic comedy (see Carroll's sixth chapter, especially page 191). But, as I will argue, the fact that Falstaff is financially rather than erotically motivated is what limits the "possibilities of change" he embodies to destruction rather than to transformation.

19. See Anne Parten, "Falstaff's Horns: Masculine Inadequacy and Feminine Mirth in *The Merry Wives of Windsor*," *Studies in Philology* 82 (1985): 192.

20. The phrase is Nancy Cotton's, in her "Castrating (W)itches: Impotence and Magic in *The Merry Wives of Windsor*," *Shakespeare Quarterly* 38 (1987): 323. See also Roberts, *Shakespeare's English Comedy*, pp. 177 and 127; Coppélia Kahn's discussion of Falstaff in *Man's Estate: Masculine Identity in Shakespeare* (Berkeley: University of California Press, 1981), pp. 147–50; and the description of Falstaff's "rapacious tendencies" in Judith Kollmann's "'Ther is noon oother uncubus but he': *The Canterbury Tales*, *The Merry Wives of Windsor* and Falstaff," in *Chaucerian Shakespeare: Adaptation and Transformation*, ed. E. Talbot Donaldson and Judith J. Kollmann (Detroit: Michigan Consortium for Medieval and Early Modern Studies, 1983), pp. 47–48.

21. See Northrop Frye, *A Natural Perspective: The Development of Shakespearian Comedy and Romance* (New York: Columbia University Press, 1965), pp. 141–42, and also J. A. Bryant, Jr., "Falstaff and the Renewal of Windsor," *PMLA* 89 (1974): 296–301.

22. Peter Evans, "'To the oak, to the oak!' The Finale of *The Merry Wives of Windsor*," *Theatre Notebook* 40 (1986): 107.

23. Kott, *Shakespeare Our Contemporary*, p. 212.

24. Carroll, *The Metamorphoses of Shakespearean Comedy*, pp. 142, 147.

25. McDonald, *Shakespeare and Jonson*, p. 55.

26. Admittedly, this claim threatens the contractual agreement Jonson proposed to his hearers in his play's induction, barring the "politic picklock of the scene, so solemnly ridiculous, as to search out, who was meant by . . . the pig-woman," etc. (lines 135ff.). But I was not in that audience.

27. Barish, *Ben Jonson and the Language of Prose Comedy*, p. 215.

28. Ibid.

29. James Bednarz notes Dekker's references to "Bear" Jonson in his "Shakespeare's Purge of Jonson," p. 196.

30. For some of these insights I am indebted to Kathleen Marley's "'A bigg fatt man, that spake in Ryme.'"

31. See Miles, *Ben Jonson,* 238.

32. Barish, *The Anti-theatrical Prejudice*, p. 151.

33. It should be noted, however, that the same did not apply to the readers of Jonson's printed folio version of the play, which contained—in customary Jonsonian fashion—extensive explanatory material.

34. Miles, *Ben Jonson,* p. 238.

35. "For sexual abstinence as an ideal in itself . . . we find no advocacy in Shakespeare" (Alfred Harbage, *Shakespeare and the Rival Traditions* [New York: Macmillan, 1952], p. 233).

36. This phrase is Peter Mercer's, from his *Hamlet and the Acting of Revenge* (Davenport: University of Iowa Press, 1987), p. 142.

37. As Nancy S. Leonard writes, Jonsonian satire and Shakespearean romantic comedy developed "in active opposition to each other, and in order for either form to realize itself, it [had to] first get rid of the other form." See Leonard's "Shakespeare and Jonson Again: The Comic Forms," *Renaissance Drama* 10 (1979): 46.

Notes to Chapter 5

1. Miles, *Ben Jonson,* p. 60. Cyrus Hoy had earlier expressed this opinion (see *Introduction, Notes, and Commentaries to Texts in The Dramatic Works of Thomas Dekker,* ed. Fredson Bowers [Cambridge: Cambridge University Press, 1980], p. 196 n. 2).

2. See David Farley-Hills, *Shakespeare and the Rival Playwrights: 1600–1606* (New York: Routledge, 1990), p. 51.

3. Henk Gras, "Twelfth Night, *Every Man Out of His Humour,* and the Middle Temple Revels of 1597–98," *Modern Language Review* 84 (July 1989): 546.

4. The quotation is from Rowe, *Distinguishing Jonson,* p. 173; also see J. B. Leishman's appendix to *The Three Parnassus Plays*, edited and introduced by J. B. Leishman (cited in my first chapter), pp. 369–70; Bednarz's "Shakespeare's Purge of Jonson," also cited earlier; and Alfred Harbage, *Shakespeare and the Rival Traditions* (New York: Macmillan, 1952). Harbage argues that Shakespeare's plays make "no overt allusion to the quarrel" (p. 113), a judgment with which James Shapiro's recent book essentially concurs (Shapiro, *Rival Playwrights: Marlowe, Jonson, Shakespeare* [New York: Columbia University Press, 1991]).

5. Rowe, *Distinguishing Jonson,* p. 175.

6. James P. Bednarz, "Shakespeare's Purge of Jonson," p. 206.

7. Ibid.

8. Leishman states that *As You Like It* "must have been acted before 4 August 1600, that is to say, almost a year before *Poetaster,* when, together with three other of 'my lord Chamberlens menns plaies,' it was entered in the Stationers' Register 'to be staied'" (*The Three Parnassus Plays,* p. 70).

9. In the introductory volume of their edition of Jonson's work, Herford and Simpson suggest that "[p]ossibly enough Jonson may be glanced at" in *As You Like It,* but conclude that the play "was clearly no 'purge'" (I:28). Arthur Gray, however, in a 1928 pamphlet, argues, as I do here, that *As You Like It* was a none-too-veiled response to Jonson's new humors method. Although apart from this shared thesis

Gray's arguments and mine do not overlap, I am grateful to him for certain additional insights made available to me through his close reading of Shakespeare's play. See his *How Shakespeare "Purged" Jonson: A Problem Solved* (Cambridge: W. Heffer and Sons, 1928).

10.   J. A. K. Thompson's *Shakespeare and the Classics* (London: George Allen & Unwin, 1952) catalogs many of Shakespeare's Ovidian references. As Jeanne Addison Roberts notes, "It is a truth universally acknowledged that Shakespeare was well-versed in Ovid and that Ovidian literature shaped and permeated his writing" (*The Shakespearean Wild*, p. 58). A recent book on this subject is Jonathan Bate's *Shakespeare and Ovid* (New York: Oxford University Press, 1993).

11.   "The English stage was a male preserve, but the theater was not. The theater was a place of unusual freedom for women in the period; foreign visitors comment on the fact that English women go to the theater unescorted and unmasked, and a large proportion of the audience consisted of women." From Stephen Orgel, "Nobody's Perfect, or Why Did the English Stage Take Boys for Women?" *South Atlantic Quarterly* 88 (1989): 8.

12.   See Anne Barton, introduction to *As You Like It* in *The Riverside Shakespeare*, p. 365.

13.   Thomas Dekker, *Satiromastix*, 1.2.289ff. These insults, obviously, were leveled before Jonson achieved Ursula size.

14.   This episode reinforces an earlier one that conspicuously associates the same country bumpkin, Sogliardo, with Shakespeare (whose purchase of a coat of arms had occurred five years before [see Peter Levi, *The Life and Times of William Shakespeare* (New York: Henry Holt, 1988), p. 149]). Encountering Buffone and Puntarvolo, Sogliardo describes his newly purchased coat of arms, whose "variety of colours" (3.4.57) associates it with the fool's motley. Puntarvolo immediately suggests the motto "*Not without mustard*" (line 86), a mocking reference to Shakespeare's motto "*Non sans droict*" ("Not without right"). (Bednarz, too, notes this Jonsonian joke ["Shakespeare's Purge of Jonson," p. 179].) Touchstone's fanciful tale of the "knight, that swore by his honor they were good pancakes, and swore by his honor the mustard was naught" but who actually "never had any honor" (*As You Like It* 1.2.62–63, 78), may have been Shakespeare's self-mocking rejoinder to Jonson's slight.

15.   Alice Lotvin Birney, *Satiric Catharsis in Shakespeare: A Theory of Dramatic Structure* (Berkeley: University of California Press, 1973), p. 124.

16.   Bednarz, "Shakespeare's Purge of Jonson," p. 207.

17.   A more detailed discussion of Cressida's acquiescence in masculine systems of valuation is offered in Grace Tiffany, "Not Saying No: Female Self-Erasure in *Troilus and Cressida*," *Texas Studies in Literature and Language* 35 (Spring, 1993): 44–56.

18.   Barton, introduction to *As You Like It*, p. 366.

19.   Again I would refer the reader to Barbara Bono's discussion of Rosalind's repudiation of Petrarchism, "Mixed Gender, Mixed Genre in *As You Like It*." Peter Erickson also demonstrates how Rosalind deflates and escapes Orlando's Petrarchism, although Erickson contends that Rosalind ultimately succumbs to other social stereotypes (see Erickson's *Patriarchal Structures in Shakespeare's Drama*, also cited earlier).

20.   The sentence is Campbell's, from his page 53; also see Bednarz, "Shakespeare's Purge of Jonson," p. 189.

21. Bednarz, "Shakespeare's Purge of Jonson," p. 189.

22. O. J. Campbell, *Shakespeare's Satire*, p. 46.

23. See Harbage, *Shakespeare and the Rival Traditions*, p. 115.

24. Gray, *How Shakespeare "Purged" Jonson*, p. 15.

25. *Twelfth Night*, probably produced, like *As You Like It*, in 1600, continued to intervene in Shakespeare's and Jonson's dramatic debate regarding the relative social values of romance and satire (as Henk Gras and Nancy Leonard have both pointed out). Among other things, *Twelfth Night* continues the association between satiric and romantic melancholy that *As You Like It* initiates. In *Twelfth Night*'s first scene, Orsino's call for a surfeit of music, the "food of love" (1.1.1), to feed his romantic obsession recalls Jaques's request for "More, more" music to "make [him] melancholy" in *As You Like It* (2.5.9–10). The solitary would-be lover and the melancholy satirist both "feed" their humors in a sensual, self-indulgent fashion: "I can suck melancholy out of a song, as a weasel sucks eggs," Jaques exults (2.5.12).

26. In a footnote, Lorraine Helms notes Rosalind's advance into "the anti-illusionistic *platea*" of the stage in the epilogue ("'The High Roman Fashion': Sacrifice, Suicide, and the Shakespearean Stage," *PMLA* [May 1992]: 563). Also, for a different perspective on the "doubleness" of boy actors in Shakespeare's epilogues, see Barbara Hodgdon's essay in the same issue of *PMLA*, "Katherina Bound; or, Play(K)ating the Strictures of Everyday Life," *PMLA*, May 1992, 538–53.

27. See Stephen Orgel, "Making Greatness Familiar," for a discussion of the complicating presence of high-paying audience members on the stage (*Genre* [Spring/Summer 1982]: 44).

28. The lines in question, which cast subtle aspersions on Jonson's overconfidence, are as follows:

> and hither am I come,
> A prologue arm'd, but not in confidence
> Of author's pen or actor's voice, but suited
> In like conditions as our argument. . . .
> (*Troilus and Cressida* , prologue, lines 22–25)

29. D. A. Beecher, "Antiochus and Stratonice: The Heritage of a Medico-Literary Motif in the Theatre of the English Renaissance," *The Seventeenth Century* (Autumn 1990): 128.

30. Thomas Dekker, quoted in R. A. Foakes's "The Profession of Playwright," in *Modern Shakespeare Criticism*, ed. Alvin B. Kernan (New York: Harcourt Brace Jovanovich, 1970), p. 160.

Notes to the Epilogue

1. See James Bednarz, "Representing Jonson: *Histriomastix* and the Origin of the Poets' War," *Huntington Library Quarterly* (Winter 1991): 7.

2. John Marston, *Jack Drum's Entertainment*, in *The Plays of John Marston*, ed. H. Harvey Wood (Edinburgh: 1939), 3:221.

3. See chapter 4 of Miles's biography for a detailed discussion of Jonson's participation in the *poetomachia* (*Ben Jonson*, pp. 49–68).

4. Quoted in ibid., p. 262.

5. Bednarz, "Representing Jonson," p. 7.

6. Belsey, "Disrupting Sexual Difference," p. 189.

7. Northrop Frye, "The Archetypes of Literature," in *Twentieth-Century Literary Criticism*, ed. David Lodge (London: Longman, 1972), p. 429.

8. Thus James Shapiro's argument that Jonson created the conflict between himself and Shakespeare, and that Shakespeare was a silent nonadversary, is one that I support in a certain sense.

9. John Aubrey, quoted in Miles, *Ben Jonson,* p. 63.

10. Levine, "Men in Women's Clothing," p. 123.

Bibliography

Aeschylus. *Aeschylus I: Oresteia.* Edited by David Grene and Richmond Lattimore. Chicago: University of Chicago Press, 1953.

Allen, Don Cameron. *Mysteriously Meant: The Rediscovery of Pagan Symbolism and Allegorical Interpretation in the Renaissance.* Baltimore: Johns Hopkins University Press, 1970.

Altick, Richard D. "Symphonic Imagery in *Richard II.*" In *Richard II,* edited by Kenneth Muir, 199–234. New York: Signet, 1988.

Ambrose, Elizabeth Ann. *The Hermetica: An Annotated Bibliography.* Special edition of *Sixteenth-Century Bibliography* 30 (1992).

Aneau, Barthelemy. *Picta Poesis ut Pictura Poesis Erit.* Lyons, 1552.

Apuleius. *Metamorphoses.* Vols. 1 and 2. Edited and translated by Arthur Hanson. Cambridge: Harvard University Press, 1989.

Aristophanes. *Four Plays by Aristophanes.* Edited by William Arrowsmith, Richmond Lattimore, and Douglass Parker. New York: New American Library, 1962.

———. *Aristophanes: The Eleven Comedies.* New York: Liveright Publishing Co., 1943.

Ashworth, William B. "Reading the Natural World." Talk given at the Folger Shakespeare Library, Washington, D.C., June 1993.

Athanassakis, Apostolos N., ed. and trans. *The Orphic Hymns.* Atlanta: Scholars Press, 1977.

Bamber, Linda. *Comic Women, Tragic Men: A Study of Gender and Genre in Shakespeare.* Stanford, Calif.: Stanford University Press, 1982.

Barish, Jonas. *The Anti-theatrical Prejudice.* Berkeley: University of California Press, 1981.

———. *Ben Jonson and the Language of Prose Comedy.* Cambridge: Harvard University Press, 1960.

Barton, Anne. *Ben Jonson, Dramatist.* Cambridge: Cambridge University Press, 1984.

———. "Falstaff and the Comic Community." In *Shakespeare's "Rough Magic,"* edited by Peter Erickson and Coppélia Kahn. Newark: University of Delaware Press, 1985.

———. Introduction to *As You Like It.* In William Shakespeare, *The Riverside Shakespeare,* edited by G. Blakemore Evans, 365–68. Boston: Houghton Mifflin, 1974.

224

———. Introduction to *The Merry Wives of Windsor*. In William Shakespeare, *The Riverside Shakespeare*, edited by G. Blakemore Evans, 286–89. Boston: Houghton Mifflin, 1974.

Bate, Jonathan. *Shakespeare and Ovid*. New York: Oxford University Press, 1993.

Beccadelli, Antonio. *L'Ermafrodito*. Milan: Studio Editoriale Corbaccio, 1922.

Bednarz, James P. "Representing Jonson: *Histriomastix* and the Origin of the Poets' War." *Huntington Library Quarterly* (Winter 1991): 1–30.

———. "Shakespeare's Purge of Jonson: The Literary Context of *Troilus and Cressida*." *Shakespeare Studies* 21 (1993): 175–212.

Beecher, D. A. "Antiochus and Stratonice: The Heritage of a Medico-Literary Motif in the Theater of the English Renaissance." *The Seventeenth Century* (Autumn 1990): 113–32.

Bellah, Robert N., Richard Madsen, William M. Sullivan, Ann Swidler, and Steven M. Tipton. *Habits of the Heart: Individualism and Commitment in American Life*. New York: Harper and Row, 1985.

Belsey, Catherine. "Disrupting Sexual Difference: Meaning and Gender in the Comedies." In *Alternative Shakespeares*, edited by John Drakakis, 166–90. London: Methuen, 1985.

Bevington, David. "'Jack Hath Not Jill': Failed Courtship in Lyly and Shakespeare." *Shakespeare Survey* 42 (1990): 1–13.

Birney, Alice Lotvin. *Satiric Catharsis in Shakespeare: A Theory of Dramatic Structure*. Berkeley: University of California Press, 1973.

Blake, Ann. "'Sportful Malice': Duping in the Comedies of Jonson and Shakespeare." In *Jonson and Shakespeare*, edited by Ian Donaldson, 119–34. Canberra: Humanities Research Centre, 1983.

Bloom, Allan. *Love and Friendship*. New York: Simon and Schuster, 1993.

Boehrer, Bruce Thomas. "Renaissance Overeating: The Sad Case of Ben Jonson." *PMLA* (October 1990): 1071–82.

Bono, Barbara. "Mixed Gender, Mixed Genre in Shakespeare's *As You Like It*." In *Renaissance Genres*, edited by Barbara K. Lewalski, 189–212. Cambridge: Harvard University Press, 1986.

Bowers, Fredson. *Introduction, Notes, and Commentaries to Texts in The Dramatic Works of Thomas Dekker*. Cambridge: Cambridge University Press, 1980.

Brown, Steve. "The Boyhood of Shakespeare's Heroines: Notes on Gender Ambiguity in the Sixteenth Century." *SEL* 30 (1990): 243–63.

Bryant, J. A. "Falstaff and the Renewal of Windsor." *PMLA* 89 (1974): 296–301.

Caldwell, Ellen. "John Lyly's *Gallathea*: A New Rhetoric of Love for the Virgin Queen." In *Women in the Renaissance*, edited by Kirby Farrell et al., 69–87. Amherst: University of Massachusetts Press, 1988.

Campbell, Joseph. *The Hero with a Thousand Faces*. Bollingen series. Princeton: Princeton University Press, 1972.

———. *The Myth of the Goddess*. In *The Story of Myth*, PBS film series, produced by Mystic Fire Video in association with *Parabola Magazine*, 1987.

Campbell, O. J. *Shakespeare's Satire*. Hamden, Conn.: Archon Books, 1963.

Carroll, Pat. Telephone interview, 1 November 1990.

Carroll, William. *The Metamorphoses of Shakespearean Comedy*. Princeton: Princeton University Press, 1985.

———. "'A Received Belief': Imagination in *The Merry Wives of Windsor*." *Studies in Philology* 74 (1977): 186–215.

Cartelli, Thomas. "*Bartholomew Fair* as Urban Arcadia: Jonson Responds to Shakespeare." *Renaissance Drama* 14 (1983): 151–72.

Cartwright, Kent. "*Gallathea*'s 'Drama of Ideas' and *Twelfth Night*." Paper presented at the annual meeting of the Shakespeare Association of America, Kansas City, Missouri, April 1992.

———. "The Humanism of Acting: John Heywood's *The Foure PP*." *Studies in the Literary Imagination* (Spring 1993): 21–46.

Chapman, George. *The Plays of George Chapman: The Tragedies, with Sir Gyles Goosecappe*. Edited by Allan Holaday. Cambridge: D. S. Brewer, 1987.

Charlton, H. B. *Shakespearian Comedy*. New York: Macmillan, 1938.

Cook, Ann Jennalie. "'Bargaines of Incontinencie': Bawdy Behavior in the Playhouses." *Shakespeare Studies* 10 (1977): 271–90.

Cotton, Nancy. "Castrating (W)itches: Impotence and Magic in *The Merry Wives of Windsor*." *Shakespeare Quarterly* 38 (1987): 320–26.

Davies, Stevie. *The Feminine Reclaimed*. Lexington: University Press of Kentucky, 1986.

The Deceyte of Women. London, 1561.

Dekker, Thomas. *Satiromastix, or the Untrussing of the Humorous Poet*. In *Jonson's Poetaster and Dekker's Satiromastix*, edited by Isiah H. Penniman. Boston: D. C. Heath, 1913.

Della Mirandola, Pico. *On the Dignity of Man, and Other Works*. Translated by Douglas Carmichael. New York: Bobbs-Merrill, 1940.

Dolan, Fran. "Taking the Pencil out of God's Hand: Art, Nature, and the Face-Painting Debate in Early Modern England." *PMLA* (March 1993): 224–39.

Dusinberre, Juliet. *Shakespeare and the Nature of Women*. London: Macmillan, 1975.

Drummond, William. *Ben Jonson's Conversations with William Drummond of Hawthornden*. Edited by R. F. Patterson. London: Blackie and Son, 1923.

Elliott, Robert. *The Power of Satire: Magic, Ritual, Art*. Princeton: Princeton University Press, 1960.

Elyot, Thomas. *The Boke Named the Governor*. Edited by Donald W. Rude. New York: Garland Press, 1992.

Erickson, Peter. "The Order of the Garter, the Cult of Elizabeth, and Class-Gender Tension in *The Merry Wives of Windsor*." In *Shakespeare Reproduced: The Text in History and Ideology*, edited by Jean E. Howard and Marion F. O'Connor, 116–40. London: Methuen, 1987.

———. *Patriarchal Structures in Shakespeare's Drama*. Berkeley: University of California Press, 1985.

Euripides. *The Complete Tragedies*. Vols. 1 and 5. Edited by David Grene and Richmond Lattimore. Chicago: University of Chicago Press, 1968.

Evans, Peter. "'To the oak, to the oak!': The Finale of *The Merry Wives of Windsor.*" *Theatre Notebook* 40 (1986):106-14.

Farley-Hills, David. *Shakespeare and the Rival Playwrights: 1600–1606.* New York: Routledge, 1990.

Ficino, Marsilio. *Commentary on Plato's Symposium.* Edited and translated by Sears Jayne. Columbia: University of Missouri Press, 1944.

Foakes, R. A. "The Profession of Playwright." In *Modern Shakespeare Criticism,* edited by Alvin B. Kernan, 141–61. New York: Harcourt Brace Jovanovich, 1970.

Freedman, Barbara. "Separation and Fusion in *Twelfth Night.*" In *Psychoanalytical Approaches to Literature and Film,* edited by Maurice Charney and Joseph Reppen, 96–119. Madison, N.J.: Fairleigh Dickinson University Press; London and Toronto: Associated University Presses, 1987.

Frye, Northrop. "The Archetypes of Literature." In *Twentieth-Century Literary Criticism,* edited by David Lodge, 422–33. London: Longman, 1972.

———. *A Natural Perspective: The Development of Shakespearian Comedy and Romance.* New York: Columbia University Press, 1965.

Frye, Susan. "The Myth of Elizabeth at Tilbury." *Sixteenth-Century Journal* 23 (Spring 1992): 95–114.

Garner, Shirley Nelson. "'Let Her Paint an Inch Thick': Painted Ladies in Renaissance Drama and Society." *Renaissance Drama* 20 (1989): 123–39.

Gras, Henk. "Twelfth Night, *Every Man Out of His Humour,* and the Middle Temple Revels of 1597-98." *Modern Language Review* 84 (July 1989): 545–64.

Gray, Arthur. *How Shakespeare "Purged" Jonson: A Problem Solved.* Cambridge: W. Heffer and Sons, 1928.

Greenblatt, Stephen. *Shakespearean Negotiations.* Berkeley: University of California Press, 1988.

Greene, Thomas F. "Ben Jonson and the Centered Self." *SEL* 10 (1970): 325–48.

Greenfield, Thelma. "The Dreaming Audience in Shakespeare's Plays." Paper presented at the annual meeting of the Shakespeare Association of America, Kansas City, Missouri, April 1992.

Guilpin, Everard. *Skialetheia.* The Shakespeare Association Facsimiles. London: Oxford University Press, 1931.

Gum, Coburn. *The Aristophanic Comedies of Ben Jonson.* Paris: Mouton, 1969.

Hall, Joseph. *Mundus ater et idem.* London, 1609.

Hamilton, Edith. *Mythology: Timeless Tales of Gods and Heroes.* New York: New American Library, 1969.

Harbage, Alfred. *Shakespeare and the Rival Traditions.* New York: Macmillan, 1952.

Hayles, Nancy K. "Sexual Disguise in 'As You Like It' and 'Twelfth Night.'" *Shakespeare Survey* 32 (1979): 63–72.

Heilbrun, Carolyn. *Toward a Recognition of Androgyny.* New York: Alfred A. Knopf, 1973.

Helms, Lorraine. "'The High Roman Fashion': Sacrifice, Suicide, and the Shakespearean Stage." *PMLA* (May 1992): 554–65.

Herford, C. H., Percy Simpson, and Evelyn Simpson. Introductions to Ben Jonson, *Ben Jonson: The Complete Works,* edited by C. H. Herford, Percy Simpson, and Evelyn Simpson. 11 vols. Oxford: Clarendon Press, 1925–52.

Hic-Mulier, or the Man-Woman: Being a Medicine to Cure the Coltish Disease of the Staggers in the Masculine-Feminine of our Times. Also Haec-Vir, or the Womanish-Man: Being an Answer to a Late Book Entitled Hic-Mulier. Facsimile edition. Yorkshire: Scholar Press, 1973.

Hodgart, Matthew. *Satire.* New York: World University Library, 1969.

Hodgdon, Barbara. "Katherina Bound; or, Play(K)ating the Strictures of Everyday Life." *PMLA* (May 1992): 538–53.

Holbrook, Peter. "Lyly, Shakespeare, and the Poetics of Gender." Paper presented at the annual meeting of the Shakespeare Association of America, Kansas City, Missouri, April 1992.

Hollander, Anne. "Dragtime: The Professor, the Transvestite, and the Meaning of Clothes." *The New Republic,* 31 August 1992, 34–41.

Homer. *The Odyssey.* Translated by Robert Fitzgerald. New York: Vintage Books, 1990.

Horace. *Horace's Satires and Epistles.* Translated by Jacob Fuchs. New York: W. W. Norton, 1977.

Howard, Jean. "Cross-Dressing, the Theater, and Gender Struggle in Early Modern England." *Shakespeare Studies* 39 (Winter 1988): 418–40.

Huebert, Ronald. "'A Shrew but Honest': Manliness in Jonson." *Renaissance Drama* 15 (1984): 31–68.

Hunter, G. K. *John Lyly: The Humanist as Courtier.* New York: Routledge, 1962.

———. "Lyly's Survival in the Boys' Theatre 1600–1610." Paper presented at the annual meeting of the Shakespeare Association of America, Kansas City, Missouri, April 1992.

Jay, Peter, ed. *The Greek Anthology.* Translated by Andrew Miller. New York: Oxford University Press,1973.

Jones, Anne, and Peter Stallybrass. "Fetishizing Gender: Constructing the Hermaphrodite in Renaissance Europe." In *Body Guards,* edited by Julia Epstein and Kristina Straub, 80–111. New York: Routledge, 1991.

Jonson, Ben. *Ben Jonson: The Complete Works.* Edited by C. H. Herford, Percy Simpson, and Evelyn Simpson. 11 vols. Oxford: Clarendon Press, 1925–52.

Juvenal. *The Satires of Juvenal.* Translated by Rolfe Humphries. Bloomington: University of Indiana Press, 1958.

Kahn, Coppélia. *Man's Estate: Masculine Identity in Shakespeare.* Berkeley: University of Californa Press, 1981.

Kimbrough, Robert. "Androgyny Seen through Shakespeare's Disguise." *Shakespeare Quarterly* 33 (1982): 17–33.

Kollmann, Judith. "'Ther is noon oother uncubus but he': The Canterbury Tales, The Merry Wives of Windsor and Falstaff." In *Chaucerian Shakespeare: Adaptation and Transformation,* edited by E. Talbot Donaldson and Judith J. Kollmann. Detroit: Michigan Consortium for Medieval and Early Modern Studies, 1983.

Kott, Jan. *Shakespeare Our Contemporary*. Translated by Beleslaw Taborski. Garden City, N.Y.: Doubleday, 1964.

Laquer, Thomas. *Making Sex: Body and Gender from the Greeks to Freud*. Cambridge: Harvard University Press, 1990.

Lattimore, Richmond, ed. and trans. *Greek Lyrics*. Chicago: University of Chicago Press, 1960.

Leggatt, Alexander. *Ben Jonson: His Vision and His Art*. New York: Methuen, 1981.

Leishman, J. B. Appendix to *The Three Parnassus Plays*, edited by J. B. Leishman, 369–70. London: Ivor Nicholson and Watson, 1949.

———, ed. *The Three Parnassus Plays*. London: Ivor Nicholson and Watson, 1949.

Leonard, Nancy S. "Shakespeare and Jonson Again: The Comic Forms." *Renaissance Drama* 10 (1979): 45–69.

Levi, Peter. *The Life and Times of William Shakespeare*. New York: Henry Holt, 1988.

Lévi-Strauss, Claude. "The Structural Study of Myth." In *Myth: A Symposium*, edited by Thomas A. Sebeok, 50–66. Bloomington: Indiana University Press, 1958.

Levine, Laura. "Men in Women's Clothing: Antitheatricality and Effeminization from 1579 to 1642." *Criticism* 28 (1986): 121–43.

Liuzza, Roy Michael. "*Sir Orfeo*: Sources, Traditions, and the Poetics of Performance." *Journal of Medieval and Renaissance Studies* 21:2 (Fall 1991): 269-84.

Lucian. *Satirical Sketches*. Edited and translated by Paul Turner. Baltimore: Penguin Books, 1961.

Lyly, John. *Gallathea*. In *Drama of the English Renaissance*, vol. 1, edited by Russell Fraser and Norman Rabkin, 126–44. New York: Collier-Macmillan, 1976.

MacCary, W. Thomas. *Friends and Lovers: The Phenomenology of Desire in Shakespearean Comedy*. New York: Columbia University Press, 1985.

McDonald, Russ. *Shakespeare and Jonson/Jonson and Shakespeare*. Lincoln: University of Nebraska Press, 1988.

Maclean, Ian. *The Renaissance Notion of Woman*. New York: Cambridge University Press, 1980.

McLuskie, Kathleen. "The Act, the Role, and the Actor: Boy Actresses on the Elizabethan Stage." *New Theatre Quarterly* 3 (1987): 120–30.

Marcus, Leah. "Shakespeare's Comic Heroines, Elizabeth I, and the Political Uses of Androgyny." In *Women in the Middle Ages and the Renaissance: Literary and Historical Perspectives*, edited by Mary Beth Rose, 135–53. Syracuse, N.Y.: Syracuse University Press, 1986.

Marley, Kathleen E. "'A bigg fatt man, that spake in Ryme': Ben Jonson and the Grotesque Dinner of Patronage." Paper presented at the annual meeting of the Sixteenth-Century Association, Atlanta, October 1992.

Marston, John. *Histrio-Mastix*. Facsimile edition. London: Thomas Thorp, 1610.

———. *The Plays of John Marston*. Edited by H. Harvey Wood. Edinburgh and London: 1939.

————. *The Scourge of Villainy.* Edited by G. B. Harrison. Edinburgh: University of Edinburgh Press, 1966.

Martial. *Epigrams.* Vol. 1. Translated by Walter Ker. London: G. P. Putnam's Sons, 1925.

Mercer, Peter. *Hamlet and the Acting of Revenge.* Iowa City: University of Iowa Press, 1987.

Meres, Francis. *Palladis Tamia: Wit's Treasury.* London, 1598.

Miles, Rosalind. *Ben Jonson: His Life and Work.* New York: Routledge, 1986.

Millard, Barbara. "'An Acceptable Violence': Sexual Contest in Jonson's *Epicoene.*" *Medieval and Renaissance Drama in England* 1 (1984): 143–58.

Muir, Kenneth. "Males as Females on Shakespeare's Stage." In *Essays on Shakespeare in Honour of A. A. Ansari,* edited by T. R. Sharma, 1–7. Meerut, India: Shalabh Book House, 1986.

Munday, Anthony. *A Second and Third Blast of Retreat from Plays and Theaters.* New York: Johnson Reprint Co., 1972.

Musgrove, Sydney. *Shakespeare and Jonson.* Auckland: Auckland University College, 1957.

Novy, Marianne. "Shakespeare's Female Characters as Actors and Audience." In *The Woman's Part: Feminist Criticism of Shakespeare,* ed. Carolyn Ruth Swift Lenz et al., 256–70. Urbana: University of Illinois Press, 1980.

O'Flaherty, Wendy Doniger. *Asceticism and Eroticism in the Mythology of Siva.* London: Oxford University Press, 1973.

Orgel, Stephen. "Making Greatness Familiar." *Genre* 15 (Spring 1982): 41–48.

————. "Nobody's Perfect: Or Why Did the English Stage Take Boys for Women?" *South Atlantic Quarterly* 88 (1989): 7–30.

Origen. *Homilies on Genesis and Exodus.* Translated by Ronald E. Heine. Washington, D.C.: Catholic University Press, 1981.

Ovid. *Heroides and Amores.* Edited by T. E. Page et al., translated by Grant Showerman. New York: G. P. Putnam's Sons, 1931.

————. *Metamorphoses.* Translated by Arthur Golding in 1567, edited by John Frederick Nims. New York: Collier-Macmillan, 1967.

————. *Metamorphoses.* Translated by Rolfe Humphries. Bloomington: Indiana University Press, 1957.

Parten, Anne. "Falstaff's Horns: Masculine Inadequacy and Feminine Mirth in *The Merry Wives of Windsor.*" *Studies in Philology* 82 (1985): 184–99.

Persius. *Satires.* In *Juvenal and Persius.* Translated by G. G. Ramsay. Cambridge: Harvard University Press, 1930.

Pigman, George. "Versions of Imitation in the Renaissance." *Renaissance Quarterly* 33, no. 1 (Spring 1980): 1–32.

Plato. *Collected Dialogues.* Edited by Edith Hamilton and Huntington Cairns. New York: Bollingen/Pantheon, 1961.

————. *Phaedrus, Ion, Gorgias, and Symposium, with Passages from the Republic and Laws.* Translated by Lane Cooper. Ithaca: Cornell University Press, 1955.

————. *The Republic.* Translated by G. M. A. Grube. Indianapolis: Hackett, 1992.

————. *Symposium*. Edited and translated by Alexander Nehamas and Paul Wood-ruff. Indianapolis: Hackett, 1989.

Prynne, William. *Histriomastix: The Player's Scourge, or Actor's Tragedy*. New York: Johnson Reprint Co., 1972.

Rackin, Phyllis. "Androgyny, Mimesis, and the Marriage of the Boy Heroine on the Renaissance Stage." In *Speaking of Gender*, edited by Elaine Showalter, 113–33. New York: Routledge, 1989.

————. "Historical Difference/Sexual Difference." In *Privileging Gender in Early Modern England*, edited by Jean R. Brink, 37–63. Kirksville, Mo.: Sixteenth-Century Journal Publishers, 1993.

Rainolds, John. *The Overthrow of Stage-Plays*. New York: Johnson Reprint Co., 1972.

Ringle, Ken. "Into the Heart—and Soul—of Africa: Laurens van der Post's Spiritual Quest as Writer, Hunter, Soldier and Humanist." *The Washington Post*, 26 June 1993.

Roberts, Jeanne Addison. "Animals as Agents of Revelation: The Horizontalizing of the Chain of Being in Shakespeare's Comedies." *New York Critical Forum* (1980): 79–96.

————. "Horses and Hermaphrodites: Metamorphoses in *The Taming of the Shrew*." *Shakespeare Quarterly* 34 (Summer 1983): 159–71.

————. *The Shakespearean Wild: Geography, Genus, Gender*. Lincoln: University of Nebraska Press, 1991.

————. *Shakespeare's English Comedy: The Merry Wives of Windsor in Context*. Lincoln: University of Nebraska Press, 1979.

Robinson, James. "*Bartholomew Fair*: Comedy of Vapors." *SEL* 2 (Spring 1961): 65–80.

Rose, Mary Beth. *The Expense of Spirit: Love and Sexuality in English Renaissance Drama*. Ithaca: Cornell University Press, 1988.

Rowe, George. *Distinguishing Jonson: Imitation, Rivalry, and the Direction of a Dramatic Career*. Lincoln: University of Nebraska Press, 1988.

Saccio, Peter. *The Court Comedies of John Lyly*. Princeton: Princeton University Press, 1969.

Sambucus, Johannes. *Emblemata*. Antwerp, 1564.

Scragg, Leah. *The Metamorphosis of Gallathea: A Study in Creative Adaptation*. Washington, D.C.: University Press of America, 1982.

Sedgwick, Eve. *Between Men: English Literature and Male Homosocial Desire*. New York: Columbia University Press, 1985.

Selden, Raman. *English Verse Satire: 1590–1675*. London: George Allen and Unwin, 1978.

Shakespeare, William. *The Riverside Shakespeare*. Edited by G. Blakemore Evans. Boston: Houghton Mifflin, 1974.

Shapiro, James. *Rival Playwrights: Marlowe, Jonson, Shakespeare*. New York: Columbia University Press, 1991.

Shapiro, Susan. "Amazons, Hermaphrodites, and Plain Monsters: The 'Masculine' Woman in English Satire from 1580–1640," *Atlantis* 13 (1987): 65–76.

Sidney, Philip. *Selections from Arcadia and Other Poetry and Prose.* Edited by T. W. Craik. New York: Capricorn Books, 1966.

Sophocles. *The Three Theban Plays.* Edited by Bernard Knox, translated by Robert Fagles. New York: Viking Press, 1982.

Spenser, Edmund. *The Faerie Queene.* Edited by A. C. Hamilton. New York: Longman, 1977.

Stallybrass, Peter. "Patriarchal Territories: The Body Enclosed." In *Rewriting the Renaissance: The Discourses of Sexual Difference in Early Modern Europe,* edited by Margaret Ferguson et al., 123–42. Chicago: University of Chicago Press, 1986.

Stubbes, Philip. *The Anatomy of Abuses.* London: Richard Jones, 1583.

Swift, Jonathan. *Gulliver's Travels and Other Writings.* Edited by Louis A. Landa. Boston: Houghton Mifflin, 1960.

Thayer, C. G. *Ben Jonson: Studies in the Plays.* Norman: University of Oklahoma Press, 1963.

Thomson, J. A. K. *Shakespeare and the Classics.* London: George Allen and Unwin, 1952.

Tiffany, Grace. "Falstaff's False Staff: 'Jonsonian' Asexuality in *The Merry Wives of Windsor.*" *Comparative Drama* (Fall 1992): 254–70.

———. "Not Saying No: Female Self-Erasure in *Troilus and Cressida.*" *Texas Studies in Literature and Language* 35 (Spring 1993): 44–56.

Traub, Valerie. "Prince Hal's Falstaff: Positioning Psychoanalysis and the Female Reproductive Body." *Shakespeare Quarterly* 40 (1989): 456–74.

Turner, Victor. *Dramas, Fields, and Metaphors: Symbolic Action in Human Society.* Ithaca: Cornell University Press, 1974.

———. *The Ritual Process: Structure and Anti-Structure.* Chicago: Aldine, 1969.

Vickers, Brian. *Appropriating Shakespeare: Contemporary Critical Quarrels.* New Haven: Yale University Press, 1993.

Walker, Hugh. *English Satire and Satirists.* New York: Octagon Books, 1972.

Westcott, Joan. "The Sculpture and Myths of Eshu-Elegba, the Yoruba Trickster." *Africa* 22 (1962): 336–54.

Whittier, Gayle. "The Sublime Androgyne Motif in Three Shakespeare Works." *Journal of Medieval and Renaissance Studies* 19 (Fall 1989): 185–210.

Williams, Bernard. *Shame and Necessity.* Berkeley: University of California Press, 1993.

White, R. S. "Metamorphosis by Love in Elizabethan Romance, Romantic Comedy, and Shakepeare's Early Comedies." *Review of English Studies* 35 (1984): 14–44.

Wind, Edgar. *Pagan Mysteries in the Renaissance.* London: Faber and Faber, 1958.

Woodbridge, Linda. *Women and the English Renaissance: Literature and the Nature of Womankind, 1540–1620.* Urbana: University of Illinois Press, 1984.

Index